D0793896

KHALAJ MATERIALS

RESEARCH CENTER FOR THE LANGUAGE SCIENCES

INDIANA UNIVERSITY

Thomas A. Sebeok *Chairman*

Andrew Vázsonyi *Associate Chairman, Publications*

Gerhard Doerfer

with the collaboration of

Wolfram Hesche
Hartwig Scheinhardt
Semih Tezcan

KHALAJ MATERIALS

Published by

INDIANA UNIVERSITY, BLOOMINGTON

Mouton & Co., The Hague , The Netherlands

INDIANA UNIVERSITY PUBLICATIONS

URALIC AND ALTAIC SERIES

Editor: John R. Krueger

Editor Emeritus: Thomas A. Sebeok

Volume 115

Copy editor: Jean Dahlquist

ISBN 87750-150-5

Library of Congress Catalog Card Number: 70-630301

All orders from the United States of American and from Canada should be addressed to Humanities Press, Inc., 303 Park Avenue South, New York, N.Y. 10010. Orders from all other countries should be sent to Mouton & Co., Publishers, The Hague, The Netherlands.

Printed in the United States of America

TABLE OF CONTENTS

1
FOREWORD

1.1 <u>The investigation of Khalaj</u>. The present volume is the first of several projected works concerned with Khalaj. Khalaj (Xäläǰ), a Turkic language spoken in central Persia, constitutes an independent branch of the Turkic group of languages. It cannot be included, for example, among the southwestern Turkic languages (the Oghuz group: Turkish, Azerbaijani, and Türkmän) nor among any other Turkic group.

In 1939 the Persian scholar M. Moġäddäm made a trip to Ą̊šteyą̊n and to other Persian districts south of Teheran primarily to gather material of the local Persian dialects. But he also gathered material of the Azerbaijani local dialect and of a Turkic language unknown up to this time: Khalaj. Since he was no Turcologist (but an Iranist), he did not realize the importance of his discovery. Furthermore, since his book was written in Persian — and modern Persian scientific books normally are disregarded in European countries (<u>Iranica non leguntur</u>) — his discovery remained unknown to Turcologists. Nearly the same academic disregard holds true for Minorsky's material, gathered much earlier but presented only in a short article (cf. bibliography, Chapter 4). Although Minorsky's report was written in English and published in an accessible journal, the material was much too sketchy to make a sensation; also, as Minorsky was no Turcologist, he failed to recognize the real value of Khalaj. Furthermore, of the three native informants upon whose speech Minorsky based his study, two spoke Khalaj well while the third, the head of Pougerd in 1917, mixed Khalaj terms with Azerbaijani (a mixture of Khalaj-Azerbaijani was at that time spoken in Pougerd; Khalaj is now extinct there). As Minorsky relied most heavily on the speech of his Pougerd informant, Minorsky's Khalaj texts had a striking Azerbaijani character. Thus Menges 1951. 278-9 qualified Khalaj ("in diaspora in the districts of Sulṭānābād and Sāva, SW of Tehrān") as "Āzerbājdžān-Turkish." [Menges informs us that Khalaj "will probably be investigated by Dr. Borecký of Tehrān University (formerly at Prague University)." To my knowledge, Mr. Borecký never has published anything about this topic.]

Thus investigation of this field came to an end for a time. In 1967, when I had to write an article for <u>Current Trends in Linguistics</u>, Volume VI, and had to consult Iranian material about Turkic languages in Persia, I found a short note in Afshar 1961, No. 4027, about Moǧäddäm's work. By the special kindness of Dr. Abbas Zaryab (Library of the Senate, Teheran) I received this book. Since the importance of this material was apparent, I began publishing several articles about Khalaj (cf. bibliography). Although I would have liked to go to Khalajistan during summer vacations, I was unable to, as I had accepted a visiting professorship at Indiana University in Bloomington, Indiana. Therefore I arranged for my three doctoral candidates— Wolfram Hesche, Hartwig Scheinhardt (both Germans) and Semih Tezcan (a Turk) — to go there with the following instructions:

(1) To define the frontiers of the Khalaj linguistic area by visiting as many villages as possible;

(2) To record some language material. To accomplish this end we planned to use as a basis for interrogations one of two lists: (a) Moǧäddäm's long list, which described the Khalaj dialect of Tälxab and which contained many Persian loanwords. This list we planned to use only in the more important villages; (b) a shorter list of words extracted from Moǧäddäm's list (we kept

only those words thought to be Turkic, not Persian), which we supplemented with other important words such as numerals. This list comprised the standard form of our language investigations.

The material which we gathered in the short period of one month is necessarily limited, but it is, I think, an important contribution to Turcology. This material (and material collected in subsequent expeditions) will be the subject matter of a projected four-volume work, of which this volume is the first. I hereby extend my special thanks to the editor of this volume.

The authors of specific sections of this book are as follows: Hesche, Scheinhardt, Tezcan (Chapters 1.2, 2, 3.1); Doerfer, Hesche, Parviz Radjabi, Scheinhardt, Tezcan (Chapter 5); and Doerfer (the remainder).

1.2 Contents of the tape cassettes. In the following section we describe briefly the contents of the tape cassettes, indicating the names of the authorities insofar as we could learn them. For statistics concerning the villages visited, consult Chapter 3. The term "Word List 1" used below refers to the short list in Chapter 5.3 entitled "Materials of Mänṣur-ạbạd and Xält-ạbạd"; "Word List 2" refers to the long list in Chapter 5.2 entitled "Material of Tälxạb." The figures I A, I B, II A, etc., refer to the tape cassettes.

I A

Mänṣur-ạbạd

Conversation with Ġolạm Reżạ, thirty-eight-year-old head of the village, upper teeth show gaps

Life in Mänṣur-ạbạd (same authority, easy to understand)

Numerals

Several words

Parts of the body

Conjugation (kål- 'to come,' va̤r- 'to go')

Several words

Animals

Fruits and vegetables

Terms of relationship

Several verbs

Some short sentences

Word List 1 (beginning)

I B

Mänṣur-a̤ba̤d

Word List 1 (continuation). Authority: Ġola̤m Reża̤

Ordinal numbers with examples (+minči not found)

II A

Mänṣur-a̤ba̤d

A short phrase (hard to understand)

Ġola̤m Reża̤ speaks with his wife (very hard to understand).

Hinz, i.e., Walther Hinz, Persisch. Leitfaden der Umgangssprache, Berlin, 1959. 234-8 (last word: dár-jāft kardän). Authority: Ġola̤m Reża̤. Only such words are asked which are thought to exist and to be important in Khalaj; such words as Benzin, Banane are omitted.

Hinz 238-46 (last word chåstän). Authority: Ruḥolla̤h, fourteen-year-old nephew (?) of Ġola̤m Reża̤. Sometimes his uncle (?) interferes.

Moujа̤n

Word List 1

Conjugation

Reża, son of the head of the village (Äṣqär) tells a fairy tale (although spoken rather swiftly, it is understandable. Reża is a pupil of the eighth grade.)

ʿÄli (from the same village) tells of something which happened the day before (rather easy to understand). In this story the form -ġalï occurs. When he had finished his story, we asked him what this form meant. He explained:

bäna šäydik varġalï : bäna kärdim räftän

bäna šäydik kälgeli : bäna kärdim amädän

bäna šäydik hayġalï : bäna kärdim goftän

Conjugation

Hinz 39-41 (list of the most important verbs)

Hinz 19-21 (interrogative pronouns, demonstrative pronouns, indefinite pronouns. Here kimdilä 'with whom' is striking; 'with whom,' Persian ba-ké, is not found in Hinz. It was asked by chance. Concerning kimdilä, cf. Xärrab bizdičä, etc.)

Conjugation (kärdän, Hinz 31)

Hinz 246 (only some words)

II B

Moujan

Word List 2

Some sentences

Some sentences constructed with -ġuluq (future participle): biz burda varġïlïq äk, vardïq balïqqa tuz alġïlïq äk

Conjugation

Hinz 247-69

Sorxädé

Word List 1

A short adventure

A complaint about poverty and the hard conditions of life (short, about one minute)

Xärrab

Word List 1 (beginning). Authorities: ʿEzzätollah, head of the village, and Yädollah, ʿEzzätollah's father, about sixty-five years old

III A

Xärrab

Word List 1 (continuation). Here we find such numerals as äkki hottuz 'sixty,' üč hottuz 'ninety.'

Some words attached to Word List 1: smell, to put on clothes, figure

An adventure (some passages cannot be easily understood, but the story shows some long and straightly constructed sentences and some very important words, e.g., yätkär-.)

Somebody else tells a story about Shah ʿÄbbas (not easy to understand).

Conjugation, several verbs

A fairy tale. Authority: Ḥosäin aġa-ye Aqali, sixty years old ("äkki hottuz")

Somebody else tells what he will do this evening.

Several sentences (Hinz 68-9)

Explanation: Khalaj buzladï = Azerbaijani buz oldi 'it became cold'

Numerals (especially üč hottuz 'ninety,' yätti hottuz 'two hundred ten,' etc.)

üšlü kün 'the day before yesterday'

A story about Shah ʿÄbbas (not easy to understand). Authority: ʿAlämdar, sixty-five years old

An adventure. Authority: Äḥmäd aġa-ye ʿÄräbgol, thirty-one

years old (easy to understand but rather mixed up with Persian)

III B

Mäzräʿä-ye Nou (Märzano)

Word List 1. Authority: the head of the village, name unknown, about thirty-six or thirty-eight years old, has been two years in his position, has lost one of his upper teeth

Ordinal numerals (+minči)

uǰa = boländ 'high'

Several sentences

Tähranda kälgilik (or kälgili) är

O här Tähranda kälgilik daġ

Conjugation

Proverbs

Several sentences and words

Hinz 278 backwards up to 269 (first word darîdän, last word bālâ raftän)

A story (spoken swiftly but easy to understand)

Several sentences

IV A

Mäzräʿä-ye Nou

Music played by ʿÄli Ḥäidäri and his companions

Several sentences

Kärdeyan

Word List 1

Colors

Some words

Explanation: Khalaj tilki = Azerbaijani tülkü 'fox'

Conjugation (several verbs and several forms)
Some sentences and words
Enumeration of villages in which the Khalaj live

IV B

Mäzrä'ä-ye Nou

Continuation of the enumeration of Khalaj villages
Some sentences

Xorąk-ąbąd

Ordinal numerals
Word List 1

Heząr-ąbąd

Word List 1
gilk 'marrow' < yilik
Colors
Conjugation
Numerals
Ordinal numerals (+minči)
An adventure (impossible to understand)

V A

Heząr-ąbąd
Dialogue (hard to understand)

Xärrąb

Mosäiyeb 'Äräbgol speaks about the Khalaj language.
He replies to several questions of ours.

He tells about the festivals of Nouruz (New Year).

He tells about some plays put on during Nouruz (plays in the form of sport):

(1) čartaġï

(2) kola̯hbärda̯r (biryäk kötürmä)

(3) ič taš (< üč taš 'three stones')

ʿÄräbgol tells how weddings are celebrated by the Khalaj.

He also describes the festival of circumcision. (Note: the conversation of ʿÄräbgol is exceptionally easy to understand but he mixes Khalaj up in a rather exaggerated way with Persian; of course, he uses some Khalaj words which do not occur in the other texts.)

Sentences constructed with -gili and -gilik (ʿÄräbgol)

A short poem by ʿÄräbgol (four misras)

Sentences constructed with -gili and -gilik (ʿÄräbgol)

ʿÄräbgol enumerates the Khalaj villages belonging to A̯šteya̯n.

Fäiż-a̯ba̯d

Word List (only the beginning)

The house-lord (brother of the head of the village, who was absent) is afraid of us and tries to drive us away (in a polite way), but this same man tells us in which of the circumjacent villages Khalaj can be found.

V B

Fäiż-a̯ba̯d

Continuation of enumeration of Khalaj villages

Our authority explains that the majority of the inhabitants of Iran consists of Turks (information which is false, by the way).

Noudeh

Word List 1. Authority: ʿÄli Äṣqär Wäfa̯i, the head of the village, has been two years in his position

We are told about Nouruz and are urged to remain for eating.

Yängiǰé

Word List 1

Several words

A short story

Conversation. Authority: Räḥimollа̯h Yängičä-ye Qäräxа̯ni, thirty-five years old

VI A

Xält-а̯bа̯d

Word List 1 (the beginning is missing). Authority: unknown, anterior upper teeth missing

Conjugation

Tälxа̯b

Word List 2. Authority: Moḥämmäd-e Tälxа̯bi, fifty-two years old

VI B

Tälxа̯b

Word List 2 (continuation)

Some words attached to it: bod 'figure,' boda- 'to color,' yid 'smell,' yitti 'was lost,' odan- 'to awake,' odat- 'to awaken (somebody else),' tašqar 'outside,' ičkär 'inside,' hay- 'to say'

Conjugation

Numerals

üšlu kün, taqïsï üšlü kün

Ordinal numerals (+minči not found)

yint- 'speak, say' (this word exists in other villages, too, < ?)

Hinz 39-41 (verbs; especially interesting: bošar- = Persian tawânestän 'to be able'< baš 'head'?)

Hinz 44 (conjunctions)

A long story about Shah ᶜÄbba̮s (spoken very swiftly but not hard to understand). Authority: Moḥämmäd (Xa̮n-)e Tälxa̮bi

Terms of relationship

Tree names: seyät 'willow,' tüt 'mulberry tree,' ġadäm 'almond'

Some words

Wa̮šqa̮n

Word List 1

Story (hard to understand)

VII A

Wa̮šqa̮n

Continuation of the story. Authority: Äḥmäd-e Wa̮šqa̮ni, thirty-five-year-old head of the village

ᶜÄli-ye Wa̮šqa̮ni, twenty-two years old, tells about Nouruz

Moḥämmäd Ḥäsän (Äsär?), fifty-two years old, originally a native of Wa̮šqa̮n but living now in Qïzïilǰa, tells a story (relatively easy to understand, but —Azerbaijani!)

Some sentences constructed with -ġalï and -ġilïq/-gülük

Ḥäsän-a̮ba̮d

Word List 1. As the man we asked turned out not to be Khalaj, we stopped in the middle of the sample.

Säfid-ạb

Word List 1. Authority: ʿÄli Reżạ, head of the village

VII B

Säfid-ạb

Several words

The mother of the head of the village complains of the hard conditions of life.

Bon-čenạr

Word List 1. Authority: Ḥạǰi Moḥämmäd, forty-year-old (about) head of the village, son of Ḥosäin

Some words attached to this list: käd- 'to put on clothes,' bod 'figure,' yid 'smell,' sanadum 'I counted'

Numerals

Zär-nušé

Word List 1

Several verbs and other words

Numerals

Several words

Verbs, conjugation (var- 'to go')

Several words

ʿÄbdollạh, forty-year-old head of the village, tells how Khalaj weddings are celebrated

A man whose name we did not learn tells about Nouruz.

VIII A

Zär-nušé

Village problems: lack of water

Dạrestạn

Word List. Authority: the petrol attendant Ḥäbibollạh-e Dạrestạni

Numerals

Conversation

Wenạreǰ

Word List 1

kăčgili yil 'last year'

Numerals

Phrase. Authority: ʿIsạ, twenty-four years old

Xärrạb

Poem, song by ʿÄräbgol

Music: näy (a kind of flute) is played

VIII B

Xärrạb

A speech is given by ʿÄräbgol on the occasion of the New Year festival (Nouruz), beginning with the words Xärrạb xalqï! Kišilär, härlär! 'People of Xärrạb! Women and men!'

Säläfčegạn

Word List 1

Numerals

Qäré-Su

An adventure

ʿÄli Ḥạǰi, nine years old (!), tells a fairy tale.

Bạġ-e yäk

Word List 1. Authority: Mortäżạ Wäfại, head of the village

Numerals
A poem
The Persian traduction thereof
About Nạder Shah and the Khalaj

Seft

Word List 1. Authority: Ḥosäin Wäfạ'i, head of the village
Several words (same authority)
Life in the village (same authority)

Ispit

Several words

IX A

Čạhäk

Word List 2. Authority: Näṣrollạh Päimi, head of the village
Some words (same authority)
Hinz 39-41 (verbs), 19-21 (interrogative pronouns, demonstrative pronouns)
Numerals
Ordinal numerals (+minči)
Several words: äta, ini, äkä, hala, dädä, tata

Mehr-e Zämin

Word List 1. Authority: twenty-year-old son of Adî Ḥämid, head of the village
Several words: yattïq~yattuq, bod, yid, tük, tiel ('curl')
Terms of relationship

IX B

Mehr-e Zämin

Continuation thereof

<u>Firuz-a̮ba̮d</u> (Qashqai!)

Word List 2. Authority: Iskändär J̌a̮hedi, the teacher of English in Firuz-a̮ba̮d

Qashqai poems

REPORT OF OUR EXPEDITION

For the Khalajistan expedition undertaken in March and April 1968 the Universitätsbund Göttingen placed DM 5000 at our disposal and the Societas Uralo-Altaica of Hamburg, DM 1800.

Contrary to our original intention to go the route of Göttingen-Teheran by train and bus and afterwards to rent a car in Persia, we bought a used Opel Caravan (1963), which the Opel agency of Göttingen thoroughly overhauled. The reason for this change of plan was, among other things, a letter from Deutsches Archäologisches Institut in Teheran informing us that this institute could not place a car at our disposal and that it would become very expensive to rent one.

We started our trip on February 28 from Göttingen. In the late evening hours of March 2 we arrived at Ankara. There we were delayed somewhat because of bad weather conditions and because of some necessary formalities (customs, visas). On March 6 we continued our journey via Samsun, Trabzon, Gümüşhane, Erzurum and Doğubeyazit. On March 9 we arrived at Tebriz, on March 11 at Sạvé, a town about seventy miles south of Teheran. Finally, on the morning of March 12, we caught sight of Dästgerd, administrative center of Khalajistan.

As soon as we arrived at this town, the vicegerent of the head of the district came to see us, inquired about the aim of our stay, and asked us to come to the office of the head of the district. There we explained our purposes and produced the letter of recommendation which the ambassador of Iran in the Federal Republic of Germany had given us. We wish to express to His Excellence our most respectful gratitude for his special kindness.

The vicegerent, himself a Khalaj, informed us about the circumjacent villages, even indicating the names of the village heads. On later occasions he was also helpful and amiable.

In Dästgerd itself we found no Khalaj. (The previously-mentioned vicegerent, Mr. Mosäiyeb ʿÄräbgol, was a native of Xärrạb.) We then went around the villages with Khalaj population by turns, always asking for further villages still unknown to us. As almost no facilities of communication exist in this region, we were, more than once, very glad that we had brought with us a car from Germany. But traveling the wild ways or mule tracks with an Opel Caravan often was rather painful. As our trip was only a provisional expedition, we may propose to use a more appropriate cross-country vehicle for the main expedition. Almost without exception we were entertained very kindly in the thirty-four villages which we visited. The Khalaj appreciated our work and their amiability contributed substantially to the success of our trip. Here is a short résumé about the Khalaj.

The Khalaj live between 49° and 51° longitude and between 34° and 35° latitude in about 46 villages. According to the data of our investigations, they number about 17,000 persons. But this number surely will diminish in the near future, as many Khalaj are leaving their native villages because of a bad water supply. Above all, most of the younger able-bodied people work in the surrounding towns; in the Khalaj villages predominantly old people and children reside. The region is rather secluded; only a few Persians and Azerbaijanis live among the Khalaj. The people are very poor. Only a few of them have landed property of their own; most of them do not possess even a small field to cultivate for themselves. The majority of the people work for the big landed proprietors. To a limited extent, goats and sheep are bred. In some villages the traditional carpet knotting is cultivated. This is the task especially of women and children. Every larger village has a school; the teachers are Persians, many of whom have to absolve their probationer time there. Scarcely any of the Khalaj — not even the heads of the villages — can read or write. Although the Khalaj are Shiites, they are tolerant towards professors of other religions. In political contrast to other Turkic nations in Iran, such as the Azerbaijani and the Qashqai, the Khalaj have always been loyal subjects of the Persian crown. Physically the Khalaj are a marked anthropological type (see the photographs at the end of this volume).

The linguistic situation is unique: the Khalaj speak (as Doerfer shows in this study) the most archaic of all existing Turkic languages (with the exception of, perhaps, Chuvash). Khalaj cannot be classified among the known six groups of Turkic languages, but is a seventh independent group. Although the material gathered by us has not yet been fully examined, some distinct features are an additional proof of the important position of Khalaj in Turcology. We were able to distinguish two main dialects of Khalaj: the northern and the southern dialects. In some especially secluded villages we found interesting words which do not exist any more in other Turkic languages. Khalaj is not a literary language. The oral traditions are scarce and presumably are often formed according to Persian or Azerbaijani patterns. The Khalaj (only the men?) are preponderantly bilingual or trilingual, i. e., apart from their native language they also master Persian and Azerbaijani. Many of them, though not able to speak Azerbaijani, understand it rather well. For this reason we had hardly any difficulties in making ourselves understood. Women in general master Khalaj better and speak it more purely than men. The western part of the Khalaj territory in particular is strongly Iranized; children there speak only Persian (though they still understand Khalaj).

We brought with us on our expedition nine tape cassettes, each lasting ninety minutes. Mr. Josef Ecker of the Hannover firm Philips Ltd.was so kind as to place at our disposal a Cassette

Recorder EL 3302 (battery operated) which stood the test very well during the whole expedition. As no electrical current exists in the region, battery-operated recorders are indispensable to Khalaj expeditions.

We tried to learn something about the history of the Khalaj, but the people were informed (to some extent) only about the immediate past. They could say nothing about their origin. To be sure, they are aware of being a special group. Hence they precisely distinguish Persians, Turks, Kurds, and Khalaj. After we had explored the territory defined in our mission, we decided to examine a reference to a Khalaj-speaking population south of Shiraz (cf. Garrod 1946.294-6). The head of Ba̮ġ-e yäk, a very educated man, told us that he himself had been there and had met Khalaj population.

On March 30 we arrived at Firuz-a̮ba̮d. This town is situated about sixty miles south of Shiraz. Firuz-a̮ba̮d is the largest town in the Qashqai territory. The Khalaj sought by us were said to live in the tribal territory of the Qashqai. During the past years, the Qashqai have engaged in several guerrilla skirmishes against the government troops. The road from Shiraz to Firuz-a̮ba̮d is, even today, closed to civil traffic after nightfall. In the daytime the road is guarded. When we arrived at Firuz-a̮ba̮d in the late afternoon, we immediately were apprehended by the police, were thoroughly questioned, and, since it was impossible to send us back at so late an hour, were finally lodged in an empty house. Because of the hostile atmosphere, it was impossible to search for the Khalaj. We also were not able to get information about them anywhere. However, accompanied by a kind officer, we succeeded in making some trips to points nearby. With his help we were allowed to stay two more days in Firuz-a̮ba̮d. During this time we occupied ourselves with the language of the Qashqai, a language which has been little explored. Then we made an important discovery. An amateur poet brought us a manuscript containing many Qashqai poems. He recited some of them on our tape recorder. Unfortunately, we could not acquire this manuscript. It indeed has been known that the Qashqai have poets, but none of their poems up to this time had been discovered. We wish only briefly to mention that the Qashqai might be interesting for ethnographs, too, for instance of women's clothes and the utensils of nomadic life.

In Khalajistan the car had been overexerted and hence was in so bad a condition that it was not capable of making the trip back to Germany. Moreover, our financial situation was more than alarming. The extension of the expedition to Firuz-ạ̄bạ̄d was possible only through the kindness of Mr. Schmidt-Dumont, vicegerent of the Cultural Attaché (Kulturattaché) and chief of the press (Pressechef) of the German embassy in Teheran, who had given us a personal loan. Among other things, the money for gasoline was lacking, as the DM 1,800 promised by Societas Uralo-Altaica had not yet arrived. As foreigners are not allowed to sell cars in Teheran or in Turkey, the only possibility of selling the Opel was in Afghanistan.

But while we were still in Iran, we had an accident. A truck ran into our car, which was considerably damaged. Thanks to the kind support of the Iranian police station, we succeeded in inducing the driver of the truck to make amends for the damage. However, the repair forced us to a longer stay in the town of Babol. Therefore we did not arrive at Kabul until April 12. Fortunately we at once found a buyer for the car, in spite of the still visible damage. The formalities of customs, etc., took several days. On April 21 we flew from Kabul via Tashkent to Moscow. As all the train tickets to Berlin were sold out, we could not leave Moscow by train until April 24. We arrived at Berlin on April 25, at Göttingen on April 26.

DISTRIBUTION AND ETHNIC MIXTURES OF THE KHALAJ

3.1 Distribution of the Khalaj. The Khalaj live, roughly speaking, in central Persia, about 120 miles SW of Teheran, cf. Chapter 2 and the maps at the end of this volume. Some Khalaj, emigrants from the same region, live now among the Qashqai of southern Persia, according to Garrod 1946; but it is unclear whether they still speak Khalaj or whether they have been assimilated by their Qashqai-speaking neighbors (the latter seems to be more likely. Garrod, speaking about the Amaleh tribe of the Qashqai, says on page 296, "the dialect differs slightly from that of the Khalaj").

I include here three lists of the distribution of Khalaj population, cf. maps at the end of this volume. In the first two lists I use the spelling of Minorsky and of Räzmạrạ̄ respectively (the sign ~ marks variants found in the works of the authors themselves.)

List A. Khalaj villages according to Minorsky 1940. (1) Kondūrūd, (2) Seft, (3) Sefīdale, (4) Aḥmadābād, (5) Nūrābād, (6) Khärrāb, (7) Espī, (8) Moshäkye, (9) Särärūd, (10) Räzābād (~ Räzäbād), (11) Khoräkābād (~ Khoräkäbād), (12) Mo^{u}jūn, (13) Kārdiyān (~ Kardejan), (14) Märzīnū, (15) Nädrābād, (16) Khorche, (17) Härīrān, (18) Sorkhedeh, (19) Āsiyābād, (20) Manṣūrābād, (21) Fo^{u}jerd (~ Po^{u}gerd), (22) Alīgān, (23) Chömänäk, (24) Tāj-Khātūn, (25) Kafshgarān.

List B. Khalaj villages according to Räzmạrạ̄ 1327. Points of reference are D = Dästgerd (or Dästǰerd), 64 kilometers west of Qom (we give the indications in kilometers because they are so given in Räzma̯ra̯), and K = Kähäk, 18 kilometers south of Qom. (1) Äna̯nǰerd (~ Nungerd) 18 km S D, (2) Ba̯ġ-e Nämäk 20 km E D, (3) J̌onda̯b 24 km S D, (4) Ča̯häk 29 km N D, (5) Čämbunäk 14 km N D (= Minorsky 23), (6) Xära̯b 12 km SW D (= Minorsky 6), (7) Xora̯k-a̯ba̯d 18 km SW D (= Minorsky 11), (8) Dästǰerd [in which, according to our investigations, Khalaj is not spoken (anymore?), cf. Chapter 2], (9) Ra̯hǰerd (~ Ra̯hgerd) 24 km SE D, (10) Zouwa̯reya̯n (~ Säwa̯reya̯n) 17 km SE D, (11) Ṣa̯leḥa̯ba̯d 18 km SW D, (12) Kordiǰa̯n 17 km SW D (= Minorsky 13), (13) Mäzrä'é-ye Nou 18 km SW D (= Minorsky 14), (14) Mušäkeyé 18 km N D (= Minorsky 8), (15) Mehr-e Zämin 33 km NE D, (16) Niǰé 24 km E D, (17) Wena̯räǰ (or Wena̯rǰ or Wena̯reǰ) 15 km NE K, (18) Häza̯r-a̯ba̯d 18 km SW D (= Minorsky 10). We see that correspondence between the lists of Minorsky and of Räzma̯ra̯ is only partial.

List C. Khalaj villages according to Doerfer and associates. This list is divided into two sections: the Khalaj villages which we visited and those which we did not visit. The order of the first section is chronological; that is, the villages are listed according to the order in which we visited them. The first entry of each village name is a form originally written down by us (which may reflect the popular pronunciation); the second entry is a purified form based on the Persian script of Räzma̯ra̯. In parentheses is Räzma̯ra̯'s Persian script followed by references to the preceding Khalaj distribution lists of Minorsky and Räzma̯ra̯. After the parentheses is a rough estimate of the number of inhabitants and the names of the heads of the villages (insofar as we could learn them).

(1) Mansurabad = Mänṣur-a̯ba̯d (منصورآباد = Minorsky 20), 400, head: Ġola̯m Reża̯

(2) Maudschân = Moujạn (موجان = Minorsky 12), 500; head: Äṣqär

(3) Surchade = Sorxädé (سرخده Minorsky 18), 360; head: Moḥämmäd ʿÄli

(4) Charrâb = Xärrạb (خراب = Minorsky 6, Räzmạrạ 6), 550, head: ʿEzzätollạh

(5) Märzâno = Mäzräʿä-ye Nou (مزرعه نو = Minorsky 14, Räzmạrạ 13), 400, head: ʿÄli Moḥämmäd

(6) Qardiân = Kärdeyạn (كرديان = Minorsky 13, Räzmạrạ 12), 800

(7) Chorâkabad = Xorạk-ạbạd (خوراك آباد = Minorsky 11, Räzmạrạ 7), 120, no head of village

(8) Hizârabad = Hezạr-ạbạd (هزار آباد = Räzmạrạ 18; another name of this village is Râzabad, Rez-ạbạd?, = Minorsky 10), 400

(9) Faizabad = Fäiż-ạbạd (فيض آباد), 400?

(10) Nûdeh = Noudeh (نوده), 450, head: ʿÄli Äṣqär Wäfại

(11) Jengidsche = Yängiǰé (ينگيجه), 120, no head of village

(12) Hâltâbâd = Xält-ạbạd (خلت آباد), 450, head is a Persian whose name remained unknown to us

(13) Talkhâb = Tälxạb (تلخ آب), 2000, head: Ḥạǰi Qorban ʿÄli Näẓäri

(14) Wâschghân = Wạšqạn (واشقان), 1300, head: Äḥmäd-e Wạšqạni

(15) Hasanabad = Ḥäsän-ạbạd (حسن آباد), 20, no head of village

(16) Sefidâb = Säfid-ạb (سفيد آب), 300, head: ʿÄli Reżạ

(17) Sarâband, Sarahband = Sär-e bänd (سر بند), 300, head: Ḥạǰi ʿÄli Äkbär

(18) Qâschä, Kâse = Kạšć, Qạšć ? (Persian script not found in Räzmạrạ), 300, head: Moḥämmäd Mirzại

(19) Buntschenâr = Bon-čenạr (بن چنار), 650, head: Ḥạǰi

Moḥämmäd Ḥosäin

(20) Mussiabad = Musi-ạbạd (موسی آباد), 200, no head of village

(21) Saghardschoq, Sïġïrdschoq - Säqärǰuq (سقرجوق , Khalaj pronunciation something like Sïġïrčuq), 600, head of village, Ḥạǰi Reżạ, on pilgrimage

(22) Zarnusheh = Zär-nušé (زر نوشه), 550, head: Äbdollạh

(23) Daristân = Dạrestạn (دارستان), 550, no head of village

(24) Muhsinabad = Moḥsen-ạbạd (محسن آباد), 120, head: Ġolạm Reżạ

(25) Nâdirabad = Näder-ạbạd (= Minorsky 15?), 1100, head: ʿÄbdollạh Ḥosäini J̌äʿfäri

(26) Wenaredsch = Wenạreǰ (or perhaps ä̱ in the last syllable, ونارج , = Räzmạrạ 17), 550

(27) Salafschigân, Salafchegan = Säläfčegạn (Persian script not found in Räzmạrạ, Minorsky mentions on p. 436 "Säläfchegān"), 700

(28) Qarasuv = Qäré-Su (قره سو), 100?, head: Ebrạhim Xošạmädi

(29) Bâghyek, Baġ-e yek = Bạġ-e yäk? (Persian script not found in Räzmạrạ), 120 (i.e., men?), head: Mortäżạ Wäfại

(30) Seft = Seft (سفت = Minorsky 2), 200, head: Ḥosäin

(31) Isbit, Ispit = ? (Persian script not found in Räzmạrạ, = Minorsky 7?), 200, head: Ạġosé ("Āghossé"?)

(32) Tschâhâk, Çehâk = Čạhäk (چاهك , = Räzmạrạ 4), 400, head: Näṣrollạh Päimi

(33) Mehr-e Zämin = Mehr-e Zämin (مهر زمين = Räzmạrạ 15), 450, head: Hämid ("Hamit" ?)

(34) Dirmenik = Dermänek? (درمنك , to be pronounced as "dormonak" according to the indication in Latin script given by Räzmạrạ), 100

Here is a list of villages which we did not visit but the population of which is, according to the people of villages nearby,

Khalaj. We include an estimated number of inhabitants and indicate the nearest village known to us (the number in parentheses refers to this list of villages). Our reasons for not having visited these villages were either lack of time, impassable muddy roads, proximity to villages already visited, or obscure location.

(35) Daghân = Dḁġḁn? (Persian script not found in Räzmḁrḁ), 700, 200 of which are Khalaj, close to Wenḁrej̆ (26)

(36) Ahmedabad = Ä̇ḥmäd-ḁbḁd (احمد آباد = Minorsky 4), number of inhabitants unknown, close to Seft (30)

(37) Sefidâle = Säfid-ḁlé? (Persian script not found in Räzmḁrḁ, = Minorsky 3), this village together with Ä̇ḥmäd-ḁbḁd (immediately above) may have 300 inhabitants, close to Seft (30)

(38) Muschäkiye = Mušäkeyé (موشکیه = Minorsky 8, Räzmḁrḁ 14), 150, close to Ispit (31)

(39) Sararûd = Sär-e Rud? (Persian script not found in Räzmḁrḁ, = Minorsky 9), number of inhabitants unknown, close to Xärrḁb (4), on the way to Hezḁr-ḁbḁd or Rḁz-ḁbḁd (8)

(40) Bachtsche Weswâr = Bḁġčé Weswḁr? (Persian script not found in Räzmḁrḁ), number of inhabitants unknown, close to Mušäkeyé (38)

(41) Tisgân = Zizgḁn ? (Persian script not found in Räzmḁrḁ), 600, head: Ḥosäin-e Bḁbḁi [information taken during the second expedition], close to Mouj̆ḁn (2) and Dästgerd

(42) Schahqulu, also Schagallu = Šḁh-qḁlu (Persian script not found in Räzmḁrḁ), number of inhabitants unknown, close to Qom (Qum)

(43) Qurqur = Qurqur, Qorqor? (Persian script not found in Räzmḁrḁ), number of inhabitants unknown, close to Qäré-Su (28)

(44) Aliâbad = ʿÄli-ḁbḁd (علی آباد), 300? close to Xält-ḁbḁd (12)

(45) Dschalilabad = J̆älil-ḁbḁd (جلیل آباد), northern suburb of Xält-ḁbḁd (12)

(46) Husseinabad = Ḥosäin-ạbạd (حسین آباد ; the form of the name is obvious, for villages having this name are spread throughout Persia), only a few inhabitants, close to Qäré-Su (28)

There are altogether forty-six villages with a population of about 17,000 persons; twenty-six of the villages have been investigated linguistically (cf. Chapter 1, contents of the tape cassettes). We must assume that even more villages exist, because in Lists A and B we find names of villages not mentioned in List C. It may be that the names of some of the villages listed in Minorsky and Räzmạrạ should be canceled because the villagers do not speak Khalaj (as we have seen, in Dästgerd, Räzmạrạ 8, Khalaj was never spoken, or at least no longer is); other names may be canceled because some villages have double names or have changed their names (without special information we should not know, for instance, that Minorsky 10 = Räzmạrạ 18, see List C, 8). However, it remains possible that Lists A and B indicate accurately the existence of other villages with Khalaj population, e.g., Pougerd (Minorsky 21), situated far from the Khalaj villages which we visited (cf. the map).

Here is a short list of Khalaj villages not found in our List C: Minorsky 1, 5, 7(?), 15(?), 16, 17, 19, 21, 22, 23, 24, 25; Räzmạrạ 1, 2, 3, 5 (= Minorsky 23), 8 (?, very doubtful, cf. above), 9, 10, 11, 16. We know that Räzmạrạ 1, 9, 11 must be canceled, for our group visited these villages on the first expedition and found that the villagers do not speak Khalaj. On the second expedition (in March 1969) we found that Minorsky 21, 24 and Räzmạrạ 3 must also be canceled (because there only Azerbaijani is spoken). Even omitting all unclear indications these make eleven more Khalaj villages. This would mean that <u>the total number of Khalaj villages is fifty-seven</u>. Furthermore, we have to assume an unknown number of Khalaj villages in the Qashqai reg

3.2 Mixture of Khalaj with other language groups. Above all, the western part of Khalajistan is under a strong foreign (mostly Persian) influence, cf. Chapter 2. Here we will include some special notes about this influence. Xält-ạbạd (12) looks very Iranized. Ḥäsän-ạbạd (15) has one Khalaj family living together with a few Persian and Azerbaijani families. Sär-e bänd (17) has half Khalaj, half Persian population. Moḥsen-ạbạd (24) has half Khalaj, half Azerbaijani population. Wenạreǰ (26) has besides 500 Khalaj about 200 Persians. Mehr-e Zämin (33) has half Khalaj, half Azerbaijani population. Dạġạn (35) has only 200 Khalaj living among many Persians. ʿÄli-ạbạd (44), according to the information of the head of Xält-ạbạd, has only old people still speaking Khalaj. Dermänek (34) has a Persian majority, with only about 100 Khalaj.

The facts indicated above — that the Khalaj language is best preserved by women, that children have forgotten their mother tongue, that many Khalaj have emigrated to adjacent towns, that the teachers are Persian — show obviously that Khalaj is a dying language. Therefore more expeditions to this country are indispensable.

The strong foreign influence is reflected by the loanwords. The situation is as follows:

(a) The Persian local dialects have influenced Khalaj to a great extent; Azerbaijani has influenced it to a lesser extent.

(b) Azerbaijani has influenced both Khalaj and the Persian local dialects.

(c) Khalaj has influenced neither the Azerbaijani nor the Persian local dialects.

Concerning (a), compare my remarks in 1968.107-8. The Persian influence is visible, for example, in the pronunciation [ạ] instead of [a] (whereas the Azerbaijani local dialect has preserved [a]); KhT. 26 Ģạ̄ᵃš 'eyebrow' = Az. gaš, 47 KhT. tạ̄lạ̄q 'milt' =

Az. dalaġ, etc. Both Azerbaijani and Khalaj have borrowed some (local) P. terms, such as KhT. 191 Kh. Az. kåm < local P. kåm, cf. Doerfer 1968. 94. But it seldom occurs that Azerbaijani borrows a Persian word in cases where Khalaj has an original Turkic word, as in KhT. 190 hȧ^{i}lȧk 'sieve' <Tu. älgäk, but Az. qälbir<P. (which is, however, an older loan, not a recent one from a local dialect). On the other hand, it often occurs that only Azerbaijani has preserved the original Tu. term whereas Khalaj has borrowed a local P. loanword, e.g., 93 sǫm 'hoof' <P. som (Az. sïrnaqx); 128 hụnd^{u}vạnä 'watermelon' < P. hendovạné (Az. g̰arpuz); 157 ạ· smạ· n 'heaven' (Az. gög, göị); 86 xịrs 'bear' <P. xers (Az. ayi), etc. See Chapter 10 for more examples.

Concerning (b), a good proof of the close contact of Khalaj and Azerbaijani are the two terms for affinity by marriage: 17 kụrȧkȧn 'son-in-law' <Az. küräkän<Mo. kürägän; 19 qa^{i}narvadụ 'sister-in-law'<Az. g̰ayïn-arvadï (Az. g̰ayïn<Tu. qādïn, which, quite normally, has become qā^{a}dụn in Kh., cf. KhT. 19, KhM., X. 57). It is well known that terms of relationship by marriage in particular are easily exchanged during contacts. See TM I. 296, 340: Mo. quda 'brother-in-law,' kürägän 'son-in-law' have become familiar in many Tu. dialects. Mo. qadum 'relative by marriage' surely is a loanword<Old Bolgar *qâdŏm (= Tu. qâdïn); also C. xuń is an old loanword from Tatar qayïn (<qâdïn), via the transitions qayïn>xayïn>xoyăn> xuyn>xuń (cf. Doerfer 1967. 64-5; this is the reason why we do not find the word in the expected form: *xurăm <*qâdăm). Finally this quotation from Puşcariu 1943. 351 is relevant: "Wenn [Rumanian] nevastă 'junge Frau, Ehefrau' slavischen Ursprungs ist, so stammt dieses Wort aller Wahrscheinlichkeit nach aus der Zeit, in der die Rumänen anfingen, sich mit Slavinnen zu verheiraten. Mi-am luat o nevastă bedeutete also anfänglich nicht 'ich habe mir eine Frau genommen', sondern 'ich habe mir eine nevastă, d.h. eine slavische Frau, genommen'." To this the editor of the German version, H. Kuen, gives the following note: "So hat jedenfalls grödn. fotər 'Schwiegervater' (aus tirolisch-deutsch fotər 'Vater') zuerst den Vater der deutschen Frau des Grödners, und vgl. bertain, friaul. brut, westrätoroman. brüt, franz. bru 'Schwiegertochter' (aus german. *brūþi 'junge Frau') zuerst die junge germanische Frau des (romanischen) Sohnes bezeichnet, bevor sie die allgemeine Bedeutung angenommen haben." As to A̯šteya̯ni qa̯yenä, see below. We also find some other loanwords from Az., such as 250 ko̦k 'thick'< Az. kök (only in Az. Tu. kök 'root, basis' has taken the meaning 'thick'). For further examples see Doerfer 1968 and Chapter 5 of this work.

The Tu. loanwords in the local P. dialects never show a typically Khalaj form. These are Wa., Aš., Ka., Am., Za., Ga. (cf. Chapter 5); we also consulted Keya̯ 1335. We find three categories of Tu. loanwords in the local P. dialects (cf. the material in Doerfer 1968):

(a) Words which are found not only in the local P. dialects but also in the written language. They often seem to be not Azerbaijani, but to be derived from an earlier period (Chagatay, etc.).

(b) Words where the Kh. and the Az. forms are identical.

(c) Obviously Az. loanwords (but never obviously Kh. loanwords).

Here is a list of Tu. loanwords in the local P. dialects (extracted from Moġäddäm, cf. 5.2): 15 'bride' Ga. a̯len <gälin? (cf. TM III headword 1700); 18 'brother-in-law' Wa. ba̯ǰa̯na̯q, Ka. ba̯ǰena̯q (TM II. 682); 28 'nose' Ga. burnaq (← burun, with suffix); 74 'cat' Za. peši, 108 'owl' Wa. ba^{i}quš, Za. ba̯^{i}qoš (TM II. 715); 126 'shrub' Wa. butä, Aš. Am. bottä, Za. bötä (TM III. 779); 151 'snow-rain' Am. a̯la̯čärpo, Za. a̯la̯čelpo; 179 'room' Wa. Aš. Ka. Za. oṭa̯q, Am. ota̯qx (TM II. 189); 192 'pot, kettle' Wa. qa̯za̯nä, Aš. qezqa̯n, Am. qäzqō̄n, Za. qäzqa̯n (TM III. 1390); 200 'bed' Aš. Ka. došäk, Za. dušäk (TM II. 697);

213 'turn' Ga. qäti (TM III. 1373); 222 'collar' Wa. Aš. Ka. Za. yäxä, Am. yexä (TM IV. 1802); 244 'beautiful' Wa. Aš. Za. qäšäng (TM III. 1498); 250 'thick' Wa. kök; 272 'stale' Wa. Aš. Ka. Za. beyąt, Am. biyąt (known in P., erroneously omitted in TM); 285 'soft' Wa. Aš. Ka. Am. Za. yomušaq. Compare even 'frog' Wa. qorbąqe, Aš. qormąqe, Za. qurbąqä (TM III. 1449), not found in our list, and other words in Moġäddäm's book. Some of these words are obviously or presumably of Az. origin, such as 74 (rather = Az. pišik than = Kh. pụšụq); 151 (a typical Az. word); 222 < Az. yäxä < yaxa, not < Kh. yaqqa; 250 kök 'thick,' a typically Az. change of meaning. I shall deal with the local Az. dialect in an article in a Širaliev-Festschrift (to appear in 1969).

Keya̯ 1335, too, has many Tu. words. Some of them are obviously Az., e.g., 122 qąyenä 'mother-in-law' (< Az. g̬ay'in, not < Kh. qā^{a}dụn); qąyen bąwą 'father-in-law'; 128 qutu, qotu 'box' < local Az. g̬utu (whereas in written P. we find only qūṭī, qūtī, cf. TM III. 1569).

On the whole, we see that Azerbaijani and the local Persian dialects show mutual influences, whereas Khalaj plays no active role; Khalaj, then, has been influenced by Azerbaijani and Persian but has not influenced either of these languages.

4

BIBLIOGRAPHY AND ABBREVIATIONS

Here is a short bibliography. I cite only linguistic works (for works of historical or geographical research see references given in body of text). I include works which are to appear. At the beginning of each bibliographical entry is a reference code (usually a name and date) before a colon. I use this code throughout the text to refer to a work listed below.

Abdullaev 1967: F. A. Abdullaev, *Fonetika chorezmskix govorov. Opyt monografičeskogo opisanija oguzskogo i kipčakskogo narečij uzbekskogo jazyka* (Taškent).

Afshar 1961: Iraj Afshar, *Index Iranicus* I, 1910-1958 (Teheran).

Azizbekov 1965: X. A. Azizbekov, *Azerbajdžansko-russkij slovar'* (Baku).

Biišev 1963: A. Biišev, *"Pervičnye" dolgie glasnye v tjurkskix jazykax* (Ufa).

Doerfer 1967: Gerhard Doerfer, "Turkisch -*n*>tschuwaschisch -*m*?" *Ural-Altaische Jahrbücher* 39. 53-70 (Wiesbaden).

Doerfer 1968: G. Doerfer, "Das Chaladsch — eine archaische Türksprache in Zentralpersien," *Zeitschrift der Deutschen Morgenländischen Gesellschaft* 118. 79-112 (Wiesbaden).

Doerfer JSFOu: G. Doerfer, "Zwei wichtige Probleme der Altaistik," *Journal de la Société Finno-Ougrienne* 69: 4 (Helsinki, 1968).

Doerfer Trends: G. Doerfer, "Irano-Altaistica (Turkish and Mongolian languages of Persia and Afghanistan)," to appear in *Current Trends in Linguistics* 6 (Mouton: The Hague).

Doerfer Würzburg: G. Doerfer, "Das Chaladsch —eine neuentdeckte archaische Türksprache," to appear in the Proceedings of XVII Deutscher Orientalistentag, Würzburg (Steiner: Wiesbaden).

Essen 1953: Otto von Essen, Allgemeine und angewandte Phonetik (Berlin).

Gabain 1950: A. von Gabain, Alttürkische Grammatik (Leipzig).

Garrod 1946: Oliver Garrod, "The Qashqai Tribe of Fars," Journal of the Royal Central Asian Society 33.294-6 (London).

Jakobson 1962: Roman Jakobson, Selected Writings I ('s-Gravenhag

Jones 1949: Daniel Jones, An Outline of English Phonetics (Leipzig

Keya̯ 1335: Ṣa̯deq Keya̯, Guyeš-e A̯šteya̯n (Teheran, h.š.)

Korkmaz 1953: Zeynep Korkmaz, "Batı Anadolu ağızlarında aslı vokal uzunlukları hakkında," Türk dili araştırmaları yıllığı, Belleten, 197-203 (Ankara).

Ligeti 1938: L. Ligeti, "Les voyelles longues en turc," Journal Asiatique 230.177-204 (Paris).

Menges 1951: K.H. Menges, "Research in the Turkic Dialects of Iran. Preliminary Report on a Trip to Persia," Oriens 4.278-9 (Leiden).

Menges 1968: K.H. Menges, The Turkic Languages and Peoples (Wiesbaden).

Meyer 1965: Iben Raphael Meyer, "Bemerkungen über das Vokal— und Schriftsystem des Runentürkischen," Acta Orientalia 29.183-202 (Havniae).

Meyer Dissertation: Iben Raphael Meyer, Vokallaengde i Tyrkisk (Dissertation, Copenhagen, not yet published).

Minorsky 1940: M. Minorsky, "The Turkish Dialect of the Khalaj," *Bulletin of the Society of Oriental and African Studies* 10.417-37 (London).

Moġäddäm 1318: M. Moġäddäm, *Guyešha-ye Wäfs wä Ašteyan wä Täfräš*, Iran-Kudé 11 (Teheran, h. š.).

PhTF: *Philologiae Turcicae Fundamenta* I (Steiner Verlag: Aquis Mattiacis, 1959).

Poppe 1965: N. Poppe, *Introduction to Altaic Linguistics* (Wiesbaden).

Puşcariu 1943: Sextil Puşcariu, *Die rumänische Sprache* (Leipzig).

Radloff: Wilhelm Radloff: *Versuch eines Wörterbuches der Türk-Dialecte* I-IV, 1893-1911 (St. Petersburg).

Räsänen 1949: Martti Räsänen, *Materialien zur Lautgeschichte der türkischen Sprachen*, Studia Orientalia 15 (Helsinki).

Räsänen 1957: M. Räsänen, *Materialien zur Morphologie der türkischen Sprachen*, Studia Orientalia 21 (Helsinki).

Räzmara 1327: Ḥosäin'äli Räzmara, *Färhäng-e ǰoġrafeya'i-ye Iran* I (Teheran h. š.).

Ščerbak 1963: A.M. Ščerbak, "O tjurkskom vokalizme," *Tjurkologičeskie Issledovanija* 24-40 (Moskva, Leningrad).

Ščerbak 1967: A.M. Ščerbak, "O proisxoždenii pervičnyx dolgix glasnyx v tjurkskix jazykax," *Voprosy Jazykoznanija* 6.34-47.

Tekin 1967: Talât Tekin, "Determination of Middle Turkic Long Vowels Through ʿarūḍ," *Acta Orientalia Hungarica* 20.151-70 (Budapest).

Thomsen 1957: K. Thomsen, "The Closed 'e' in Turkish," *Acta Orientalia* 22.150-3 (Havniae).

TM: Gerhard Doerfer, Türkische und mongolische Elemente im Neupersischen I-III, 1963, 1965, 1967 (Wiesbaden).

Vasmer 1955: Max Vasmer, Russisches etymologisches Wörterbuch II (Heidelberg).

Yüknekī 1951: Edib Ahmed b. Mahmud Yüknekī, Atebetü ʾl-Hakayik, ed. Reşid Rahmeti Arat (Istanbul).

Abbreviations

Am.: local Persian dialect of Ạmoré

Aš.: local Persian dialect of Ạšteyạn

ATu.: Ancient Turkic

Az.: Azerbaijani

C.: Chuvash

CTu.: Common Turkic (all Turkic languages except for Chuvash and sometimes Yakut and Tuvinian)

Ga.: local Persian dialect of Ġärbät

K.: al-Kāšġarī, according to Divânü lûğat-it-türk, ed. Besim Atalay I-III, 1140-3 (Ankara): volumes of Tercümesi

Ka.: local Persian dialect of Kähäk

Kh.: Khalaj

KhM.: Khalaj, dialect of Mänṣur-ạbạd (shorter: M.)

KhT.: Khalaj, dialect of Tälxạb (shorter: T.)

KhX.: Khalaj, dialect of Xält-ạbạd (shorter: X.)

Mo.: Mongolian

P.: Persian

PTu.: Proto-Turkic

QB: Qutadġu Bilig, according to Reşid Rahmeti Arat, Kutadgu Bilig I, 1967, Metin (Istanbul) and to Tekin 1967

RTu.: Runic Turkic

T.: Türkmän (Turkmen, Turcoman)

Tu.: Turkic

Tuv.: Tuvinian

Wa.: local Persian dialect of Wäfs

WOD.: Western Osman (Anatolian) dialect according to Korkmaz 1953

Y.: Yakut

Za.: local Persian dialect of Zänd

Grammatical signs

. before a nominal inflectional suffix

: before a verbal inflectional suffix

+ before a nominal derivational suffix

- before a verbal derivational suffix

5
MATERIALS OF THREE DIALECTS

5.1 Introduction. In this chapter we present the materials of three dialects: Tälxa̯b, Mänṣur-a̯ba̯d, and Xält-a̯ba̯d.

(a) A word list in the dialect of Tälxa̯b. Since material about KhT. had been published by Moġäddäm previous to our expedition, we thought it would be useful to ask our authorities to verify Moġäddäm's word list. As the reader will see, our list gives many corrections of Doerfer 1968, e.g., 74 pu̯šu̯q 'cat' (not púšük), 95 pü̯f^{i}läk 'urinary bladder' (not pufläk), 188 qa̯rġọ 'reed' (not qa̯rq), 218 ī̯^{e}m 'trousers' (not 'im), etc. This dialect belongs to the northern group, having preserved ö, ü.

(b) A shorter word list of the dialects of Mänṣur-a̯ba̯d and Xält-a̯ba̯d. The first of these dialects belongs to the southern group, the second to the northern group (though ö, ü is not so fully labial as in KhT., but slightly delabialized. We indeed find many transitions in the Kh. dialects, but we did not think it useful always to write ö̯^{6}, ü̯^{6} in the KhX. material, especially as the delabialization is very slight). Tu. *kǖn 'day,' for example, is kü̯n in KhT., kü̯n (or kü̯^{6}n) in KhX., ki̯n in KhM. Northern dialects, that is, those which have preserved ö, ü (or which have delabialized these vowels slightly as in ö̯^{6}, ü̯^{6}, which are respectively ę^{5}∼i̯^{5}, i̯^{5}, but not ę∼i̯, i̯) are, apart from KhT. and X., those of Mehr-e Zämin and Ispit (but not, for example, those of Wa̯šqa̯n nor of Ča̯häk). According to Minorsky, Kondurud also has preserved ö, ü (e.g., tört 'four,' yüz 'one hundred,' hürün 'white'); also Pougerd (e.g., hürün; but Xora̯k-a̯ba̯d has e, i, not only according to our material but even according to

Minorsky's: Kondurud has hatïmï hündüm 'I mounted my horse,' whereas Xoraķ-ąbąd has hatï hindim 'I mounted the horse,' cf. 14.7, headword ûn-).

The following lists were compiled during the summer semester of 1968 by one of my classes. The members of this class were the members of the expedition plus one other participant, Mr. Parviz Radjabi, an instructor of Persian. We compiled the lists in the phonetic laboratory by listening to the tape cassettes and writing down and comparing what we heard. We checked our results again and again, so that for compiling only 541 words we had to work for a total of twenty-four hours.

5.2 Material of Tälxąb. For the etymologies cf. 14.6 and Doerfer 1968; the items enclosed in slashes (/ ... /) are less sure alternatives which our authorities identified as being Khalaj terms, but only after our investigators suggested them.

No.	Persian	German	English	KhT.	(Moġäddär
1	pedär	Vater	father	baba, dȧdȧ	(bąbą)
2	mądär	Mutter	mother	nȧnȧ	(nänä)
3	berądär	Bruder	brother	lala	(lälä)
4	xąhär	Schwester	sister	bą̄ǰų	(bąǰi)
5	pesär	Sohn	son	ǫġųl	(oqlan)
6	doxtär	Tochter	daughter	qị̄^{i}z, p^{e}i̯īz	(qïz)
7	nävé	Enkel	grandchild	nȧvȧ	(nävä)
8	nätiǰé	Urenkel	great grandchild	——	(nätiǰé)
9	bäčé	Kind	child	qą̄l	(kąl)
10	pedär-e bozorg	Großvater	grandfather	tą˙tą˙, bą˙bą˙	(tątą)
11	mądär-e bozorg	Großmutter	grandmother	ȧbȧ	(äbä)
12	märd	Mann	man	hȧr	(här)

13 zän	Frau	woman	kịšị[5]	(kši)
14 šouhär	Gatte	husband	——	(här)
15 ʿärus	Braut	bride	kåli̦n	(kälîn)
16 ʿärusi	Hochzeit	wedding	kụ̈dån	(kůdän)
17 da̬ma̬d	Schwieger-sohn	son-in-law	bå[i], båg, båG /kụråkån/	(kůräkän)
18 ba̬ǰänäq, hämriš	Schwager	brother-in-law	ba̬·ǰanax	(ba̬ǰäna̬q)
19 ǰa̬ri	Schwägerin	sister-in-law	qa[i]narvadụ, qā̬[a]dụn kịssi̦	(qäyn-a̬rva̬-di)
20 hävu	Frau desselben Mannes	wife of the same husband	——	(kůni)
21 pedär-e zän	Schwiegervater der Frau	wife's father-in-law	kịšị̌ babasụ	(äbä)
22 madär-e zän	Schwiegermutter der Frau	wife's mother-in-law	——	(äbä)
23 sär	Kopf	head	bo̬·š	(boš)
24 čäšm	Auge	eye	kö̬[2]z	(kôz)
25 možé	Wimper	eyelash	mọžä, kịprịk	(kiprik)
26 äbru	Braue	eyebrow	Ģā̬[a]š	(qa̬š)
27 guš	Ohr	ear	Gụlā̬q, Gụlā̬qʿ	(qula̬q)
28 bini	Nase	nose	bụrụn	(burun)
29 läb	Lippe	lip	å·rịn/ånnẹ/	(änne)
30 ka̬m	Gaumen	palate	qā̬m	(ka̬m)
31 zäba̬n	Zunge	tongue	tịl	(til)
32 dända̬n	Zahn	tooth	tị·š	(tiš)
33 ča̬né	Kinn	chin	ča̬·nå	(čänä)
34 riš	Bart	beard	såqqål	(säqqäl)
35 säbil	Schnurrbart	mustaches	sịbịl	(säbil)
36 mu	Flaum	down	tū̬[ü]·k, qịl	(tůk)
37 gis	Haar	hair	sa̬č	(sa̬č)
38 zolf	Locke	curl	bị[r]čåk	(birčäk)

39	gärdän	Hals	neck	bọyụn	(boyun)
40	gälu	Kehle	throat	bọġụz	(boquz)
41	siné	Brustkorb	chest	tọ̄^{ö}ˑš, Dọ̄^{ö}ˑš	(tȯš)
42	pesta̮n	Busen	bosom	mȧmȧk	(mämäk)
43	šekäm	Bauch	bellow	qa̮ˑ rụn	(qa̮ron)
44	na̮f	Nabel	navel	kụ̈ndụ̈k	(kȯndu̇k)
45	rudé	Darm	bowels	bọġa̮rsa̮ˑq	(boqa̮rsa̮q)
46	ǰegär	Leber	liver	ǰịgȧr	(ǰegär)
47	seporz	Milz	milt, spleen	tā̮lā̮q	(ta̮la̮q)
48	kämär	Taille	waist	bị̄^{e}ˑl	(bil)
49	kir	Penis	penis	čụ̈lụ̈k	(čuč)
50	kos	Cunnus	cunnus	hā̮^{ə}m	(ha̮m)
51	kun	Anus	anus	kọ̈t	(kȯt)
52	däst	Hand	hand	ȧˑl	(äl)
53	ba̮zu	Arm	arm	(cf. 223)	(qul)
54	a̮renǰ	Ellbogen	elbow	tịˑ^{r}sȧk	(tirsäg)
55	moč	Handgelenk	wrist	moč, mụ^{r}č, zụmrụq, d̄ụmrụq	(moč)
56	ängost	Finger	finger	ba̮rma̮q	(ba̮rma̮q)
57	šäst	Daumen	thumb	šā̮ba̮rma̮q	(ša̮ba̮rma̮q
58	na̮xon	Fingernagel	nail	tị^{2}rnaq	(tirna̮q)
59	pa̮	Fuss	foot	ha̮da̮q	(ha̮da̮q)
60	ra̮n	Schenkel	thigh	bụ̄^{u}ˑt	(but)
61	za̮nu	Knie	knee	tị̄z	(tiz)
62	sa̮q-e pa̮	Unter-schenkel	shank	ha̮da̮qị̄̃ a̮^{6}sDọ /qịč/	(qič)
63	qa̮b-e pa̮	Knöchel	ankle	tā̮^{ə}pā̮n, tọpụq	(topoq)
64	ru-ye pa̮	Spann	instep	ha̮da̮qị̄̃ ịụ̈zụ̈	(u̇sdȯ)
65	käff-e pa̮	Fusssohle	sole	ha̮da̮qị̄̃ a̮sDọ	(a̮sdo)
66	pust	Haut	skin	tȧrị	(täre)
67	gušt	Fleisch	flesh	ȧt	(ät)
68	pih	Fett	fat	pị̄ /ya̮ˑġ/	(pih)

69 ša̮š	Urin	urine	sị̄dȧk	(sidäk)
70 goh, än	Exkrement	excrement	ha̮rq	(ha̮rq)
71 äsb	Pferd	horse	ha̮t	(ha̮t)
72 xär	Esel	donkey	ȧšGä	(äškä)
73 säg	Hund	dog	ị̄t	(it)
74 gorbé	Katze	cat	pu̦šu̦q	(pu̇šu̇k)
75 muš	Maus	mouse	si̦čg̮ā̮n [g̱ almost ġ̱]	(sičqa̮n)
76 ga̮v	Kuh	cow	sị^{4}ġị^{4}r	(sïqïr)
77 gusfänd	Hammel	wether	yịlqï	(yilqä)
78 miš	Schaf	sheep	Çụ^{o}·n	(qun)
79 bärré	Lamm	lamb	bu̦zu̦ (sic!)	(quzû)
80 boz	Ziege	goat	ȧ^{k}či̦	(äče)
81 bozġa̮lé	Zicklein	kid	———	(oqla̮q)
82 a̮hu	Gazelle	gazelle	ǰä^{i}la̮·n [-l̲- hardly understand-able; may be r̲, d̲]	(ǰeyra̮n)
83 xärguš	Hase	hare	ta̮vụšġa̮·n	(ta̮vušqa̮n)
84 xuk	Schwein	pig	to̦n̦g̦u̦z	(dunquz)
85 gorg	Wolf	wolf	bị̄^{e}·ri̦	(bere)
86 xers	Bär	bear	xi̦rs	(xers)
87 ruba̮h	Fuchs	fox	tụ̈lkụ̈	(tu̇lkȯ)
88 šir	Löwe	lion	šị̄r	(šir)
89 bäbr	Tiger	tiger	bȧbr, pȧlȧn̦G	(bäbr)
90 päläng	Leopard	leopard	palan̦G	(päläng)
91 päšm	Wolle	wool	yụn̦^{k}	(yu̇nk)
92 dom	Schwanz	tail	qu̦d^{u}ʾru̦q	(qudruq)
93 som	Huf	hoof	so̦m, sü̦m	(som)
94 pehen	Mist	dung, manure	pẹịịn	(pehen)
95 ša̮šda̮n	Harnblase	urinary bladder	pụ̈f^{i}·läk	(pufläk)
96 äfsa̮r	Halfter	halter	afsa̮r	(a̮fsa̮r)

97 morġ	Huhn	hen	kịtʿịkᶜ	(kitik)
98 xorus	Hahn	cock	xọrọ˙ s	(xorus)
99 ǰuǰé	Küken	chicken	ǰụǰä, ǰịrịk, fȧrịk [the first word means 'pullet'; the best word is said to be ǰịrịk]	(ǰirik)
100 käbutär	Taube	dove	kọ̄^{ö}˙kȧrčịk	(kůka̯rčik)
101 käbk	Rebhuhn	partridge	qa̯˙ q^{u}˙lụ̦q	(ka̯kuluk)
102 käla̯ġ	Rabe	raven	Ç̭ā̯^{a}q	(qa̯q)
103 gonǰešk	Spatz	sparrow	Ç̭ụ̦š	(quš)
104 sa̯r	Star	starling	qaraġa̯˙ ġ, sïġirčin, sïġirčịġọ, sïġirčịu̯ọ	(sa̯r)
105 hodhod	Wiedehopf	hoopoe	hụpapaq	(hupa̯pa̯k)
106 ba̯l	Flügel	wing	qȧnȧt	(pär)
107 pär	Vogelfeder	bird's feather	yȧlȧk/ pȧr/	(yäläk)
108 ǰoġd, bum	Eule	owl	ba^{i}ġụ̦š, baị̯^{a}ġụ̦š	(ba̯yquš)
109 mägäs	Fliege	fly	qụ̦d^{u}ġụ̦	(sičäk; mis print: must be mičäk)
110 päššé	Mücke	gnat	pašša	(päššé)
111 kerm	Wurm	worm	Ç̭ū̦^{u}t	(qurt)
112 ma̯r	Schlange	snake	yịlā̯n	(ila̯n)
113 deräxt	Baum	tree	ha̯ġa̯č	(ha̯qa̯ǰ)
114 čub	Holz	wood, timber	ha̯ġa̯č	(ha̯qa̯ǰ)
115 sib	Apfel	apple	a̯^{6}lụ̦mla̯	(älomla̯)
116 gola̯bi	Birne	pear	amrū̦^{u}t	(a̯mrut)
117 a̯lu	Pflaume	plum	a̯˙ lụ	(a̯lu)
118 zärda̯lu	Aprikose	apricot	ȧrịk	(ärik)
119 šäfta̯lu	Pfirsichart	a kind of peach	šäfta̯˙lụ, hụlụ	(holu)

120	holu	Pfirsichart	a kind of peach	_____	(holu)
121	ängur	Weintraube	grape	hụḋụ̈m [d̲ almost y̲, like -d̲- in Danish gade]	(hużüm)
122	gerdu	Walnuss	walnut	yaġā̤q	(ya̤qa̤q)
123	fondoq	Haselnuss	hazelnut	fi̦ndïq̦, fi̦ndi̦⁴q	(fondoq)
124	pesté	Pistazie	pistachio	pe̦stä	(pesté)
125	ba̤da̤m	Mandel	almond	gā̤ᵃdā̤m (sic)	(ga̤da̤m)
126	buté	Strauch	shrub	pu̦˙ta	(bottä)
127	ka̤läk	Zucker-melone	sweet melon	qa̤˙lȧk	(ka̤läk)
128	hendo-va̤né	Wasser-melone	watermelon	hu̦ndᵘ̦va̤nä	(hendova̤né)
129	xeya̤r	Gurke	cucumber	xi̦ya̤r	(xeya̤r)
130	kädu	Kürbis	pumpkin	qu̦du̦	(kädu)
131	ǰuy	Bach	rivulet	aĠĠa̤˙r, aqĠa̤˙r	(a̤qa̤r)
132	kärt	Beet	bed (of a garden	qardu̦	(kärdu)
133	estäxr	Teich	pond, pool	gö̤ᵒ̈l, gȫ̤ᵒ̈l	(gül)
134	xärmän	Schober	stack, rick	xarman	(xarman)
135	da̤s	Sichel	sickle	hō̤ġraqᶜ, hō̤ġrax	(hura̤q)
136	ga̤v-a̤hän	Pflugschar	coulter	ga̤˙va̤i̤in	(ga̤väyen)
137	čärx-e xärmän-kub	Dreschgöpel	a kind of threshing machine	_____	(ča̤n)
138	xiš	Pflug	plough	xi̦š /a̤vǰa̤r/	(a̤vǰa̤r)
139	yuġ	Joch	yoke	bu̦ndᵘ̦ru̦q, bo̦ⁱndïru̦q	(bundroq)
140	čärm-e yuġ	Jochleder	yoke leather	lā̤yu̦n /lā̤yi̦n/	(la̤hin)

141	čäha̯r-ša̯x	Heugabel	pitchfork	yā̯vašịn	(ya̯väšin)
142	xa̯k	Erdboden	ground, soil	tu̦rpā̯q‘	(turpa̯q)
143	säng-e bozorg, kämär	Fels	rock	tā̯^{a}š	(ta̯š)
144	kuh	Berg	mountain	tā̯^{a}ġ	(ta̯q)
145	däšt	Steppe	steppe	dȧšt	(däšt)
146	a̯b	Wasser	water	sụ·^{v}, sụ·v	(su)
	täšné äm	ich bin durstig	I am thirsty	sụ^{v}sụzȧm	cf. 269
147	rudxa̯né	Fluss	river	čā̯^{ai}	(ča̯y)
148	bärf	Schnee	snow	Ġā̯^{a}r	(qa̯r)
149	ba̯ra̯n	Regen	rain	ya̯^{6}ġu̦š	(ya̯quš)
150	tägärg	Hagel	hail	tụ^{o}lo̦	(tolo)
151	šola̯b	Schneeregen	snow-rain	ha̯·lȧčȧlpa̯^{ġ}, a̯·lȧčȧlpa̯^{g}	(a̯läčärpo
152	äbr	Wolke	cloud	bu̦lu̦t	(bolut)
153	ba̯d	Wind	wind	ye̦·l	(yel)
154	a̯täš	Feuer	fire	hū̦^{o}t	(hot)
155	a̯hän	Eisen	iron	tȧmịr	(tämer)
156	mes	Kupfer	copper	mi̦s	(mes)
157	a̯sma̯n	Himmel	heaven	a̯·sma̯·n /kȫ̦ö̦k/	(a̯sma̯n)
158	xoršid	Sonne	sun	kụn	(kün)
159	ma̯h	Mond	moon	hā̯^{ai}	(ha̯y)
160	mähta̯b	Mondschein	moonshine	hā̯^{ai} ịšqi̦^{4}	(ha̯y išekä
161	seta̯ré	Stern	star	yu̦ldụZ	(yuldus)
162	ruz	Tag	day	kụn /kụndụz/	(kündüz)
163	šäb	Nacht	night	kī̦^{e}čä	(kečä)
164	sa̯l	Jahr	year	yịl, i̯il	(yil)
165	emruz	heute	today	bẹi̯in	(boyn)
166	diruz	gestern	yesterday	ȧ́ŋ̦gịr	(ängir)
167	dišäb	gestern Nacht	last night	ȧ́ŋ̦gịr kī̦^{e}čä	(ängir keč

168	färda̮	morgen	tomorrow	sẹbẹ	(sebe)
169	pa̮rsa̮l	letztes Jahr	last year	bị́ldịr	(bildir)
	sa̮l-e digär	nächstes Jahr	next year	yẹṇgị	______
170	säfidé-ye ṣobḥ	Morgenröte	dawn	t̯ẹ̄zdä	(sebe tezdä)
171	ẓohr	Mittag	midday	čā̮št	(ča̮št)
172	ʿäṣr, ġorub	Abend	evening	kụn ba̮tȧr	(ʿäṣr, ġorub)
173	šärq	Osten	east	kụn ča̮lȧr	(künča̮la̮r)
174	ġärb	Westen	west	kụn ba̮tȧr	(künba̮ta̮r)
175	šema̮l	Norden	north	qọllịsịyá̮˙	(kolessiya̮)
176	ǰänub	Süden	south	qị[4]blä	(qeblä)
177	xa̮né	Haus	house	hȧv	(häw)
178	ḥäya̮t, ḥeṣa̮r	umfriedeter Hof	patio	hȧsa̮˙r	(häsa̮r)
179	oṭa̮q	Zimmer	room	ọtaĠ	(oṭa̮q)
180	där	Tür	door	ī[e]˙šịk	(išik)
181	diwa̮r	Mauer, Wand	wall	dụva̮˙r	(duu̯a̮r)
182	pänǰäré	Fenster	window	pänǰȧrä	(pänǰäré)
183	sura̮x	Loch	hole	tọ̈plụ̈k	(töblik)
184	pošt-e ba̮m	Dach	roof	dā̮[a]m ịstụ̈	(da̮m)
185	pelläka̮n	Leiter	ladder	pȧläka̮˙n	(päläka̮n)
186	ḥouż	Bassin	basin, pool	hau̯ụz	(ḥäuż)
187	lulé	Röhre	tube, pipe	lụ˙lä	(lulä)
188	näy	Schilfrohr	reed	qa̮rġọ	(qa̮rq)
189	la̮nǰin	Tontrog	earthen trough	na̮˙nǰị˙n (sic)	(la̮nǰin)
190	ġärba̮l	Sieb	sieve	hȧ[i]lȧk	(häyläk)
191	kȧm	Siebrand	wooden border of the sieve	kȧm	(käm)
192	dig	Topf, Kessel	pot, kettle	ā̮šbȧ? [last consonant hardly understandable; may be č̲ or x̲́] yẹkȧlȧk	(qa̮zqa̮n)

193	dizi	Kochtopf	cooking pot	čọlmȧk	(čůlmäk)
194	sepa̯yé	Dreifuss	tripod	ȧštȧda̯·q	(äštäda̯q)
195	oǰa̯q	Herd	hearth	hụ̄^{o}·ča̯q (sic)	(hučaq)
196	kuré	Ofen	stove	kụ·rä	(kuré)
197	tänur	Backofen	oven	tụnnụ·r	(tänur)
198	xa̯kestär	Asche	ash	kụ̈l	(kůl)
199	čera̯ġ	Lampe	lamp	čịra̯ġ	(čera̯ġ)
200	došäk, tušäk	Bett	bed	dọšȧk	(tůšäk)
201	leḥa̯f	Decke	blanket	yọrġā̯n	(yorqa̯n)
202	ba̯leš	Kissen	cushion	ya̯·sDụq	(ya̯sdoq)
203	nämäd	Filz	felt	käčä	(käčä)
204	gelim	Teppich	carpet	gịlị·m	(gelim)
205	ǰa̯ru	Besen	besom	sụ̈pụ̈rǵä	(sȯpůrgä)
206	na̯n	Brot	bread	hịkmȧk	(hikmäk)
207	nämäk	Salz	salt	tụ̄^{u}·Z	(tuz)
208	a̯š	Suppe	soup	ā̯š	(a̯š)
209	šir	Milch	milk	sụ̄^{ü}·t	(sůt)
210	xa̯mé	Rahm	cream	xa̯·matọ, qā̯^{a}naq (šire poxté?)	(xa̯mätu, qa̯näq)
211	käré	Rahmbutter	cream butter	———	(kärä)
212	pänir	Käse	cheese	pẹnị·r	(penir)
213	ma̯st	saure Milch	sour milk	qa̯tụq	(qa̯toq)
214	käšg	Trockenmilch	dried milk	tụ̄^{o}·ra̯q (sic)	(tora̯q)
215	räxt	Kleidung	clothing	kȧsịk	(käsik)
216	qäba̯	langes Männergewand	long clothes of men	kȧsịk /a^{r}xa̯lụq, arqa̯lụq/	(a̯rxa̯loq)
217	pira̯hän	Hemd	shirt	tụ̄^{o}n	(toun)
218	ǰälva̯r	Hose	trousers	ị̄^{e}·m	(ím)
219	ǰoura̯b	Strumpf	stocking	ǰọ·ra̯·b	(ǰoura̯b)
220	kola̯h	Hut	hat	bọ̈^{ö}·k	(bůrk)

221	käfš	Schuh	shoe	u̦rsu̦q, ha̮da̮q qā̮^{a}bo̮	(ha̮da̮qqa̮bo)
222	yäqé	Kragen	collar	yaqqa	(yäxä)
223	a̮stin	Ärmel	sleeve	qụ^{o}·l	(qul)
224	da̮män	Saum	seam	ḣȧṫȧk	(hätäk)
225	a̮stär	Futter	lining	a̮stȧr	(a̮stär)
226	näx	Faden	thread	bị̄^{e}·š^{i}·mi̦	(boyšimä)
227	risma̮n	Schnur	cord	qa̮tma	(yiplik)
228	ṭäna̮b	Seil	rope	ṫȧna̮˙f, ṫȧna̮˙B	(täna̮f)
229	tišé	Beil	hatchet	kȧsȧr	(käsär)
230	ärré	Säge	saw	harra	(ha̮rra̮)
231	mätté	Bohrer	drill, borer	mättä, mịyä	(miyä)
232	täxté	Brett	plank	taxDa	(täxté)
233	tišé-ye xa̮r-käni	Axt	axe	tavarču̦q^{c}	(ta̮va̮rčuk)
234	ma̮lé	Kelle, Spatel	ladle, trowel	ma˙la	(ma̮lé)
235	bil	Schaufel	shovel	bị^{e}·l	(bil)
236	xešt	Ziegel	brick	xịšt	(xešt)
237	pa̮ru	Ruder	oar	kụrǵȧk, kụryȧk	(kürgäk)
238	xub	gut	good	ha̮vụl	(ha̮vol)
	xub nist	ist nicht gut	is not good	ha̮vụl da̮^{6}ġ	______
239	bäd	schlecht	bad	______	(pis)
240	ra̮st	gerade	straight	to̦ǧru̦	(ra̮st)
241	käǰ	krumm	crooked	äyri̦	(käǰ)
242	roušän	hell	bright	ị^{4}šị^{4}q	(išiq)
243	ta̮rik	dunkel	dark	qa̮rā̮lu̦x	(qa̮ra̮loq)
244	xušgel	schön	beautiful	qȧšȧn̦G	(qäšäng)
245	zešt	hässlich	ugly	pī̤s	(pis)
246	när	männlich	male	hị˙rkȧk	(hirkäk)
247	ma̮dé	weiblich	female	tịšị	(tišé)
248	pir	alt	old	______	(qa̮rri)

249	ǰävḁn	jung	young	ǰävḁ˙n /ǰḁ˙hi̦l, ǰḁ˙i̯o̯l/	(igit)
250	čḁq	dick	thick	kọ̈k	(kȯk)
251	lḁġär	dünn	thin	hḁrqā̰n, i̦dbḁ˙r	(hḁrqḁn)
252	kučäk	klein	small	balla	(bḁllḁ)
253	bozorg	gross	big	bidik, yäkGä [hardly understandable]	(yekgä)
254	säbok	leicht	light	yü̦n̦gü̦l	(yu̇ngu̇l)
255	sängin	schwer	heavy	qu̦ʳs	(qurs)
256	tär	feucht	wet	họ̈ᵒ·l	(hȯl)
257	xošg	trocken	dry	qu̦rru̦Ġ	(qurruq)
258	tiz	scharf	sharp	tu̦nt, yi̦tDi̦	(yitti)
259	kond	stumpf	blunt	ku̦nt, kü̦nt, ko̯nt	(kond)
260	derḁz	lang	long	u̦zā̰q	(uzḁq)
261	kutḁh	kurz	short	qïsqȧ	(qïsqä)
262	bḁrik	schmal	narrow, thin	nḁ˙zu̦q /hȧnsi̦z [said to be Az. by an authority]/	(häniz)
263	pähn	breit	broad	hȧnli̦Ġ	(hänlix)
264	täng	eng	narrow, tight	tā̰ᵃr	(tḁr)
265	dur	fern	far	?i̦rā̰q [anlaut hardly understandable]	(yirḁq)
266	näzdik	nah	near	yo̦ġu̦q	(yuvoq)
267	sir	satt	satisfied, having eaten one's fill	to̦x, to̦q	(toq)
268	gorosné	hungrig	hungry	ā̰ᵃč	(ḁǰ)
269	täšné	durstig	thirsty	su̦˙ᵛsu̦z	(susus)
270	tḁzé	frisch, neu	fresh, new	tḁ˙zä	(tḁzé)

271 kohné	alt	old	kọ˙na	(kohné)
272 beya̯t	altbacken	stale	bẹyā̯t	(beya̯t)
273 sur	salzig	salty	šọ˙r, hā̯^{a}čụx	(ha̯čöx)
274 širin	süss	sweet	šịrịn	(širin)
275 čärb	fett	fat	yā̯^{a}glụx	(ya̯qlo)
276 tälx	bitter	bitter	hā̯^{a}čụx	(ha̯čöx)
277 tond	gewürzt, scharf	bitingly seasoned	tụnt	(tond)
278 torš	sauer	sour, acid	tụ^{r}š, tụš	(turš)
279 särd	kalt	cold	bụ̄^{u}˙z	(buz)
280 gärm	warm	warm	hịssị^{y}	(hisdi)
281 xonok	kühl	cool	sȧrịn, bụ̄^{u}˙z	(xonok)
282 säxt	hart	hard	sọụ̂ụq	(säxt)
283 seft	stark	strong	bȧk	(bärk)
284 šel	schwach	weak	čọla̯q	(boš)
285 närm	weich	soft	narm /yụm^{u}ša̯q/	(yomuša̯q)
286 por	voll	full	tụ^{o}la	(tola̯)
287 ǰelou	vorn	before	yịlġȧr [g̲ spoken almost as y̲]	(ilgär)
288 ʿäqäb	hinten	after	ha̯˙ġa̯	(ha̯qa̯)
289 säfid	weiss	white	hụ̇rụ̇n	(hu̇ru̇n)
290 seya̯h	schwarz	black	G̬a̯ra	(a̯ra̯)
291 zärd	gelb	yellow	sā̯^{a}rụx	(sa̯rox)
292 säbz	grün	green	yā̯^{a}šụl	(ku̇k)
293 a̯bi	hellblau	light-blue	______	(a̯bi)
294 käbud	blau	blue	kụ̄^{ö}˙k (cf. 157)	(gu̇y)
295 sorx	rot	red	G̬ị^{4}rmïzị^{4}	(q̈irmïz)
296 benäfš	lila	violet	bȧnȧ^{f}š	(benäfš)
297 bala̯	oben	above	kọ̄^{ö}˙k, ụǰa̯ /yọqqa̯r/	(yoqqa̯r)
298 pa̯ʾin	unten	beneath	ị̄^{e}˙nä	(enä)

299	yäk	eins	one	bī
300	du	zwei	two	ȧkkụ̈
301	se	drei	three	ụ̈̄š
302	čähạr	vier	four	tọ̄ᵒ·rt
303	pänǰ	fünf	five	bị̄ᵉ·š
304	šäš	sechs	six	ạltạ
305	häft	sieben	seven	yättị
306	häšt	acht	eight	säkkịz
307	noh	neun	nine	tọqqụz
308	däh	zehn	ten	ᵘ̂ọ·n
309	yạzdäh	elf	eleven	ọn bị̄
310	bist	zwanzig	twenty	yịịirmị
311	si	dreissig	thirty	họtDụz
312	čehel	vierzig	forty	qị⁴rq
313	pänǰạh	fünfzig	fifty	ȧllịʸ
314	šäst	sechzig	sixty	altmụš
315	häftạd	siebzig	seventy	yätmịš
316	häštạd	achtzig	eighty	ḣȧštạ·d, sẹⁱ̂sȧn [hardly understandable; may be sẹⁱ́xsȧn]
317	näväd	neunzig	ninety	nȧvȧd, Dọxsan
318	ṣäd	hundert	a hundred	yụ̈̄z
319	häzạr	tausend	a thousand	mịn

5.3 Materials of Mänṡur-ạbạd and Xält-ạbạd.

No.	Persian	English	Mänṡur-ạbạd	Xält-ạbạd
1	seyạh	black	Ǧạra	______
2	boz	goat	ȧččị	ȧkk´ụ̈
3	däst	hand	ȧ·l	ȧl
4	sib	apple	ạ⁶lụmlạ	ạ⁶lọmlạ
5	diruz	yesterday	ȧ´ṇgịʳ	ȧ´ṇᵍụ̈r
	dišäb	last night	ȧ´ṇgịʳ kị̄ᵉ·čä	ȧ´ṇᵍụ̈r kị̄ᵉ·čä

6	läb	lip	ȧ· rịn	lȧb, lọ^{u}
7	bud	it was	———	———
8	äsb	horse	hḁt	hḁt
	xär	donkey	ȧšGä	ȧškä, ȧšGä
9	sepḁyé	tripod	ȧštȧdḁq	ȧštädḁq
10	xodḁ	God	xụdḁ	———
11	gorg	wolf	bī̤^{e}ri̤^{l}	bī̤^{e}·rị^{l}
12	kämär	waist	bī̤·^{e}l	kȧmȧrbȧnd /bī̤·^{e}l/
13	rudé	bowels	bọġḁrsụq	ru· dḁ
14	gärdän	neck	bọġụZ	bọġzụm, bọġụz
15	sär	head	bḁ· š	bḁ· š
16	emruz	today	bệi̤n	bṳ́i̤^{ü}·n
17	näx	thread	bī̤·^{e}šmị	bē̤š^{i}·mị
18	kolḁh	hat	bi̤· riȧk	bịriȧk
19	xub nist	is not good	hḁ^{6}vụl dḁġ	hḁvụl dḁġ
20	tälx	bitter	hā̤^{a}čụ^{q}x	zȧ·r (<P. zähr) [in the discussion we heard hā̤^{ə}či̤^{q}x dḁġ, širịn är]
21	deräxt	tree	hḁġḁč	dịräxt/hḁġḁč, hụ̈ʔtụn [the last word explained as čub 'wood']
22	pḁ	foot	hḁdḁG	———
23	lḁgär	meager, slack	ịdbḁ·r	ịdbḁ·r, lḁ·gär
24	ärré	saw	hḁrrḁ	ȧrrä
25	äsp	horse	———	hḁt
26	xub	good	hḁvụl	hḁvụl
27	goftän	to say	hḁ·^{i}d^{u}lḁ^{6}r	hḁ^{i}maq (sic)
28	bḁrik	narrow	nḁ·zụq	nḁ·zụq [hȧnsịz explained as ụzāq dḁġ 'not long']
29	pähn	broad	kī̤·^{e}n̦^{k} /hȧnli̦^{g}x/	———
30	xḁné	house	hȧv	họ̈^{ü}
31	ġärbḁl	sieve	hȧlyäk′	hä^{i}lȧk

32	sa̭xtän	to make	ị̄^{e}·tt·^{i}lä^{l}r, ị^{e}t^{i}ṛäk	———
33	na̭n	bread	hịk′mäk′	hịkmȧk
34	gärm	warm	hịssị	hịssị^{ǵ}
35	a̭täš	fire	hụ̄^{o}·t	hụ̄^{o}·t
36	tär	wet	hị̄^{e}·l	hị̄^{e}·l
37	oǰa̭q	hearth	hụ̄^{o}·ča̭·q	kȧlȧk
38	da̭s	sickle	dȧsġa̭lä	dȧsġa̭lä, dȧsġa̭lä[5]
39	säfid	white	hịrịn	hụrụn
40	ǰelou	before	ịlyä^{l}r	ị^{l}lgär
41	där	door	ị̄^{e}·šịk	ị̄^{e}šịk
42	ferestȧdän	to send	sịrd·^{i}lä^{l}r	yo̭·lla̭[6]maq /sụrmȧk/
43	šälva̭r	trousers	ị̄^{e}·m	ị̄^{e}·m
44	bäčé	child	qā̭l	qā̭l
45	nämäd	felt	———	———
46	ʿärus	bride	kȧlịn (and kịdȧ̂ịi 'bride-groom')	kȧlụn
47	šäb	night	kị̄^{e}·čä	kị̄^{e}·čä
48	na̭f	navel	kịndịkʿ	kụndụk
49	čäšm	eye	kị^{l}z	kö̭z
50	suxtän	to burn	kị^{e}·ndị	kö̭·nmäk
51	säbz	green	kị̄^{e}·k	kȫ̭^{o}k
52	xoršid	sun	kịn	kụn
53	pa̭ru	oar	kịryäk	pa̭·ro̭
54	ʿärusi	wedding	kịdȧn	kụdȧn
55	käbutär	dove	gȧ^{5}uȧ^{r}čịn [?, almost gȧlȧ^{r}k′ịn]	kȧftȧr
56	zän	woman	kịšị (and hȧr 'man')	kịšị
57		affinity by marriage		
	pedär-e zän	husband's father-in-law	kịšịm dȧdȧsị	kịšị babasị

	ma̯där-e zän	husband's mother-in-law	qā̯^{a}di̦n ȧbä̇	qā̯^{a}d̈in ȧbȧ, qā̯^{a}du̦n ȧbȧ
	bera̯där-e zän	husband's brother-in-law	qā̯^{a}du̦n	kịšị lalas̈i
	xa̯här-e zän	husband's sister-in-law	———	kịšị ḋȧdȧsị
	pedär-e šouhär	wife's father-in-law	———	hȧrị babas̈i
	ma̯där-e šouhär	wife's mother-in-law	———	qā̯^{a}d̈in ba̯ba̯
	bera̯där-e šouhär	wife's brother-in-law	———	qā̯^{a}d̈in hȧrịm
	xa̯här-e šouhär	wife's sister-in-law	———	———
58	deräxt-e bozorg	big tree	bịdịk ha̯ğa̯č	———
59	ẓolm	angry	bȧdî̦ẹtmä, a̯za̯˙b	———
60	koda̯m	which	qā̯^{a}nị	qā̯^{a}ni̦
61	za̯mé	cream	xa̯˙mȧtu̦, qā̯^{a}-naq [for the last word ru-ye šir was also given, as was sịlt 'milk']	xa̯˙ mȧtu̦, qā̯^{a}naq
62	šekäm	bellow	qa̯˙ru̦n	qa̯˙r̈in
63	pir	old	qa̯rrị	———
64	sa̯q-e pa̯	shank	mụ^{r}č	———
65	doxtär	daughter	qī̤^{4z}	———
66	kuta̯h	short	qu̦la̯ (cf. 90)	———
67	dom	tail	qu̦rdu̦q	do̯m [another person interferes: qu̦rdu̦q]
68	ba̯zu	arm	qo̯l	qo̯˙l
69	guš	ear	qu̦la̯q	qo̯lā̯qʿ
70	miš	sheep	qo̯n	qo̯˙n
71	xošg	dry	qu̦rru̦^{ġ}	qu̦rru̦ġ
72	gonješk	sparrow	Gu̦š	Gu̦š

73	zärd	yellow	č̬aqụr	sā̬^{a}ro̬^{g}, sā̬ro̬^{g}
74	mägäs	fly	qụdġị^{4}	mȧgȧs
75	ša̬š	urine	sị˙däk	sị˙däk
76	muš	mouse	sịčġā̬n	sị^{4}čġā̬n
77	ga̬v	cow	sị^{4}ġị^{4}r	sïġïr
78	a̬b	water	sụ˙v	sū̬
79	kuh	mountain	tȧBȧ	tā̬^{a}ġ
80	täng	narrow	tā̬^{a}r	tā̬^{a}r
81	xärguš	hare	to̬vụšġā̬n	to̬^{u}ụšġā̬n
82	zäba̬n	tongue	tị˙l	tị̬l
83	käšg	dried milk	tụ^{o}ra̬˙q	tụ^{o}ra̬˙q
84	pira̬hän	shirt	tū̬^{o}n	tū̬^{o}n
85	siné	chest	k^{i}ẹ^{i} [hardly understandable]	tō̬^{ü}š
86	xa̬b räftän	to (go to) sleep	yā̬tma	ya̬tmïš, ū̬ča̬, ū̬qa̬ ɓa̬rmịš
87	piya̬dé	on foot	ī̬^{e}nȧ^{k}	______
	säva̬r šodän	to mount	hī̬nȧk	______
88	gärdu	nut	yo̬ġa̬˙q	yaġa̬˙q
89	sa̬l	year	yị˙l	yị˙l
	emsa̬l	this year	______	bụ̂ịl
	sa̬l-e digär	next year	______	kȧlȧn yịl
	sa̬l-e goza̬šté	last year	______	kȧšgụ̈lị (? kȧ^{t}šgụ̈lị) ịịl, bụldụr
90	dur	far	hịrā̬q	tụ̈rkä^{r} [? 'is far'], yịrā̬q
	näzdik	near	qo̬la̬^{i} (cf. 66)	yo̬^{u}q
91	yäk	one	bī̬	bī̬
92	do	two	ȧkkị	ȧkkị
93	se	three	ī̬č	ṻ̬š
94	čäha̬r	four	tī̬^{e}rt	tō̬̈^{o}rt
95	pänǰ	five	bī̬^{e}š	bī̬^{e}š

96	šäš	six	a̯lta̯, a̯⁶lta̯	a̯lta̯
97	häft	seven	yätti̤	yätti̦
98	häšt	eight	säkki̦z	säkki̦z
99	noh	nine	to̦qqu̦z	to̦qqu̦z
100	däh	ten	ṳ̄o̦n	o̦ˑn, ᵒō̦n
101	ya̯zdäh	eleven	o̦²ˑ n bī̤	o̦n bī̤
102	bist	twenty	yī̤ⁱˑrmi̤	yi̤gi̤rmi̦
103	si	thirty	ho̦ttu̦z	ho̦ttu̦z
104	čehel	forty	qi̤⁴ rq	qïrq
105	pänǯa̯h	fifty	à'lli̤	àlli̤ᵍ́
106	šäst	sixty	a̯¹ tmi̤š	a̯ltmi̤š /àkkⁱ-o̦ttu̦z/
107	häfta̯d	seventy	yätmi̤š	hàfta̯ˑd /àkkⁱ-o̦ttu̦z-o̦ˑn/
108	hašta̯d	eighty	saⁱ̂san	hàšta̯ˑd
109	näväd	ninety	to̦ᵠxsan	nàvàd
110	ṣäd	a hundred	yi̤ˑ z	yṳ̄z
111	häza̯r	a thousand	mi̤n̦ᵏ	———

This list includes, of course, the mistakes so typical of first investigations of languages. For example, KhT. 63 tāᵃpā̯n presumably is not 'ankle' but 'sole'; KhT. 65 ha̯da̯qī̤ a̯sDo̦ presumably is not 'sole' but 'shank'; KhT. 184 dā̯ᵃm i̤stṳ̈ presumably is not 'roof but 'on the roof' or 'the upper side of the roof'; KhT. 284 čo̦la̯q presumably is not 'weak' but 'cripple'; KhX. 14 bo̦ǧzu̦m is not 'neck' but 'my neck' or even 'my throat'; KhX. 57 seems to contain many misunderstandings; KhX. 86 ṳ̄ča̯ is not 'to sleep' or 'to go to sleep' but 'in sleep, during sleep'.

6
MOĠÄDDÄM'S MATERIAL

On the following facsimile pages we publish Moġäddäm's Khalaj material (only this, not the whole book), since it can be obtained only with difficulty, yet will always have some historical value in the development of our knowledge of Khalaj. For the transcription, (German) translation, etc., cf. Doerfer 1968. We omitted the list of misprints, because it contains very few Khalaj corrections, already noted and considered in Doerfer 1968. We have rendered: (1) Moġäddäm's remarks about his stay among the Khalaj (p. 22); (2) Moġäddäm's explanation of his transcription and the dictionary itself (pp. 25-92; we do not include the whole dictionary, which continues giving verbs up to p. 108, but here Moġäddäm's record of Khalaj words has stopped); (3) Moġäddäm's remarks about the difference between Azerbaijani and Khalaj (pp. 152-156).

۲۲

خلج

چون برای نگارنده فرصت دست نداد که بمرکز خلج ها در قاصی خلجستان بروم نمونهٔ این گویش را از چند نفر خلج که در تلخاب فراهان رعیت بودند بدست آوردم . بررسی دامنه دارتری در بارهٔ این گویش بی ارزش نخواهد بود .

غربت

غربتها چادرنشین هستند وخودرا "ایلِ فیوُج" می خوانند . از بیست سال پیش برای گرفتن شناسنامه ناچار شده اند که ملک یا کشتزاری بخرند و رعیت آن محل بشوند. اکنون ۵ ماه در ملک هستند و

هفت ماه دوره گردی
میکنند. غربتها بمردم دیگر
دختر نمیدهند ولی از دیگران
زن میگیرند. دسته ای که
به آنها در خنجین برخوردیم
۱۲ خانوار بودند و اصل
خود را از شیراز میدانستند.
مرکز آنها در اُشُق در
بلوک چَرّا (یا شَرّا) میان
همدان و اراک است.

غربتها در ایران بنامهای
گوناگون شناخته میشوند.
در بیشتر جاها آنها را کولی یا
غربیل بند یا قِرِشمال مینامند.
در مازندران آنها را جوکی
و در شیراز غربتو و لولی
میخوانند.

لولیان در سراسر جهان
به خنیاگری شهرت دارند.
(حتی لیست Liszt موزیک
ملی مجار را از اصل لولی میداند)
از اینرو در برخی جاها آنها را
چنگی و چنگیان و چنگنه یا

چگانه (چغانه ؟) مینامند. در ترکیه و یونان بهمین نام خوانده میشوند و این واژه بصورتهای Atzigan و Tsigane و Czigany و Zigeuner و Zingari به کشورهای بالکان و مجارستان و آلمان و ایتالیا و فرانسه رفته است. (کولیها در اروپا خود را رُم میخوانند.) بررسیهائی که در اروپا انجام گرفته بستگی گویش کولیهای اروپا را با گویشهای هندی آشکار ساخته است.

کار کولیها در اروپا مانند ایران غربیل بندی و بافتن توری و دام و آهنگری و مسگری است و زنان کولی برای جادو و سحر و کف بینی شهرت دارند.

کولی های ایران دیگر انرا "تاتاش" میخوانند و بگفته دُرگان جوکیهای استراباد دیگر انرا "تَنِش" مینامند.

~~~

چند نشانه که در جدول واژه ها بکار رفته

= بجای واژه در ستون هر گویش نشان میدهد که در آن گویش همان واژهٔ فارسی را بکار میبرند.

X بجای واژه در ستون هر گویش نشان میدهد که آن واژه را در آن گویش ندارند و بکار نمیبرند.

— بجای واژه در ستون هر گویش نشان میدهد که آن واژه در آن گویش پرسیده نشده است.

رقم های پیش از واژه های فارسی در هر ردیف نشان میدهد که آن واژه در "واژه نامهٔ طبری" (شمارهٔ ۹ ایران کوده) آمده و خواننده باید به آن شماره در "واژه نامهٔ طبری" برگردد.
~~~

نشانه‌هائی که در جدول واژه‌ها بکار رفته

کخ میان ک و خ خوانده شود. (درگویش آمره شنیده میشود.)

قخ میان ق و خ خوانده شود. (درگویش آمره و ترکی شنیده میشود.)

ق مانند ق (= غ) فارسی خوانده شود.

غ فقط درگویش ترکی بکار رفته و صدای آن به ۊ نزدیک میشود.

چ میان ج و چ خوانده شود. (درگویش آمره شنیده میشود.)

ۊ مانند و کُردی و عربی و درفارسی در "جو" و "نو". (ﺳ روی حرف مانند فارسی خوانده شود.)

زبر (اَ) و زیر (اِ) و پیش (اُ) مانند فارسی خوانده شود. نشانهٔ پیش (د) هرگاه زیر حرف باشد (اِ) اُخوانده شود با میل بسوی اِ (مانند ö آلمانی).

آ (اول) و ا (آخر) کشیده و مانند فارسی (آب - با) خوانده شود.

ا (آخر) همان صوت است کشیده ولی بُریده و درگویش ترکی شنیده میشود.

ی ی ی کشیده و مانند فارسی (بی - نیز) خوانده شود. ی ی ی همان صوت است کشیده ولی بریده و درگویش ترکی شنیده میشود.

وُ سوُ کشیده و مانند فارسی (او - بو) خوانده شود. وِ سوِ همان صوت کشیده است با میل بسوی زیر (مانند ü آلمانی).

آُ مانند آ فارسی کشیده ولی باکمی غنّه و میل بسوی اُ خوانده شود.

خط – روی صوت نشانهٔ اینست که روی آن صوت باید درنگ بیشتری بشود.

حرفها و نشانه‌های دیگر مانند فارسی خوانده شود.

		وفس	آشتیانی	کهک	آمره	زند	غربت	خلج	ترکی
۱۹۰.	پدر	بُوَ (باوَ)	پُوا / اشُووَ	پپیَ	شپیَ	بُوَ	بهانگ	بابا	دَدَ
۷۰۷.	مادر	نَنَ	نَنَ / نا	مُو	ما	نَنَ	ماقپس	نَنَ	نَنَ
۱۰۵.	برادر	برا	براز / آقِ	برا	برا	برا	برانگ	لَلَ	قارداش
۳۲۳.	خواهر	خاکَ	خووِاکَ	خاکَ	خوواخَ	خوویشک	خاهانگ	باجی	باجی
۳۹۸.	پسر	لازَ / لیلِ	پور / لازِ	لیلَ / پور	پور	کُر	پُشتر	اُقلان	اُغلان
۳۴۰ و ۶۳۱.	دختر	کِلِ	دِت	دِت	دِتک	دووَت	دیهپر	قیز	قیز
	نوه	رُووِزا	رُووِزا	نَوَ	—	نَوَ	×	نَوَ	نِوَ
	نتیجه	رُووِزا اُوزا	رُووِندِ	=	—	—	×	=	=

٢٧

٠٧٨٠	بچه	زارو	لازک	رند	روودند	جقل	جاد	کال	اوشاخ
٠٦٣٩	پدربزرگ	باپور	{بابا ژان / بابا مسدر}	پیی مسدر	شپی مسدر	بووگوور	بهانگ	بهانگ تاتا	بابا
٠١٥٢	مادربزرگ	خان نن	{نن ژان / نن مسدر}	ماما مسدر	ماسدر	دای	ماقیس	ماقیس اب	خان
٠٥٠٨	عمو	آمو	آمو	آمو	آمو	امو	لامو	—	ام
٠١٦٤	عمه	امه	امّ	ام	امه	پیپی	X	—	{امه / بی بی}
٠٥٤٣	دائی	دای	دائی	دائی	دای	خالو	X	—	دائی
٠٧١٦	خاله	{لاله / دیز}	خالک	خالک	خوواخما	پیپی	لاخ	—	خال
٠٧١٨	مرد	مرد (مرد)	مرد	میرکرد	مرد	پیاک	تک	هر	کیشی
٠٤٠٧	زن	{زن / زنک}	زنی	زن	زن	ژن	ندو	کشی	آزواد

		وفس	آشتیان	کهک	آمره	زند	غربت	خلج	ترکی
۴۹۷.	شوهر	شُو	شُو	شُو	شو		مک	هر	ار
۵۰۶.	عروس	ویوَ	آروش	اروسَ	اروسَ	ویو	آرِن	گلین	گلین
۸۰۱.	عروسی	تووی	آروسی	اروسی	تووی	اروسی	آلِندی	کودَن	قی
۴۱۲.	داماد	زاوا	زاما	زاما	زما	دامادَ	X	کورکن	کورکن
	باجناق (همریش)	باجناق	همباجناق / همپاچ	باجناق	—	هامپاچ	—	باجناق	باجاناق
	جاری	هیوَرزن	هماروش	هماروش	—	هام ویو	—	قیناروادی	قاین خاتونی
	هوو	هوَ	خوَ	خوَ	خوی	هوو	دزنا	کونی	گونی
	خواهرشوهر	وپیت	—	—	—	خوونگ شو	X	—	یزنَ

	پدرزن	—	—	پپی زَن	شپی زنر	بوژن	بهانگ ندو	اَبَ	قاین آتا
	مادرزن	—	—	موزَن	مازنر	دالک ژن	ماقس ندو	اَب	قاین نَنَ
	کله { سر	{ سرک / گل / (کودوء)	{ = / =	{ گل / مَن	=	{ = / =	گلور	بش	باش
۲۸۴.	چشم	چم	=	=	=	چو	نهور	کز	وگز
۷۱۳.	مژه	رمز	موچشم	مجی	پچ	مج	×	کبترک	کبترک
۱۰۷.	ابرو	اَترو	=	=	ابرو	=	×	قاش	قاش
	پیشانی	=	=	=	پیشی	پوشانی	×	—	آتی + آل
	گوش	=	=	=	=	=	کن	قولاق	قلاق
۸۱۱.	بینی	ونیی	ونی	داماق	ونیی	لوت	بورناق	بورون	{ بورن / بورون
۶۹۸.	لب	لو	لو	لو	لو	لچ	×	اَن	دوداق

		وفس	آشتیانی	کهک	آمره	زند	غربت	خلج	ترکی
۳۷۳.	دهان	دان	=	دوون	دن	دم	دشنا	–	آغز آغز
	کام (سق دهان)	ساک	ساک	ساق	ساکخ	ساق	×	کام	ساق
	زبان	زووان	زووان	زووان	زن	زووان	×	تپل	دیل
	دندان	دندان	دندان	=	دندن	دپیان	دندری	تیش	دیش
۵۵۱.	زنخ (چانه)	چان	چان	=	زنخ	چن	×	چن	چن
	ریش	=	=	=	=	=	والی	سقل	سقل
۱۱۰(۲).	سبیل	سفیل	=	=	=	سیول	×	=	بغ
	مو	=	=	=	مو	مو	پتکائی	توک	توک

		وفس	آشتیان	کهک	آمره	زند	غربت	خلج	ترکی
	جگر	=	=	جیگر	=	جگر	×	=	جیگر
۸۰۰.	قلوه (گرده)	وک	وک	قلب	وک	گرچال	×	—	گربک، گردال
	سپرز	اسپز	اسپرز	اشفرز	اسپز	رسپل	×	تالاق	دالاغ
	کمر	=	=	کمر	=	=	×	بیل	بل
۳۰۴.	کیر	کر	کر	کر (کل)	کر	=	گرگون	چوچ	سیک
۵۷۳.	کس	=	=	= (وک)	=	=	هرت	هام	آم
۶۳۲.	کون	کون	=	فون	افون	کپنگ	نیک	کت	گت
۸۴.	دست	=	=	=	=	=	خت	ال	ال

	گیس	گیسَ	=	=		=	والی	ساچ	ساچ
	کاکل	=	=	=	کاکُل	کوکُل	والی		کوکول
	زلف	=	=	=	زُلف	=	والی	پرچک	پرچک
	گردن	=	=	=	گردن	دل	×	بیون	بین
۶۵۶.	گلو	{گُل / گُل}	گلو	نو	نا	گلو	×	بقوز	بغاز
	سینه	سینَ	=	=	سینَ	سینک	سینکی	تُش	دُش
	پستان	چِز	=	=	ننگ	ممک	×	ممک	اَمجک
۳۷ و ۱۲۲.	شکم (دل)	تَلّ	{تل / اشکم}	اشکم	تله	{زک / دل}	پیتو	قارن	{قارن / قارن}
۶۳۵.	ناف	ناف	=	=	=	نوک	×	کندوک	گبک
۳۸۹.	روده	لووال	=	=	=	رود	×	بقارساق	باقرساق

	بازو	=	=	=	=	بال	×	قول	قل
۰۴۵	آرنج	کیلیزن	=	کل‌وشت	=	نارنج	×	تیرسنگ	دیرسنگ
	مچ	مرنج	مرنج	مرنج	مرنج	مچ	×	مچ	بیلک
	کف‌دست	{ = نان‌مشت	=	=	=	=	×	×	اوج
۰۵۶	انگشت	انگشت	انگشت		انگشت	کلیک	×	بارماق	بارماخ
	شست	{ شانگشت شاهنگشت	شاانگشت	=	شاهنگشت	=	×	شابارماق	بیک‌بارماخ
	ناخن	=	=	=	نخن	ناخن	×	تیرناق	درناق
۰۷۰۵	پا	=	=	=	=	=	پاقلم	هاداق	ایاقخ
۰۳۹۷	ران	ران	=	=	رن	=	×	بوت	بود

۳۴

		وفس	آشتیان	کهک	آمره	زند	غربت	خلج	ترکی
۴۰۹.	زانو	ارزانِ	=	=	=	زانو / کُنگُک	×	تیز	دیز
۴۱۷.	ساق پا	قَلَمبَ	قَلَم	ساقِ پو	قَلَم پا	قَلَم	×	قیج	قلم / اولار
	(قوزک) قاب پا	قاپ پای	قاپ پا	قاپک	قافک	قاپق	×	تپق	تپق
۵۳۸.	پاشنه	=	=	=	پشن	=	×	–	دیابان
	روی پا	دپوپای	اَبری پا	پشتِ پو	دم پا	بان پا	×	اوشد [رو]	ایاق اوزی
	کف پا	زرپای	–	زیرپو		=	×	آشد [زیر]	ایاق آستی
	پوست	پوشد	=	پوشدی	=	پوش	چمی	تَر	دری
	گوشت	=	=	=	=	=	ذهوت	اَت	اَت
	پیه (پی)	=	=	پپی	=	=	×	=	=

۳۵

	رگ	رپی	=	=	رگ	=	X	—	دامار
	خون	=	=	=	خون	خون	لیپن	—	قان
	عرق	ازاق	=	=	ارغ	=	×	—	ترک
۵۷۵.	شاش	{پیشو / زراب}	چر	چر	چر	میز	شلوک	سیدک	اپشک
۶۶۸.	گه (آن)	{گو / چر}	آن	گو	آن	گو	گاز	هارق	بخ
	قی	قیپیان	—	=	=	قیان	×	—	قیان
۴۰۴.	آب بینی	اودینی	نک	نک	بیک	نک	×	—	برن سوی
۵۹۳.	سرفه	کلکل	=	{کل / کلک}	که	کووک	ترف	—	اسکرم
۵۱۰.	عطسه	سزن	=	—	—	پشم	{پک / ترب}	—	{آشقرم / آقرم}

	دفس	آشتیان	کهک	آمره	زند	غربت	خلج	ترکی
۳۷۴. دهان دره	دانزِلِ	دنانزر	دُدُنزر	دهندر	آثارگی	×	—	{آنگمگ / آشماق}
جان	گان	=	=	گیپی	گیان	جونکام	—	=
تن	{= / بدن}	جان	=	=	لش	×	—	{بدن / جان}
۳۸۵. (دیم) صورت	دیو	دیم	دیم	دیم	سورت	م	—	اوز
تخم (خایه)	خای	{تخم / خای}	تخم	{خای / ترمش}	تخم آدم [تخم آدم]	×	—	داشاق
اسب	=	=	=	=	=	گرا (اسب) / ماقیذی (مادیان)	هات	آت
خر	=	=	=	=	=	گیر	آشک	اشک

٥٧٣.	کُرّه	کُرّهَ	=	=	کُرّهَ	کُرّی	جادَ	–	کُرّهَ / تودلون [اسب] / قُدُق [خر]
	کرّه الاغ یکساله	هُوَلی	هُوَلی	هُوَلی	–	هُوَلی	کُرگی	–	هوَلی / شتیا [دوساله]
	قاطر	=	=	=	=	=	×	–	=
	سگ	اَسْبَ	اِسْبَ	اِسْبِی	اِسْبَ	=	سُنفتا	ایت	کیک / ایت
	توله	=	=	تولِی	تولَ	تونَک	تُلقا / جادَ	–	تَل
٨٦.	گربه	کوگَ	کوء	کوء	مالَک	پشی	×	پوشوک	پیشیک
٦٥١.	موش	=	=	=	موش	موش	×	سیچقان	سیچان
	شتر	اُشتُر	اُشتُر	=	اُشتُر	=	×	–	دَوَ
	شتر نر	–	–	–	–	لوک	–	–	لِک
	شتر ماده	–	–	–	–	آروان	–	–	آروان

		وفس	آشتیان	کهک	آمره	زند	غربت	خلج	ترکی
	بچه شتر	—	—	—	—	دیلاق	—	—	دیلاق
	شتر جوان نر	—	—	—	—	لوچ	—	—	لوچ
	شتر جوان ماده	—	—	—	—	مجی	—	—	مجی
	شتری که هنوز بار نکشیده	—	—	—	—	—	—	—	کشک
	شتر سواری	—	—	—	—	جامباز	—	—	—
۶۵۹.	گاو	گا	گا	گاه	گا	گو	تپرنگ	سقر	سقر
۶۶۴.	گوساله	گول	=	گووار	=	=	جادتپرنگ	—	بزو
۲۷۱.	گاو جوان	ایوان گا	نوبند	جوان (نر) نوبر (ماده)	جوان	جووان	×	—	دان جنگ
	گوسفند	چروا	=	چرواي	گو	پز	لپور	پیلق	داوار
	میش	میش	=	میش	میش	میی	×	قون	قین

۷۹. (برّه) گوسفند یکساله	وَرَ	وَرِّ	ورِی	وَرّپِی	برَخ	لپورْ	قوزو	قوزی
۲۱۹. (تقلی) « یکساله	—	تقلی	تقلی	—	تقلی	×	—	تخلی
۴۷۸. (شیشک) « دوساله	شیشک	شپشک	—	شپشک	شک	بگل	—	شیشک
« سه ساله (نر)	اوگج	اوگج	اوگج	اوگج	اوگج	×	—	اوگج
« چهارساله ؟	ارگج	—	—	—	—	×	—	—
« پنجساله (نر)	ازمان	آزمان	ازمان	ازمان	{آزمان / دزّپی میی	×	—	آزمان
« شش ساله ؟	دپژمان	دپژمان	—	دپژمان	{دپژمان / سرزی میی	×	—	دیژمان
۱۱۲. بز	بزَ	=	بزی	بزَ	بزن	×	اچ	گچی
۱۱۳. بزغاله	بزلَ	=	بزقالی	—	کرّ	لپور	اوقلاق	{بچی / اولاخ

۴۰

		وفس	آشتیان	کهک	آمره	زند	عزبت	خلج	ترکی
	آهو	=	=	=	=	=	×	جیران	جیران
	خرگوش	خروش	=	=	=	=	×	تاووشقان	دووشان
۰۳۳۳	خوک	=	=	=	خوگ	گراز	×	دونقوز	دنقز
۰۷۸۲	گراز	=	=	=	=	=	×	–	قابان
۰۷۸۵	گرگ	ورگ	ورگ	=	ورک	=	سنقتابرا	بر	قورت
۰۳۶	خرس	=	=	=	=	=	×	=	آیی
۰۶۹۶	روباه	لوواش	روبا	روبو	روبا	روئی	×	تولک	تولکی
	شیر	=	=	=	=	=	×	=	=
	ببر	=	=	=	=	=	×	=	=
	پلنگ	=	=	=	=	=	×	=	=

۴۱

پشم	پرَزمَ	=	=	=	خرِي	پتکائي	یونک	یونگ
چرم	=	=	قیش	=	=	×	—	{گن / قیش [ابدجری]
دُم	=	=	=	دِنب	دو	×	قودروق	قویروق
دنبه	دُنبِ	دُمبِر	دُنبي	دِنبَ	دو	×	—	قویروق
سُم	=	٦	=	سُمب	سِمب	=	×	=	سرناوخ
پهن	پرَّ	پقَرَ	پگرِ	پقرَ	پَن	خشمک [سوخت]	=	پپین
شاشدان	چُردان	چُردان	چُردان	شاشدون	میزلدان	×	پوفلک	قوُق
کوهان	کوُ	=	کوکان	=	کوُوآن	×	—	کوَن
پالان	=	جُل	جُل	چِل	جُلکا		—	{جُل =

	وفس	آشتیان	کهک	آمره	زند	غربت	خلج	ترکی
۶۷. افسار	اُوسار	اُوسار	اُوسار	اِوسار	اُوسار	×	آفسار	اُوسار / تخت
مِهتر	مِتَر	=	مِتَر	مِتَر	میتَر	×	–	مِتَر
۵۶۵ و ۶۳۶. چوپان	=	=	=	چوپون	شووان	×	–	چُپان / چُپان
آخور	آهُر	آخُر	آخُری	اوخُر	=	×	–	آخُر / اوخُر
۲۸۷ و ۵۹۵. طویله	تُوَل	=	پاگا	توپل	توپل	×	–	تُوَل
۵۶۷. مرغ	کرگ	کرگ	کرگ	کرگ	تامِر	چماری	کِتیک	تیق / تیوق
۲۲۴. خروس	=	=	=	=	=	چماری	=	خروز

۳۰۵. جوجه	جوجی	جیجی	لیج	جوج	جوج	جوجک	×	جریک	جوج
۶۱۸. کبوتر	کتور	کفتر	=	کفتر	کفتر		×	کوکارجیک	گلگرجین
۶۲۵. کبک	کوک	کوک	کوک	کوک	کوک		×	کاکولوک	کلیک
۵۹۱. کلاغ	قالاق	قلاق	قلاق	قلاق	قلاق		×	قاق	قارق
۷۴۲. گنجشک	ملوچ	میلیچ	ملیچوء	ملیچی	ملوچک		×	قوش	سرچ
۴۸۱. سار	سیلک / ملوچکا	=	سیاداراق	سیاملیچ	ملوچک سیی		×	=	سقرچین
دارکوب	دارشکل	—	—	دارتوق	—		×	—	دمردوندوک
۴۹۵. (شانه‌سر) هدهد	شان‌سلک / بوبوکلک	—	—	هدهد	ملوچ کوکلی		×	هوپاپاک	بوبوبوک / بوبود
بال	پال	پال	پال	پال	=		×	پرک	قنت

۴۴

		وفس	آشتیان	کهک	آمره	زند	غربت	خلج	ترکی
	پر	=	=	=	=	=	×	یلک	یارپاق / پرش
۷۲۰.	تخم (مرغ)	کرگاخا	ترمق	تخم کرگ	ترمق	تخم امر	گکری	—	یومورت
۱۸۸.	(بوم) جغد	بیقوش	=	بوو	بوء	بایقش	×	بایقوش	بایقوش
۷۰۹.	مگس	مس	مقس	مقس	پخش		×	میچک	میلچک
۶۸۴.	پشه	=	=	=	=	پخش کور	×	=	میلچک / پشه
	کیک	کک	گک	گک	کیک		×	—	بیره
	کنه	کن	کن	گرا	کن	کن	×	—	کن
	صاص	سرخک / انگن	انگن	انگن / جیو	انگن	انگن	×	—	جوجو

۰۲۳	شپش	اِشْبِزَ	اِشْبِزَ	اِشْبِجَ	رِسْپِیْ		جپکا	—	بپث
	سِن	سپِنْ	=	سِنَ	سِنَ	=	×	—	=
	ملخ	مَلَقْ	مِلاقْ	مَلَقْ	مَلَقْ	مَلَقْ	×	—	=
۰۱۳	کرم	کِرْمَ	=	=	=	=	×	قورْتْ	قورْدْ
۰۷۳۹	مار	=	=	مُوْرْ	=	=	رِسْکائی	ایلانْ	ایلانْ
۰۷۹۸	قورباغه	قُرْباقِ	قُرْماقِ	دُزْوُزاقَ	وِزْوِزاقَ	قورْباقَ	×	—	قُرْباقَ
۰۶۶۶	جُعَل	ماچِسَ	بَلْچونِ	—	چُسْنی	رودچولِکَ	×	—	چُسَنَ
۰۳۳۵	درخت	دارْ	=	=	=	=	رِدَخْتْ	هاقاج	آغاجْ

		وفس	آشتیان	کهک	آمره	زند	غربت	خلج	ترکی
۳۰۰.	چوب	چوُوَ	چوُوَ	چوُءِ	چوُ	چوُ	هوُترا	هاٰقاج	آقاج
۳۱۲.	شاخه	=	=	شاخی	شاخ	=	×	—	{شَقّ / گلَ
۶۵۲.	برگ	وَلگ	وَلگ	وَلگ	وَلک	بَلگ	×	—	یارپاق
	گل (بمعنی عام)	=	=	گلِ	گل	=	×	—	گول
	گل (بمعنی خاص) گل سرخ (ورد)	دِل	=	=	دِل	=	×	—	گول
۵۲۱.	بید	وِیدار	ویذ	وی	ویذ	=	×	—	سوگد
۶۲.	نارون	{ناژوند / وِژم	=	نارِبند	نارِبند	=	×	—	=
	چنار	شاچنار	=	=	=	=	×	—	شاچنار
۴۴۸.	سرو	=	=	=	=	=	×	—	=
	کاج	=	=	=	=	=	×	—	=

۴۷

	ارژن (بادام وحشی)	ارجین	ارجن	ارج	ارجن	ارجن	×	—	ارجین
	میوه	میو	=	میو	مو	میو	×	—	میو
۷۲۸.	مو	میو	مو	میی	میو	می	ردخت رزک	—	میو
	باغ میوه (بجز انگور)	چال	—	—	—	—	×	—	—
	باغ	رز	رز	باغچی	رز	=	بالکوواز	=	=
۴۵۴.	سیب	{ سیو / سی	سی	سی	سوء	سیف	لیب	الملا	آلم
۲۲۷ و ۷۵۰.	گلابی	{ گلوپی / کیرپزپی		=	=	گلوی	×	آمروت	آرموت
۴۲۲.	آلو	آلوو		=	آلوی	آلو	×	=	آل
	زردالو	شیلان	شیلانک	شیلانو	شیلنک	زردالو	×	اریک	اریک

		وفس	آشتیان	کهک	آمره	زند	غربت	خلج	ترکی
	آلوبالو	آلوچ سور	گیلاسک	آلووکک	آلبالو	آلبالو	×	—	آلبالو
۱۷۲.	شفتالو	اشتالود	—	هلو	هولوء	آلوچرگک	×	هلو	—
۱۷۲.	هلو	هلود	خلک	هلو	هولوء	هلو	×	هلو	هول
۵۷.	انگور	انگور	انگور	اینگور	انگور	انگور	زرک	هوزدم	اوزوم
۴۱.	(گوز) گردو	ویژ	گردک	گردک (قال)	گردک	گردو	آقوز	یاقاق	قز
	فندق	=	=		=	فندق	×	=	فندق
	پسته	=	=	پشتی	=	پس	×	=	پشت
	بادام	واود	وام	ویم	وام	بایم	×	گادام	=

	باداشان	واوزار	{وانزار / وانشان}	ویمشان	وانزار	بایمسان	×	—	{بادام لیک / بادام لوق}
	سنجد	شینجی	سنجی	سینجی	سینجی	سرنجک	×	—	اید
۸۰۶.	زالزالک	جبلوء	—	—	—	—	×	—	گیویج
	هسته	تند	تخم	تندی	خت	تند	×	—	{دند / چنج}
۶۱۶.	بوته	بوت	{بت / لنک (موختر)}	درمب	بت	بت	×	بت	بت
۵۴۵.	(خربزه) کالک	کالک	کالک	کالک	کلاک	خربز	ختک	کالک	قوون
۳۳۱.	هندوانه	{هندووان / همدووان}	هندووان	همدیان	هندیوون	شامی	×	=	قارپوز
	خیار	خیار	=	=	=	{= / بادرنگ}	×	=	=
۵۳۵.	کدو	کدو	کدو	کوتوء	کودوء	کدو	×	=	کودی

		وفس	آشتیان	کهک	آمره	زند	غربت	خلج	ترکی
۰۸۳	باقلا	باقالی	باقالی	بقالی		باقالی	×	–	باقال [گاهی به لوبیا گفته میشود]
	ماش	=	=	=	ادس	=	×	–	=
۰۷۱۵	عدس	=	نشک	=	مرجوو	نژرو	×	–	مرجی / نوجی
	نخود	نخو	نخپی	نخوء	نخوو	رخ	مرجنگی	–	=
۰۳۷۱	برنج	=	=	=	=	=	رزم	–	دوگی
	گندم	گندو	=	گمّ	گندم	گنم	داهان	–	بغد
	جو	یو	=	جو	ج	جوو	کورز	–	آرپ
	خوشه	هوش	=	خوش	خوش	خوش / سنبل	×	–	سالخم / ساخلم

۵۱

	ینجه	=	=	ینجی	ینج	ینج	همیش	–	ینج
	حاصل	=	=	=	=	=	×	–	آکین [کشت
	چمن	چمن	=	چمند	چمن	چمن	×	–	چمند
۲۸۲.	چراگاه	–	=	–	–	=	×	–	چرانگا
	گرمسیر	گرمسیر	گرمسیر	گرمسیر	کلمسیر	گرمسیر	×	–	قشلاق
	سردسیر	ییلاق	سردسیر	سردسیر	ییلاخ	ییلاق	×	–	یایلاق
۳۳۲.	چشمه	خانی	=	چشمی	چشم	=	×	–	بولاق
۴۵۳.	قنات	کریز	=	قنات	کریز	=	×	–	کریز
۵۹۸.	جوی	مو	جوء	نهر	جوء	جو	×	آقار	آرخ

		وفس	آشتیان	کهک	آمره	زند	غربت	خلج	ترکی
۶۷۸.	گرت	گردِ	گردَ	گردِ	گردَ	=	×	گردو	گردِ
	دیم	=	=	=	=	=	×	–	دیم
۸۳۹.	استخر	اِستِلَ	اَشتِل	اَشتَلِ	اِشتِلَ	اَسَک	×	گول	گل / آسیل
۶۱۵.	خرمن	=	=	خرمن	خرمن	=	برمن	خارمان	=
	درو	دُرِی	=	دِرُو	=	دِرَو	رِگو	–	بیچین
۳۷۲.	داس	داتره / داخر / داخرِ	دسخالیِ	دسخالودِ	دسقالیِ	دسقال	×	هوراق	اُراق
۱۹.	گاد آهن	گِستن	گوئن	گوئن	گوهن	گواهن	×	گاوین	گوهان
	چرخ خرمن کوب	جلجل	چان	چرخ	چوین	چان	×	چان	چان / جنجل

خیش	اُوجار	اُوجار	اُوجار	اِوجار	اُوجار	×	آوجار	اُوجار / هیش
یوغ	وی / ویَ	یُوْ	یو	یوَ	یُوْ	×	بونْدرُق	بیندرق
چرم یوغ	لائپنَ	لائپنْ	لایپنْ	لائپنَ	یُوجپنْ	×	لاهپنْ	لایپنْ
ماله تخته‌ای که بگرمی بندند و بکشند	کولکی / کولی کرش	مالَ	پیمالَ	مالَ	—	×	—	—
چهارشاخ	یَواشپنَ	یُوَرشْ	یَوُرشَ	یُواشَ	یَواشپنْ	×	یاوَشپنْ	یابا / یاواشپنْ
گواز (گاوران)	وَلپنَ	گُوْرانْ	گُوْرانِ	گوْرُوْ	گُوْرانْ	×	—	گُوْرانْ
۳۵. آسیاب	آهْرِ	آسوءِ	آسیُوْ	آشدسوَ	آسیُوْ	×	—	دگرمان / دیزمان
آسیاب دستی	دِستاهْرِ	دَسْتارْ	دَسْتارْ	دَشتَرَ	دَسَرَ	×	—	دَستارْ
۱۰۶. رعیت (برزگر)	برزیگر / آکار	=	زارپکار	=	=	×	—	=

	وفس	آشتیان	کهک	آمره	زند	غربت	خلج	ترکی
۱۳۷. زمین	زُوین	زِمین	=	زِیو	چکلی	—	یِر
خاک	خا	=	خاش	خاکخ	=	چکلی	تورپاق	تُرپاقخ
گَرد	گَرد	=	=	گَرت	گَرت	×	—	تُز
سنگ بزرگ (کمر)	گوَر	کَمَر	کِمَر	کَمَر	کَمَر	کُلوت	تاش	داش [سنگ] قَیَ [کمر] جاو [سنگ بزرگ]
قلوه سنگ	لُرد / اَل	-	—	—	—	—	—	چانقِل [تلاشه]
سنگ کوچک (ریگ)	ری / ریچ	ریگ	ریگ	ریگ	رِخ	×	—	ریر
شِن	= / پشن	=	=	شَن	شَن	×	—	قُم [ماسه]
کوه	کو	کو	کوء	کو	کوءَ	×	تاق	داغ

۵۵

۵۵۸.	تپّه	تُپّل	تَپ	تَپي	تَپ	مُودِر	کوتي	–	قالاق (اپته)
۵۴۴.	دره	دَرَ	دَرَ	دَري	دَرَ	دَرِگ	×	–	دَرَ
	دشت	=	=	=	=	=	×	=	=
۸۴۶.	ہامون	هِموار	–	هَموار	هِموار	هامار	×	–	هامار
	راه	=	=	جَر	را	ري	واتي	–	يل
	جاده	جَد	جَتر	جَر	را	جَر	واتي	–	جَد
۵۹.	آب	اَوَوَ	اوَوَ	اوَوَ	اُوَوَ	اُو	ميو	سو	سو
	رودخانه	روخان	روخان	روخاني	رُخن	روخان	×	چاي	چاي
۷۸۴.	برف	قَرف	وَرف	وَرف	وَرف	=	×	قار	قار

		وفس	آشتیان	کهک	آمره	زند	غربت	خلج	ترکی
۷۷۳.	باران	واران	واران / وشند	واران	وارون / وشند	=	×	یاقوش	یاقش
۴۴۳.	تگرگ	تیرس / ترس	تیرک	گرزلک	تیرس	تگر	×	تل	دلی / چلی
۴۸۲.	شلاب	دیلی	ورفل	ورفل	آلاچرپ	آلاچلپ	×	آلچرپ	آلچلپ
۷۳۸.	ابر	اور	اور	=	اور	اور	×	بلوت	بلوت
۷۷۰.	باد	وا	واد	باد	واث	=	×	یل	یل
۲۱۲.	آتش	آیر	=	=	=	آگر	منگل	هت	ات
	آهن	=	=	=	=	آهن	لووی	تمر	دمر
	مس	=	=	مشث	مشث	=	×	=	=

آسمان	آسُوان		=	آشتُمون	=	×	=	{گگی / گُگک}
۳۲۴. خورشید (آفتاب)	خرُ	آفتو	آفتو	{آفتو / تیغ}	خوُر	×	کوُن	گوُن
ماه	ما	ما	موُ	ما	مانگ	×	های ـ	آی
مهتاب	مفتو	مافتو	=	مافتو	مانگشو	×	های ایشک	آیدین
ستاره	{اِستاهره / اِستاخر / اِستارخ}	=	=	اِستار	=	×	یولدوش	اولدوز
روز	=	=	=	=	روژ	رات	کوندوز	{گوندوز / گونوز}
شب .(۴۸۵)	شو	شِو	وشوَ		شَو	لیل	کیج	گجَ
سال	سال	=	سال	سال	=	×	پیل	ایل
۲۲. الآن (ایسا)	اَرتن	اَلان	اَلان	{اِسا / اَلان}	–	هالاشتی	–	ایندی

		وفس	آشتیان	کهک	آمره	زند	غربت	خلج	ترکی
	امروز	آهروُ آخروُ آرخوُ	=	اَمروز	اَمروُ	=	راثرات	بیَن	بوگون
۰۳۸۷	دیروز	هَزیری	هِزیری	هِزَر	هِزِر	دووَک	دپرات	انگیر	دونین
۰۱۶۹	پریروز	پَرَش	پِرِش	پَرِ	پَر	پپرَک	پَرپرات	—	اپرلیگون
۰۳۸	دیشب	هَزیری شو	هِزِرشو	هِزَرشَو	هِزِرشو	دووِشو	دپلیل	انگیرکیج	دونین گیج
	فردا	سُواش سوبِی	سُوا	سُوا	سُب	×	سِب	سَهَر سابا	
	پس فردا	پَس سُواش	پَس سُوا	پَس سُوا	پَس سوا	دُسُب	×	—	پپری گون
	اسال	اِسال	=	اَسال	اَسال	=	×	—	بوئیل
	پارسال	پار	=	پار	پار	پارَک	پارات	پپلدیر	بیلدیر

	سفیدهٔ صبح	سِفیدَ	سِفیدِ	سِفیدَی	سِفیدَ	شُب زو	×	سِب تِرْدَ	اِرْتَ
٥٠٢.	صبح	سُبی	سُباهی	{ سُوای / سُبَی } سُبَی	سُب	سَکال	–	{ سابا / سَهَر }	
	ظهر	چاشت	چاشت	زوُر	زِرمو	زُر	×	چاشت	گون اُرْتَ
	عصر ـ غروب	{ نوشاوان / نوواشان }	نمازگر	=	=	=	×	=	{ آقشام / گون باتن }
	شرق (مشرق)	=	=	=	=	خوورداگ	×	کونچالار	گون چخر
	غرب (مغرب)	=	=	=	=	خوورقروب	×	کونباتار	گون باتر
	شمال	{ کلپا = }	=	=	{ کلپا = }	کلیسیا	×	کلستیا	کلپا
	جنوب	{ قبل = }	=	=	=	قبل	×	قبل	قبل

		وفس	آشتیان	کهک	آتره	زند	غربت	خلج	ترکی
۴۲۳.	خانه (کده)	کِ	کِپیَ	کِپی	کِپیَ	ئالْ	دِپلَ	هوَ	اِوْ
	حیاط (حصار)	هَسارْ	هسارْ	هِسارْ	هَسارْ	هسارْ	لِقا	هسارْ	هَسارْ / هَیات
	عمارت	یُرْت / رُت	-	اُمارَت	-	اَمارَت	x	-	اَمارَت
	فضا، جا	رُت	یُرْت	جا	پِرْد	مِیدانْ	تاگا	-	یِر
	اطاق	=	=	=	اُتاقْ	=	دِپلَ	=	اُتاقْ
	دَر	برَ	برَ	برَ	برَ	=	دُدرکی / بَرَکی	اِشیک	قاپی
۵۵۰.	دیوار	دُوارْ	=	دُووارْ	دُووارْ	دیوارْ	x	دُووارْ	دُووارْ
	پنجره	=	=	پنجرَ	=	=	x	=	=
	شیشه	=	=	شیشی	=	=	x	-	شوشَ

(دریچه) روزنه	بَرِیزَ	بِلیچَ	—	—	—	×	—	درجَ / پاجَ
سوراخ	هُلَّ	خُلَ	سُولاخْ	خُلَ	کُنا	×	تُبْلِیکْ	دَلیک
سکو	=	بِکوُ	=	اِیْوُ	سَرکوُ	×	—	تَکَ
طاقچه (دولاچه)	دوُلاْ	دوُلِپی	دِلُوْ	دوُلوُءَ	تاقْچَ	×	—	تَخْچَ
تیر	دارْ	= / دِرَخْتْ	=	دِرَخْتْ	=	×	—	=
سقف	بِنْداری	=	سَفْتْ	دانوُ	= / بانْ	×	—	دامْ
پشت‌بام	بانْ	بانْ	بانْ	بُ	بانْ	×	دامْ	دامْ
پلکان	پالاکانَ	پِلکانْ	پِلّی	پَلّکوُنَ	پَلّکانَ	×	پَلّکانْ	=
هره	شَرَفَ	شَرَفِ	هَرَّ / شَرَفَ	لُوْ / شَرَفَ	شَرَفَ	×	—	هَرَّ

		دفس	آشتیان	کهک	آتره	زند	غربت	خلج	ترکی
	(معجر) نرده	مَنْجَر	مَنْجَر	مَنْجَر	مَنْجَر	مَنْجَر	×	–	مَنْجَر
۱۶۳.	پرچین	=	=	=	پَرْدو	=	×	–	=
	نردبان	سِرْدَ	نَرْدووان	نَرْدُوان	پِرْدون	نَرْدَوان	لاباجا	–	پِلْکان
	ناودان	سوَلَ	اوُسْتولپیار	نوُدانِ	اوشدول	نوُدان	×	–	نوُخَ / نوُچَ
	حوض	=	=	=	هَیوز	=	×	=	=
	لوله	=	لوُلَ	=	لولَ	لولَ	×	لوُلَ	لوُلَ
۶۸۵.	نی	=	=	=	=	=	×	قارق	قَمیش
	حمام	=	=	هُمامْ	هَمومْ	هَمومْ	کورِسی	–	هامامْ
۲۹۴.	چاه	=	چا	=	چا	چا	چائوتا	–	قویی

۶۳

	سطل	سَلْتَ		=	=	سَلْتْ	×	–	سَتِلْ
۵۹۰.	کوزه (بزرگ) (سبو)	یُوْنَ	سُوْ	سِوْ	نُوسِوْ	–	×	–	{بَتُوْ / بِشْتِ}
	کوزه (کوچک) (تنگ)	دُوْرَ	=	کُوْزَ	کُوْزَ	کُوْزَ	×	–	{تُونْگْ / کُوْزَ}
۳۸۰ و ۷۰۰.	سبد	{کَلَکْ / سِیَ [بزرگ] / تِیزَ [پهن]}	سَفْتْ	=	سُوپِیَ [بزرگ] / بِرْشِیالْ [کوچک]	سَوَاتْ	×	–	سَبَتْ
	سینی	لَنْگِرِی	{لَنْگِرِی / =}	{لَنْگِرِی / =}	=	=	×	–	سِپِنْ
	لانجین	تَکِدِ	سِپِلِ	=	اوشدونِیَ	=	×	=	=
	غربال	هَلْبالْ	کَمِ	=	آزْدُوجَ	بِرْزِنْگْ	پَرْوُنِی	هَیْلَکْ	قَلْبِرْ
	کم	کَوَ	کَمِ	کَمَ	کَمَ	=	لَکَرْ	=	=
۶۹۳.	دیگ	قازانَ	قِزْقانْ	تِپیانْ	قزْقانْ	قرْقانْ	×	قازْقانْ	قازانْ

		وفس	آشتیان	کهک	آمره	زند	غربت	خلج	ترکی
	دیزی	دیز	دیزی	تینگورو	دیگ	دیز	×	چولمک	چلمک
۳۸۲.	سه‌پایه	دیزوان	دیزندان	=	دیزندو	=	×	اشتداق	=
۵۹۶.	اجاق	کلک	ازاق	گلگ	کلن	کودانک	×	هوجاق	=
	کوره	کور	=	کور	کور	کور	×	=	کور
۲۳۷.	تنور	تندر	تیور	تن	کل	تنور	×	=	تندر
۸۴۷.	هیزم	هیزد	چوب	ایزم	هوزم	ستن	خشمک	-	ادن
۳۸۸.	ذغال	=	=	=	=	زغال	×	-	=
	جرقه	برقل	=	-	-	بورک	×	-	جرق

۶۵

	دود	دُو	دُو		دُو	دودْ	×	–	توتونْ
	دوده	=	=	دُودُو	دوءَ	دودَ	×	–	دُودَ
۵۱۸ و ۶۰۱.	خاکستر	هُلَ	=	خاکپسر	خاخَرَ	خاشگر	چکلي	کولْ	کولْ
	انبر	=	=	اَنْبُرُ	اَنْبَرَ	=	×	–	مَقّاش
	چراغ	چرا	چرا	چرا	چرا	=	لراق	=	چراغ
	شمع	شَوَ	شَمَ	شَمِي	شَمْ	شَمَ	جلوندني [سوناندني]	–	شَمْ
۱۲۷.	شعله	شُلَ	=	شُوْلِ	شُئُلَ	شُوْلِ	×	–	اَلُو
	دُشک (توشک)	نالي	دُشک	دُشک	نالي	دوشک	×	توشک	دُشِک
۳۶۴.	لحاف	جووانخا	لاهاف	لوف	حومخو	لاف	پوش	يرقان	يرقان

		وفس	آشتیان	کهک	آمره	زند	غربت	خلج	ترکی
(۴۳۲).	بالش	بالِشم	بالِشم	بالِشم	بالِشم	بالِشت	×	یاسدق	{یاستق / یاسوق}
۶۸۹.	نمد	نِوَ	=	=	=	=	×	کیجَ	کیچ
	گلیم	گلیوَ	=	گلیم	گلیمَ	=	رِلگیم	=	=
۴۱۸.	جارو	سپزدَ	=	جاروء	=	=	×	سپورگ	سوپورگ
	غذا	=	نان	غذای	=	=	تپیاک	–	=
	صبحانه	{زف / زفِ قلیان}	زفِ قلیان	زفَ قلیان	–	زفِ قلیان	×	–	{قیلان آشی / ناشتالیک}
	نهار (ناهار)	=	=	لور	=	=	×	–	=
	شام	=	=	=	شم	=	×	–	=

نان	=	=	کوِرا	ن	=	مِنا	هپکمک	چرک
خمیر	هوپر	خمیر	=	=	خیر	بمپر	–	=
نمک	نوک		=	نمک	خووآ	شورکا	توز	دوز
۷۶۹. آش	=	=	=	=	=	پرس	=	=
۷۳۲. (مویز) کشمش	کپشمپش	=	=	میوج	کپشمپش	میتو	–	کپشمپش / ییمیش
(دوشاب) شیره	دوشا	دوشو	دیشو	دوشو	شیر	شیلدا	–	شیر
شیرهٔ انگور نیم پخته	باقالی	–	–	–	–	–	–	–
شراب	شردو	=	شراب	شراب	شردو	لراب	–	=
شیر	=	=	=	=	=	شفت	سوت	سوت
خامه	خاواتو	خامتو	توج	خمتو	خامتو	×	خامتو / قاتوق	خاماتو

	وفس	آشتیان	کهک	آمره	زند	غربت	خلج	ترکی
کره	=	=	کَرَ	کَرَ	کَرَ	رَکَ	کَرَ	کَرَ
۳۹۳ . روغن	رُن	=	=	روُغَن	روُن	تِپل	—	یاغ
پنیر	=	پِنیر	=	=	=	لِپیر	پِنیر	پِنْدِر
ماست	=	=	=	=	=	قَتی	قاتُق	قاتُوخ
۳۶۳ . دوغ	دوُ	دوُ	دوِء	دوُ	دوُ	دوُکی	—	ایران
۱۵۵ . کشک	=	=	=	=	=	کِلالی	تُراق	قوُروُت
۴۲۴ . زج (قرقوروت)	سِزَ	سِزَ	رِسَج	زَجّ	تَرَف	×	—	قَرَقوُروُت
مزه	مَزَ	مِزَ	مَزَ	مَزَّ	مَزَ	×	—	داد
طعم (تَم)	تاو	=	=	=	=	×	—	تام

	درد	=	=	=	=	=	×	—	آقر
۱۰۸.	گریه	بِرَم	بَرَم	بَرَم	بِرَم	گیریون	شنگک	—	آقلماق
۴۰۶.	ناله	=	=	نال	=	=	ناسنگنا	—	×
(۴۰۶).	زاری	=	=	=	نالبی	=	×	—	=
	عزا	{شیون =	=	=	=	{شیون =	×	—	یاسش = }
	آفت	=	=	=	=	=	×	—	×
	زخم	=	=	=	=	=	×	—	یار
۴۶و۱۲۹و۲۸۶.	ورم	واش	{واد =	=	—	باد	×	—	شیش
۲۴۰.	تب	=	تو	توی	تو	تو	نارنگنا	—	اپستم
	سردرد	سَردرد	سَردرد	سَردرد	—	سرشی	(کلوزدک)	—	باش آقری
	دلدرد	دلدرد	دلدرد	دلدرد	—	دلشی	(پتودک) [درد سکیند]	—	اورگ آقری

		وفس	آشتیان	کهک	آمره	زند	غربت	خلج	ترکی
	آبله	اُوِلَ	اُوِلِ	اُوِلِی	اُوِلَ	اُوِلَ	×	–	چیچک
	دوا (دارو)	دَوا	دَوا	دَوای	دُئا	درمان	رادی	–	دَوائی / دار
	رخت	=	=	=	=	=	پوش	گَییک	یالتار / اِرتیک
۱۷۱ .	قبا	قَوا	قووا	قاوا	قوا	قَوا	×	آرخالق	دُن
۲۶۶ .	پیراهن	شی	شیوی	پیرهن	شوی	کِرواس	پیرفتا	تون	کینک
	شلوار	پوَوار / پوَر / شِلوار	شِلوار	شلوار	شِلوار	شووال	دُلنکا	اِم	تُمان / دیزدنی
	جوراب	گورَدَ	=	=	گوردوَ	جرو	×	=	جُراب
۵۸۹ .	کلاه	=	=	کلو	=	کلو	لُکا	بورک	برک
۶۲۳ .	کفش	لاق (نعلین)	گوش	گوش	گوش	–	چلکین / پیلری	هاداق تاب	اَیَق قابی (یاشماق)

	گیوه	هاسوءَ	—	گیوَ	گوءَ	گیوَ	×	–	کَلاش
	یقه (یخه)	یَخَ	یَخَ	یَخَ	یَخَ	یَخَ	×	یَخَ	یَخَ
۰۱۷۶	جیب (کیسه)	جیوَ	کیسَ	کیسَ	کیسَ	گیرفان	برک	–	=
۰۶۸	آستین	اَنگَل	اِشتووَ	اوشدیَ	اوِشدیَ	بال	×	قول	قُل
۰۶۹۰	دامن	داوان	دامان	دامان	دُموَن	دُوان	× .	هَتک	اَتک
	آستر	آشور / آستار	=	=	=	آستر	×	=	آستار
	پنبه	چلَ / لوکَ [نرده]	=	گندو / لوکِ	گندیَ / لوکَ	پمک	×	–	پمبق
	پارچه	جشن	=	پارچ	پارچ	پارچ	×	–	پارچ
	کرباس	جاوَ	=	=	=	جوو	×	–	ربز
۰۳۴۸	سوزن	دِرزن	-	-	-	-	×	-	اپن

		وفس	آشتیان	کهک	آتره	زند	غربت	خلج	ترکی
۰۱۹۴	نخ	دِسِّ	رِسْمان	رِسْمان	اِیْوا	دِرْزِک	رِشْکائی	یُشِیم	اِیپْلیک
۰۳۹۲	ریسمان	رِیِش =	=	=	رِیِشُم	بَن	رِشْکائی	پِیپْلیک	اِیپ
	طناب (رسن)	رَسَن	رَسَنِ	رَسَنی	رَسِن	گُرِیش	رِشْکائی	تَناف	تَنَف
۰۲۴۵	تار	تان اَرِشْک	=	تان	تُن	تان	رِشْکائی	-	اَرِش
۰۱۸۳	پود	پوءِ	=	پو	پوءَ	پو	رِشْکائی	-	آرْقاج
	کارگاه	دارْبار	=	کارْگو	دارْبار	دارْکول	جَلال	-	دارْبار
	نجار (درودگر)	دُلوگَر	=	=	=	=	x	-	=
۰۱۹۶	تیشه	تَرِشَد تَرِشَت	=	=	تِیش	=	تِیشْکی	کَسَر	تیش
۰۸۳۶	اره	وِیشَد وِهِشت	=	اَری	اَرّ	اَرّ	ارکی	هارّا	اَرّ

٧١۴ .	متّه	میَ	متّه	مئیْ	میَ	مَتَ	×	نپیَ	میَ
	میخ	مِخْ	=	=	=	=	×	–	مِخْ
٦٧٧ .	تخته	تَخْتَ	=	=	=	=	×	=	تَخْتَ
	تیشهٔ خارکنی (تبر)	تُرَ	تَوَرْ	تَوَرْ	تیوَرَ	–	×	تاوارچوکْ	–
٢۴١ .	تبر	دارْبَخْنَ / دارْزَنْ	نَرْتَوَرْ	نَرْتَوَرْ	تَرْکَبِرْ	تَوَرْ	×	–	تیوَرْ
	ماله	تالَ / تالاَ	=	تالِیْ	تالَ	=	×	=	تالَ
	بیل	بَهْرَهَ / بَخْخْ / بَرْکَخْ	=	بالَ	بیلَ	=	×	=	بِلْ
٢۵۴ .	گِل	=	=	گِلِ	=	=	چِکِلی	–	پالْچوخ / پالْچوخ
۵۴ .	کاه‌گل	=	=	کُوْگِلْ	=	کیگِلْ	×	–	سووْاوْخْ
٦٠۵ .	کاه	=	کَا	کَا		کَی	تمنا	–	ساتانْ

	دفس	آشتیان	کهک	آمره	زند	غربت	خلج	ترکی
خشت	هِشتَ	=	خِشتَ	خِشتَ	=	×	=	گرگبیچ
گچ	گرَچ	=	=	=	=	×	—	=
آهک	=	=	=	=	=	×	—	=
خدا	=	=	=	=	=	پاوِری	—	تاری
دُعا ،	=	=	دُوْ	=	=	×	—	دودوا
۱۴. نفرین	دووانِ	نُفرین	نُفرین	نُفرین	نپرفن	نارسَگِنا	—	قارقِش
نماز	نوواز	نُماز	مَن	نُماز	=	شوودا	—	=
روزه	روزَ	=	روزَ	روجَ	=	شوودا	—	اُرج
دوست	=	=	=	=	=	آشکی	—	دُش
دشمن	دِشمن	=	دشمن	دِشمن	=	ناکِنا	—	دِشمن

٨٤٩. فحش | شوردن = فوش شماردن فاش گاليون - سيگش
دعوا | دوا دوا دوا جنگ جنگ گالوتي - التشماخ
مهمان | مهمان = مهمان مهمن ميوان گجا - قناخ
شكارچي | اشكارزن شكارزن شكاروان اشكارچي شكاروان × - اوچي
٦٧٠. لاشه | لاش لش لش لش لش × - لش
قبر | = = = گور قور × - گر
٢٣١. خار، تيغ | تيك تيك تيك تيكخ دريك × - تيكان
زنجير | زنجير زنجر زنجيل زنجر = خشگرو - زنجير
٥٢٢. پارد | فيي = = = = × كورگك كورك

		وفس	آشتیان	کهک	آمره	زند	غربت	خلج	ترکی
۸۰۹.	آواز (صدا)	{ = / سزا }	{ = / (=) }	=	آواز	اوواز	دناش	—	{ اواز / سس }
	فریاد	هاوار	سدا	داد	فریاد	داد	دادتا	—	داد
	خبر	خور	=	=	=	خور	×	—	=
	فرمان	=	=	=	فرمون	فرمن	×	—	=
۵۳۷.	بازی	کاوا	وازی	وازی	بوازی	=	×	—	اوین
	چادر	—	—	—	—	چاپر	رخلو	—	چادر
	سایه	ساین	=	سایی	سای	سای	×	—	کولک
	همسایه	همسپا	=	=	همای	هوسا	همسوک	—	قنشی
	رنگ	=	=	رنگ	=	=	رنگتا	—	=
	بو	بوء	=	بوء	بوء	=	قح	—	{ قخی / ای، ایس }

١٩١.	پول	=	=	=	پول	پول	گما	–	=
	گدا	=	=	=	=	گیا	منگنا	–	دیلنچی
	پیمانه	کپل	کپل / کپل	پیمانو	پیمون	= / کپل	×	–	کپل
١.	ذرع	زر	زر	زر	گز	زر / گز	×	–	آرشین
٧٤٦.	مشت	مشت	چنگ	=	مشت	=	×	–	اوج
	بار	=	=	=	=	=	پور	–	یوک
٣٨٤.	دکان	=	دوکان	دوکان	ذکون	=	×	–	دکان
	نانوا	=	=	=	نونوا	نانود	بناپک	–	ننوا
	قصاب	قسو	=	=	=	قسو	ذهوت میتون	–	=
	خط	=	=	=	=	=	×	–	جزق
	نقطه	نخت	=	=	نقت	نخت / نکت	×	–	نقت

		وفس	آشتیان	کهک	آمره	زند	غربت	خلج	ترکی
۲۲۱.	تُک (نوک)	=	=	=	تُک	=	×	—	اوُج
۱۳۴.	بیخ (بُن)	بِن	=	=	=	تَ	بِنْخام	–	دیب
	حَدّ	=	=	=	=	هَدِسَدّ	×	—	=
	نصف (نیم)	نیوَ	=(=)	نِسْم	نِسْم	=	نِسموتا	–	یاری
(۸۴۰).	جفت	=	—	—	=	=	داهات	–	جوت
	عجب	=	اَزَب	=	=	=	×	–	= } پ
	یکهو	پیرای	یهو	یهو	یدو	یهو	پی بیلی	–	بیردن
۳۱۱.	خوب	نَخ	=	=	نیچکخ	= / خاس	دَخ	هادل	یاخچی
	بد	گکت	=	= / اپر	پیس	=	ناچکو	پیس	پیس
	راست	=	=	رُوِشت	=	راس	دَخ	–	گرکچک
۳۵۰.	دروغ	درو	درو	درو	درو	درو	نادخ	–	یالان

	راست	=	=	رُوُسْت	=	=	×	=	دوُز
۸۰۵	کج	هُل	=	=	خُلّ	=	×	=	اَیْر
	روشن	روُشَن	روُشِن	روُشَن	روُشِن	روُشِن	×	اِشِق	اِشِق
	تاریک	=	=	=	=	=	×	قارالُق	قَرَنقُلُق
	پاک (پاکیزه، تمیز)	=	=	=	=	{ = / تَمیس	دَخیا	–	{ = / تَمیش
	چرک	=	=	=	=	چِرکِن	ناکِنا	–	چیرْک
	نجس	نَجِس	=	=	نَجِسْت	=	ناکِنا	–	نَجیس
۳۱۳	خوشگل	قَشَنگ	{ = / قَشَنگ	رَشید	نیچَک خ	قَشَنگ	دَخیا	قَشَنگ	{ گِنجِک / قِزِل
	زشت	گَشت	=	=	زِج	بَد	ناچکو	پیس	پیس
	نر	نِر	=	=	=	نیر	×	هِرکِک	اِرکِک
	ماده	{ ماما / مایِل	=	مادی	{ مای / مایی	ما	×	تیش	دیشی

		دفس	آشتیان	کهک	آتره	زند	غربت	خلج	ترکی
	پیر	=	=	=	=	=	پیرقات	قاری	قج
	جوان	=	جووان	=	جاهل	=	×	ایگیت	جاهال
	چاق	کک	=	=	=	=	بردو	گک	کک
	لاغر	= / بی پا	=	=	=	= / بیپا	×	هارقان	آروخ
۳۲۵.	کوچک	وریج / وجیل	کستر / کستر	خورد	کوسترک	بوچک	قلیل	بالا	کوچک
۶۳۸.	بزرگ	مزن	مدر	مدر	مدر	قیو	تلو	بگ	بیک
	سبک	سک	سوک	=	=	=	×	یونگول	یونگول
	سنگین	=	سنگین / سقت	سنگین	سقت	=	اپول	قورس	آقر / قورس
	تر	=	=	=	=	=	×	هل	یاش
۱۰۱.	خشک	هشک	=	=	=	=	×	قوروق	قوری

۱۹۹.	تیز	=	=	تند	تیج	تیرش	×	پیتی	اپتی
	کند	=	=	=	=	=	×	=	کیند
	دراز	{بلند	=	دروز	= {بلند	دیریش	رداز	اوزاق	{اوزاخ اوزون
۵۸۷. (۲۱۱)	کوتاه	{کوتا کل کپل	{کوتا کل کپل	{کوتا کوتول	کلک	کوتا	×	قیق	قس
	باریک	=	=	=	=	–	×	هنیز	اینچ
۶۷۵.	پهن	فراخ	=	فراخ	پن	پیین	×	هنلیغ	انل
	نازک	=	=	نازک	=	نازک	ناتک	–	نازیک
	تنگ	=	=	تنگ	=	=	×	تار	دار
۳۸۱.	دور	=	=	=	دور	دور	×	پیراق	ایراخ
	نزدیک	=	نزدیک	=	نزپک	=	×	یووق	{یاخون یاووخ
	زود	{زود زودی	=	=	زو	زو	زوکم	–	رتز

		وفس	آشتیان	کهک	آمره	زند	غربت	خلج	ترکی
	گم	ماک	=	=	گینیپا	=	مَخ	–	اپت
۳۷۹.	پیدا	دیپار	=	=	دیپار	دیپار	×	–	بِل
۳۲۲.	خواب	خُو	خُو	خُو	خُو	خُو	نوف	–	یُخی
۸۱۵.	بیدار	=	=	=	=	=	×	–	آیوخ / اُیاق
	سیر	=	=	=	=	=	رُپ	تُق	تَخ
۷۹۵.	گرسنه	گُشن	=	گُشن	گُشن	بِرْسی	بُکا	آج	آج
۲۱۵.	تشنه	تِشن	=	تَشن	تِشن	تَنِگ	×	سوسوش	سوسوز
	ناشتا	=	=	=	=	=	×	–	آناشت
	خوش	=	=	=	=	خووَش	×	–	=
	ست	=	=	=	=	=	×	–	=
	خام	خاو	=	=	خوم	نورشیاک	×	–	بیش‌کمیز

	پخته	پت	—	—	پت	ورشپاک نکوئید		—	بیش میش
	تازه	=	=	تازی	تاز	=	×	=	پینگی
	کهنه	کفر	=	کونی	کونی	کن	×	=	کین
	بیات	=	=	=	بیات	=	×	=	=
	شور	=	= } تل	=	=	=	×	هاچخ	شر
	شیرین	=	=	=	=	=	شیلدا	=	شیرین
	چرب	چرپ	=	چرب	=	چور	×	یاقل	یاقلی
۰۲۲۲	تلخ	تل	تل	تل	تل	=	×	هاچخ	آجی
	تند	=	=	=	وتند	تن	×	=	وتند
	ترش	=	=	=	وترش	=	×	تورش	تورش
۰۲۷۴	سرد	=	=	=	یخ	=	سپلک	بوز	سیخ
	گرم	=	=	=	=	=	×	هیشدی	ایسی

		وفس	آشتیان	کهک	آمره	زند	غربت	خلج	ترکی
	خنک	هُنُک	خُنِک	خُنُک	کپی	خُنِک	×	=	سَرِن
۷۹۲.	دِلرم	دُلُرم	=	دُلُرُم	=	–	×	–	مُحْنَت
	سخت	=	=	=	=	=	×	=	بَرکَ
	سفت	{ قرس / = }	=	=	سَخت	=	×	بَرکَ	بَرکَ
	سفت بمعنی کشیده	تِرنَک	تِرِنگ	سِفت	–	سِفت	×	–	تَرینگ
	شُل (روان)	چول	چول	چول	شُل	=	×	–	دوری
(۶۸۰.)	شُل (لخت)	شُل	=	=	شُل	=	×	بُش	{ شُل / بُش }
	نرم	=	=	=	=	=	×	یموشاق	نَرم
۶۸۰.	سست	سُسْت	=	=	سُست	شُل	سُستوتا	–	شُل
۸۴۱.	خسته	ماندَ	مانِد	ماندَ	مُندِ	هپینگ	×	–	یُرولمیش
	بیمار (ناخوش)	ناخُش	{ ناخش / = }	ناخش	ناخُش	{ ناخش / = }	نارنگنا	–	{ ناساز / ناخُش }

۶۸۷ .	تنبل	=	اَلْشِم	=	تَنْبَل	=	×	-	تَلْنَد
۱۹۵ .	تنها	تَنْهای		=	تَینا	تَنیا	تَنهوتا	-	یالقز / یالقوز
۶۶ .	آبستن	اُودُشتن	اودوشت	اُشتن	اُدِشتی	اُودُرن	بَرده	-	بُخاز / ایکی جانلی
۵۱۷ و ۵۲۸ .	نازا	قِیر / نزا (برای حیوان) / نجا (برای مردم)	نزا / قیر	قیر	نزا / قیر	نزدوک / قیر نزا	×	-	قیر / دُغمیین
	خراب	خراو	=	خراب	=	خرو	نادخ	-	یخلمیش
	آباد	اُودان	=	=	=	=	دَخیا	-	اُوادان
	گران	=	=	=	گرون	=	رِگون	-	باها
	ارزان	=	=	=	ارزون	=	×	-	اُوجوز
	مفت	=	=	=	مفت	=	مُفتوتا	-	مفت
	بیشتر	ویشتر	ویشتر	=	ویشتر	-	اپوپل	-	آرخ

		دفس	آشتیان	کهک	آمره	زند	غربت	خلج	ترکی
۰۷۲۴	پُر	پُرْ	=	=	پُرْ		رُپْ	تُلاْ	دُلی
	سرازیر	سَرازیرَ	=	سَرازیر	{سَراشوءَ / سَرادم}	بُرُوخُوُرِی	×	–	باش آشاقی
	سربالا	سَرابالا	سَربالا	رُوبالا	سَرابالاگی	بُرُوزُرِی	×	–	{باشیخاری / یقش}
	جلو (پیش)	پُرْوانَ	=	=	جلو		پیشتام	ایلگر	قاباق
۰۳۶۰	عقب (پس)	دُمْبَ	دُنْبالْ	دُمَ	پُشْتْ	دُمْبالْ	×	هاقا	دالْ
۰۳۰	سفید	اِسْپی	=	=	اِسْپیکْ	چَرَگْ	سِفِینْ	هورُونْ	آقْ
۰۴۶۰	سیاه	سیا	سیا	سیا		سیی	سوتَ	آرا	قَرَ
	زرد	=	=	=	=	=	×	سارخ	ساری
۰۴۴۹	سبز	سُوْزْ	=	=	سُوْزْ	سُوْزْ	×	گوکْ	یاشِلْ
	آبی	=	=	=	=	=	×	=	=
۰۵۳۴	کبود	کُوکْ	کَبُوتْ	کَبُوتْ	کُوکْ	کُوکْ	×	گُوی	{گُوی / اَبلَک}

سرخ (قرمز)	سور	=	=	قرمز		×	قرمز	قرمزی
بنفش	بنوش	بنفش	بنفش	بنوش	بنوش	×	=	بنوش
من	ازمن	از من	آ از من	از من	من	خکیم	–	=
تو	ت اشت اشد	ت	ت	ب	تن	خکیت	–	سن
او	آن تان تانی	آن	اون	ی	او	اوری	–	ا
ما	آدان تادان	ایم امان	ایما	ما ما	ایم	خکیاسون	–	بیز
شما	سوان سوادان	ایشم	ایشما	=	اود	خکیاتون	–	سیز
ایشان	آن تانان	آنکل	آنند	انکل	آدانا	اوریا	–	الار الرك

	وفس	آشتیان	کهک	آمره	زند	غوبت	خلج	ترکی
(اَ)م	(اَ)م / (اُ)م	(اَ)م / (اُ)م	(اُ)م	(اُ)م	(اِ)م	(اُ)م	–	(اِ)م
(اَ)ت (اِ)	(ا)ي	=	=	(اِ)ت	(اِ)ت	(اِ)ت	–	(ا)پن
(اَ)ش (اِ)	(اِ)ش	(اِ)ش	=	=	(ا)ي	=	–	اِ
(اِ)مان	(اُ)وان	=	=	(اِ)مون	=	(اُ)مون	–	(اِ)میز
(اِ)تان	(ا)پیان	=	=	(اِ)تون	=	(اِ)تون	–	(ا)پیز
(اِ)شان	(اِ)سان	(اِ)سان	=	(اِ)ش	(ا)پیان	(اِ)شون	–	لَری
خود (خویشتن)	اِشتن	خشتن	خشتن	خ	خ	خک	–	اِز
همه	هَوپی	=	=	هَم	گشت	هَمشدیک	–	هامی
هر	=	=	=	=	=	×	–	=

۱۰. يک	{ = / اِي	-	{ يَک / تي	-	يِ	يکاتْ	-	بِرْ
دو	=	-	دوُ	-	=	دُهاتْ	-	اِکی
سه	=	-	=	-	=	سِهاتْ	-	اوُچْ
چهار	=	-	چوُرْ	-	چووآرْ	چارْهاتْ	-	دُرْدْ
پنج	پنْجْ	-	پنْجْ	-	=	پَناتْ	-	{ بيشْ / بيسْ
شش	=	-	شَشْ	-	شَشْ	شِشاتْ	-	آلْتی
هفت	=	-	=	-	=	هَفاتْ	-	يِدی
هشت	=	-	=	-	=	هَشاتْ	-	سَکِزْ
نه	=	-	نوُ	-	=	نيي	-	دُقُزْ
ده	=	-	=	-	=	دَئي	-	اُنْ

		وفس	آشتیان	کهک	آمره	زند	غربت	خلج	ترکی
	اینجا	{اینْدی / ایندْیینَ	اِنّا	ایندْیَ	اِنْدْوْ	گِرَ	اینْ تال	–	{بُرَ / بورَ
	آنجا	آندی، آندیَنَ	اُدْنا	اوبْ [باغنه]	اُدْنَ	ورَ	اونْ تال	–	اُرَ
۲۶۷.	بالا	=	=	=	{وَسَرَ / =	باآنْ	لاٰبا	یُقار	یُخاری
۲۶۰.	پائین	زِرْ	=	=	{هاچال / هادِم	خووار	پائینْ تام	اِنَ	آشاقی
	زیر	زِرْ	=	=	واشتو	زیرْ	زیرْ تام	–	{آشت / آلت
	رو	سرکـ....دَ	=	دیمْ	وَسَرَ	باآنْ	مْ	–	{اوزْ / اوسْت
۳۷۸ و ۱۱۱.	بیرون	بَرَ	بَرَ	=	بَرَ	دیشْت	بَرا	–	{یازی / دیشخاری
۳۵۱.	درون	{نانَ / نانْتِل....دَ	آندَرونْ	=	بِـ....دَ	نوْ	تُکامْ	–	ایچَری
۳۵۶.	میان	نانَ	میانْ	میانْ	نیموْم	نُوراش	x	–	ایچ
۷۸۱.	کنار	{کَلْ =	{کُلْ =	=	=	=	x	–	قِراق

اين	=	یانْ	یَنْ	یُ	یُیَ	اپری	- بُ / بوُ
آن	=	=	اوُنْ	اِنوُ	اَوَ	اوُری	- اد
کدام	کانْ	کامِنْ	=	کیمی	کامِنْ	کدُنری	- هانْسی
که (کی)	کِ	کی	کِ	کی	کمی	کپرپزْ	- کیمْ
چه (چی)	چی / چِزْ / چِزِی	جیشی	چیچی	چی	چَ	چکمْ	- نَمَ
۳۰۳. چرا (واسۀ چی)	چرا	=	=	=	=	×	- یاوِوُزْ
برای (واسۀ)	ـرا	بَرا	داشدِیْ	وا	آرِ	بَکی	- رِچِنْ
کو	=	=	=	=	کوءَ	کورِیزْ	- هانی
کجا	کانی / کاندِیا	کونا	کبِ	کِ	کورَ	کتالْ	- هارَ
چندبار	چِنْ پکدا	=	چِن دَفَ	چِن را	چِن دَفَ	چِن وِلیک	- رَنَخ پی / رَنَخ ویل
اگر	=	=	=	=	=	×	- اگَ

	وفس	آشتیان	کهک	آره	زند	غربت	خلج	ترکی
۱۱. دیگر	هِتی	هینی	دیگَ	هِنی	دیتَ / دیِرْ	دیگَ چیگْ	–	داها / داهِ
۷۲۲، ۲۰۰. از	=	=	جِ	جِ	لَ	آ	–	...دَنْ
بی	=	=	=	=	=	=	–	...سِزْ
با	...را	=	= / هَمْرَدْ	بَ / هَمپا	= / اَوَلْ	=	–	...نَنْ
۷۵۱. نه	=	نیَ	=	=	=	نَئیکْ	–	یُخْ
بله (آری)	لا	لا	لا	لا	اَری	هَوی	–	هَینْ / هَیَ

			وفس	آشتیان	کهک	آتره	زند	غربت	ترکی
٦٠٦ . کردن	بکن / کرد	×	هاکر / هارِش کرد	بکَ / بَش کرد	بک / بِش کرد	بَکر / بَش کرد	بک / اکرِد	بنار / هِناشت	اِلماق
٧٨ . گفتن	بگو / گفت	واتن	بوواز / بِش وات	بوواز / بَش وات	بوواچ / بِش وات	بتا / بَش وات	بوژ / وِت	بیامار / هماشت	دیماق
صداکردن یازدن (بانگ زدن)	صداکن / صداکرد	×	وانگ زن / وانگِش زَ	وانگزی کَ / وانگزِ بِش گرد	وول بزن / وولش بزی	ویلکر / ویلش زِنا	ربچر / چرچی	تاگابوین / تاگاویذ	شش لزماق ،، (الماق)
٨١٦ . دیدن (٣٨٥)	ببین / دید	دیین	بوپن / بپش دی	= / بش دی	بین / بپش دی	بوی / بش دی	بون / دی	برق / رقید	گرماق
١٢٠ شنیدن	بشنو / شنید	×	بشنو / بپشن	بشنو / بشنفت	= / بشنفت	بشنو / بشنفت	= / شنفت	بلان / سلاند	اِشماق

رِجا : برو (۹۷) .
عربی "جاءَ" : آمد ، هزوارش [illegible] : آمدن .
سنسکریت گا = جا ، اوستا [illegible] - = [illegible] از ریشهٔ [illegible] بمعنی آمدن و رفتن .

رِمیت : بمیر ، رِمیتون : بکُش (۹۶).
هزوارش [illegible] : کُشتن .

پسوند هات ، هُذ ، هُت ... برای عددها (۸۹ و ۱۴۸) .
این پسوند در عدد ۱ در عربی دیده میشود : اَحَد ، وَحَد (اوستا [illegible] - [illegible]) + پسوند "حد" . (نیز نگاه کنید به ایران کوده ۴ : ص ۱۷) .

گویش خلج

[دربارهٔ گویش خلج در ایران تنها چیزی که بنظر نگارنده رسیده نمونه هائی از واژه ها و جمله های خلج است که مینورسکی گردآورده و ذیل عنوان "گویش ترکی خلج" نشر داده است :
The Turkish Dialect of the Khalaj, by V. Minorsky, Bulletin of the School of Oriental Studies, Vol. X, Part 2.
گفتار مینورسکی بیشتر در پیرامون حدسی است که دربارهٔ اصل خلج ها و کوچ کردن آنها زده است (ص ۴۲۴ تا ۴۳۷) . نمونه های جمله ها و چند واژهٔ خلج و بررسی آنها را در صفحه های 424-418 داده است .]

اینجا درباره گویش خلج فقط از نظر همبر کردن آن با گویش ترکی بلوک وفس چند نکته را یادآور میشود.

واژه‌های بسیاری در خلج در برابر ترکی بکار میرود که همریشه نیست. واژه‌های ذیل برای نمونه داده میشود:

خلج	ترکی	صفحه	خلج	ترکی	صفحه
کَلَ	قارداش	۲۶	قازق	تمیش	۶۲
کال	اوشاق	۲۷	هیکمک	چرک	۶۷
اَب	خان	۲۷	تراق	قورود	۶۸
هَرَ	کیشی	۲۷	گمک	ارتیک	۷۰
کشی	آرواد	۲۷	تون	کتنک	۷۰
کودَن	نی	۲۸	اِم	دیزدنی	۷۱
اَنِ	دداق	۲۹	کَرَ	تیش	۷۲
کام	ساق	۳۰	هادل	یاخچی	۷۸
چوچ	سیک	۳۲	قادی	قچ	۸۰
سیدک	آیاک	۳۵	هل	یاش	۸۰
هازق	آغز	۳۵	هتز	اینج	۸۱ (؟)
پیلق	داداز	۳۸	بوز	سیخ	۸۳
بر	قورت	۴۰	ایلگر	قاباق	۸۶
توش	سرچ	۴۳	هاقا	دال	۸۶
یاقاق	قز	۴۸	هورون	آق	۸۶
آنگر	دونیش	۵۸	آرا	قر	۸۶
آپیک	قاپی	۶۰	کودک	یاشل	۸۶

افزوده شدن "هـ" بر سر واژه‌هائی که در ترکی با صوت آغاز میشود. (مینورسکی نیز این نکته را یادآور شده است.) نمونه:

خلج	ترکی	صفحه	خلج	ترکی	صفحه
هَرْ	اَرْ	۲۸	هَوْ	اِوْ	۶۰
هامْ	آمْ	۳۲	هوچاقْ	اُجاقْ	۶۴
هاداقْ	اَیاقْخ	۳۳	هَتَکْ	اَتَکْ	۷۱
هاتْ	آتْ	۳۶	هارّا	اَرّا	۷۲
هاقاجْ	آقاجْ	۴۵	هیرْکَکْ	اَرْکَکْ	۷۹
هوزومْ	اوزومْ	۴۸	هارْقانْ	آرُقْخ	۸۰
هوراقْ	اُراقْ	۵۲	هَتْلیغْ	اَتْلِ	۸۱
هُتْ	اُتْ	۵۶	هاچْخْ	آجی	۸۳
هایْ	آیْ	۵۷	هیشْدی	ایسْتی	۸۳

ولی در سه واژهٔ ذیل در خلج "هـ" افزوده نشده است:

خلج: اَلْ، اَتْ، آجْ (ص ۳۲ و ۳۴ و ۸۲).

"ک" آغازی در خلج برابر است با "گ" ترکی. (این نکته را مینورسکی نیز یادآور شده است.) نمونه:

خلج	ترکی	صفحه	خلج	ترکی	صفحه
کَلینْ	گَلینْ	۲۸	کوکارْچینْک	گُگَرْچینْ	۴۳
کونی	گونی	۲۸	کونْ	گونْ	۵۷
کُزْ	گُزْ	۲۹	کِچَ	گِجَ	۵۷
کُتْ	گُتْ	۳۲			

در دو واژهٔ ذیل "ک" آخر خلج نیز برابر "گ" ترکی است:

خلج : یونگ و اَریگ برابر ترکی : یونگ و اَرپگ (۴۱ و ۴۷).

"ت" آغازی خلج برابراست با "د" ترکی. (این نکته راسینورسکی نیزیادآورشده است.) نمونه :

خلج	ترکی	صفحه	خلج	ترکی	صفحه
تیل	دیل	۳۰	تاش	داش	۵۴
تپش	دپش	۳۰	تاق	داغ	۵۴
تش	دش	۳۱	تمر	دمر	۵۶
تالاق	دالاغ	۳۲	تنلیک	دلیک	۶۱
تیزنگ	دیزنگ	۳۳	توشگ	دشک	۶۵
تیزناق	دزناق	۳۳	توز	دوز	۶۷
تیز	دیز	۳۴	تیش	دیشی	۷۹
تر	دری	۳۴	تار	دار	۸۱
تاووشقاق	دوشان	۴۰	تلا	دلی	۸۶

ولی دردو واژهٔ ذیل "ت" آغازی خلج برابر با "ت" ترکی است:
خلج تولک و توزپاق برابر ترکی: تولکی و تزپاقخ (۴۰ و ۵۴).

افزوده شدن "ی" برسرواژه‌هائی که در ترکی با صوت آغازمیشود. نمونه :
خلج : ییل (۵۷) ، ییتلیک (۷۲) ، ییتی (۸۱) ، ییراق (۸۱) برابر ترکی : اپل ، اپتلیک ، اپتی ، اپراقخ .

دردو واژهٔ ذیل "د" خلج برابر "ی" ترکی دیده میشود:

خلج: هاداق (۳۳) و قوذرذوق (۴۱) برابر
ترکی: اَیاقخ و قویردوق.

در سه واژهٔ ذیل پسوند خلج "قان" برابر است با ترکی "ان":
خلج: سیچقان (۳۷)، تاودشقان (۴۰)، قازقان (۶۳) برابر
ترکی: سیچان، دوشان، قازان.

"ق" خلج در بیشتر واژه‌ها برابر است با "ق" ترکی ولی گاهی "ق" خلج برابر است با "قخ" یا "خ" یا "غ" ترکی. نمونه:

خلج	ترکی	صفحه	خلج	ترکی	صفحه
قولاق	قلاقخ	۲۹	اقلان	اغلان	۲۶
بقارساق	باقرساقخ	۳۱	بقوز	بغاز	۳۱
بارماق	بارماقخ	۳۳	تالاق	دالاغ	۳۲
تورپاق	ترپاقخ	۵۴	تاق	داغ	۵۴
قانق	قانوخ	۶۸	اوزاق	اوزاخ	۸۱
ییراق	ایراقخ	۸۱	تق	تخ	۸۲
یووق	یاووقخ	۸۱	یقار	یخاری	۹۰

اوقلاق اوقلاقخ ۳۹ (ق = و و ق = قخ).

"گ" برابر "ب" فارسی خلج "گادام" = "بادام" (۴۸) در گویش خور بیابانک دیده میشود.

دربارهٔ گویش ترکی

۱ـ صوت شناسی

شمارهٔ واژه‌های ترکی که در جدول واژه‌ها داده شده برای بررسی کلی در صوت شناسی ترکی یا برای یافتن فرقهائی که میان گویش ترکی بلوک وفس و مثلاً گویش ترکی آذربایجان پیدا میشود بسنده نیست. اینجا فقط چند نکته را دربارهٔ صوت شناسی همین گویش بلوک وفس که نمونه‌هائی از آن داده شده یادآور میشود.

بجای صوت ـ نیز ا شنیده میشود.

نمونه: بجای پمبق، پامبق (۷۱).

بجای صوت ي نیز ی شنیده میشود.

نمونه: بجای باجي وتاري، باجی وتاری (۲۶ و ۷۴).

وبرعکس: بجای گلین، گلین (۲۸).

بجای صوت ا نیز آ شنیده میشود.

نمونه: بجای باش وقاش، باش وقاش (۲۹).

بجای صوت ؤ نیز و شنیده میشود.

نمونه: بجای گؤزگول وتورش، گؤگول وتورش (۳۱ و ۸۳)

آنجائیکه درستون ترکی = داده شده وواژهٔ ترکی مانند فارسی است آخر واژه را باید با ـ خواند.

نمونه: کتیع (۲۶) و نتت (۴۹). (بتت درست نیست.)

صوت ـ همان ی است واگر فرقی دارد ازهم شناختن این دو آسان نیست.

(رویهمرفته باید نفوذ صوتهای فارسی را درهمه جا درنظر گرفت.)

7
PHONOLOGY, CONSONANTS

7.1 *Pure consonants*. In this chapter we shall discuss the consonants of Khalaj. It must be emphasized that this study is a provisional survey only of the dialects of KhT., KhM., and KhX. The sequence of consonants is about the same as that of the Sanskrit alphabet, that is, it is not alphabetical in our sense. We have found this system to be more natural than that of the regular alphabet. For the examples compare the dictionary in Chapter 14.7.

The phonemes of Khalaj are almost the same as those of ATu. and perhaps those of PTu. with the following exceptions: /ņ/ may originally have been */ņ/ and */ņ́/ (cf. Räsänen 1949.200-3, a rather doubtful interpretation as */ņ́/ may be explained as */ņ/ under certain conditions). We find no traces of */ņ́/ in Khalaj; /ņ/ very often has become /n/. Kh. /n/ is both ATu. /n/ (e.g., *kü̦n* 'day' < *kǖn*) and ATu. /ń/ (e.g., in *qọ˙n* 'sheep' < *qōń*). /f/ is found in foreign words in Khalaj. ATu. -/b/ has become /v/ (or a diphthong, e.g. *hȧv*, *hö̦̂ü* 'house' < *äb*). Kh. /h/ is a special sound not found in ATu. but presumably belonging to a very old Tu. layer (cf. 9.8). On the whole, Kh. is quite close to ATu. We shall deal with some of the peculiarities of Kh. in Chapter 9. So much for the historical development of Khalaj consonants. The following is a description of the consonants (the numbers refer to the language lists given above).

/k/ [k] and [q] velar voiceless fortis stop. *k* and *q* (both of which are slightly, or sometimes a little more than slightly, aspirated) are hardly distinguishable (in contrast to other Tu. languages); that is, a distinction between a prevelar and a postvelar voiceless fortis stop is hardly perceptible. This is especially obvious in such loanwords as T. 262 na̤˙zu̜q 'thin' ← P. na̤zok or T. 132 qardu̜ 'bed (of a garden)' ← P. kärdu, where /k/ is not pronounced so forward as in Persian. On the other hand, /k/ in, for example, M. 70 qo̤n 'sheep' or T. 43 qa̤˙ru̜n 'bellow' is not just pronounced back. The difference between the *k and *q of other Tu. languages is not stronger than in English, where /k/ before front vowels (as /i/) is spoken more to the front than before back vowels; cf. Jones 1949. 134: "Taking the k in come kʌm as the principal member of this phoneme, we find that a more forward k is used before i: (as in keep ki:p) and a more backward k before ɔ (as in cottagé kɔtidʒ); other intermediate sounds are used before other vowels according to their nature." (The same, by the way, is true of German and other languages. It is possible that Khalaj has preserved in this respect the system of PTu., making no genuine distinction between the allophones [k] and [q] of the PTu. phoneme /k/.) To speak frankly, then, a distinction between [k] and [q] is hardly justified in Khalaj (neither from the phonetic nor from the phonologic viewpoint). However, we make this distinction for the following reason

(a) Comparison with other Tu. languages is facilitated. For a Turcologist qa̤˙ru̜n 'bellow' looks somewhat more familiar than ka̤˙ru̜n (in spite of Turkish karin).

(b) [k] < CTu. [k] before /i/ is a bit palatalized; such palatalization never happens with CTu. q (of course ki- >k′i- is nothing more than a kind of secondary assimilation).

(c) CTu. [q-] often becomes, or alternates with, [G] (transcribed G̬ by us); CTu. [k-] always remains a fully voiceless [k-] (with the exception of ATu. k̂öl 'lake' >Kh. gọ̈̄ᵒ·l, but this word may be a loan from older Azerbaijani). Even this viewpoint is semi-diachronic.

(d) CTu. [-q] often becomes, or alternates with, [qx], [x] (e.g., T. 135 'sickle' họ̄ġraqᶜ, họ̄ġraqx, họ̄ġrax), whereas [k] never shows such alternances.

(e) In the vicinity of [q] and [ġ] instead of [i̤], [i̦] we sometimes find [ï] or a slightly more back variant of [i̤], [i̦], similar to Evenki /i̦/.

The above considerations show that the distinction between [k] and [q] is not so much in pronunciation (which differs only slightly, just as in the English /k/ before /i/ or /o/) but in the fact that CTu. [q-] has a tendency to become (semi-)voiced and [-q] has a tendency to become affricative (the old /ï/ before it tending to be preserved), whereas [k] has a tendency to become palatalized.

[k'] a palatalized [k], especially before [i̤] (and before [ṳ] < [i] as in T. 300 ȧkk'ṳ 'two' < äkkī); e.g., kī̤ᵉ·čä is indeed k'ᶜī̤ᵉ·čä. This [k'] seldom occurs in other cases, as in auslaut (M. 31 hȧlyäk' 'sieve').

[G̬] CTu. [q], very often [G̬], respectively voiceless or semi-voiced media lenis, mainly in anlaut; e.g., M. 1 G̬ạra 'black,' seldom in auslaut (M. 22 hạdạG̬ 'foot'). (It would be better to write [G] because [G̬] is not pronounced very far to the back; this situation is the same as /k/ = [k] and [q].)

[x] postvelar voiceless fricative as in Scotch loch (or in German Loch), often used as an alternance of [qᶜ], cf. above;

sometimes used in foreign words (in this case it is better regarded as an independent phoneme /x/).

[x́] palatal voiceless fricative as in German ich 'I' (only one doubtful example exists: T. 316.

[^{q}x] affricate of a slight [q] (somewhat back /k/) and [x] (cf. M. 20); alternance of [q], [q^{c}], [x]. Also [qx] (T. 135).

[^{k}] slightly (hardly audibly) pronounced [k] (M. 87, T. 80).

[k^{c}] and [q^{c}] aspirated (more to the front or back) /k/, [q^{c}] often alternating with [qx] or [x] (e.g., T. 135). Since /k/ normally is slightly aspirated (though not so strongly as in some northern German dialects, cf. Jones 1949. 135 141), we have noted the aspiration only when it is stronger

/g/ [g] and [g] the normal English [g] as in gone. (Diachronically, */g/ has been partly preserved, e.g., T. 17 bàg, bàG 'son-in-law' < bäg 'prince' and has partly developed to various zero-grades, such as [y] in T. 241 äyrį 'crooked' <ägrē.)

[ǵ] palatalized [g] (T. 205), sometimes pronounced almost as [y] (T. 287), and dialectically alternating with [y]: T. 287 yįlǵàr 'before' = M. 40 įlyä^{1}r = X. 40 į^{1}lgär.

[G] voiceless (semi-voiced) media lenis (T. 17 bàG ~ bàg).

[ġ] postvelar voiced fricative (as in New Greek); in T. 75 a sound intermediate between [g] and [ġ].

[^{g}x] affricate of [^{g}] and [x] (M. 29).

[Ġ] approximately voiceless (semi-voiced) affricative media lenis articulated between [x] and [ġ] (T. 179, 257).

[^{Ġ}] slightly pronounced [Ġ] (T. 263 hànlį^{Ġ} 'broad').

[^{g}] slightly pronounced [g] (X. 5).

[$^{\dot{g}}$] slightly pronounced [ġ].

[$^{\acute{g}}$] slightly pronounced palatal voiced fricative (sounding almost like [^{y}], with which it alternates: X. 34 *hịssị$^{\acute{g}}$* 'warm' = T. 280 *hịssị^{y}*).

[ṛ] French *r* grasseyé (uvular rolled) in M. 32 *ị̄^{e}t^{i}ṛäk* < older *êtgäk* 'we shall do.' Since it alternates with [g], this [ṛ] is an allophone not of /r/ but of /g/.

/ŋ̦/ [ŋ̦] velar nasal sonant. Apparently without allophones; never occurring in isolation but always before /g/ and /k/; could be regarded as an allophone of /n/. Cf. M. 111 *mịŋ^{k}* 'a thousand' (T. 319 *mịŋ*), etc.

/č/ [č] palatal voiceless affricate with the components [t] and [š]

/ǰ/ [ǰ] palatal voiced affricate with the components [d] and [ž] (occurring only in loanwords).

/t/ [t] dental voiceless fortis stop.

[tʿ] aspirated [t] (T. 97).

[D] voiceless (semi-voiced) dental media lenis (diachronically mostly < */t/, more seldom <*/d/, e.g., T. 41. Often occurring after consonants and used in foreign words, cf. T. 311 *họtDụz* 'thirty,' but *yättị* 'seven'; also 202 *ya̯ˑsDụq* 'cushion' and 232 *taxDa* 'plank'< P. *täxté*, i.e., ← older local P. **taxDa*. The same phenomenon is found, for example, in Aš., cf. Keya̯ 1335, 27 *täxdä* = P. *täxté*).

[^{t}] slightly pronounced [t] (X. 89).

[ṯ] a sound between [k] and [t] (diachronically developed

from [t] before front vowels, mainly [i], but never [í] <[ü]). The same sound is found in southern Karaim, cf. PhTF 329 (and even here it is < t, just as in such languages as Samoan or Hawaiian, where older mata 'eye' has become maṭa, written mata, maka, respectively).

/d/ [d] dental voiced lenis stop.

/n/ [n] dental nasal sonant.

/p/ [p] bilabial voiceless fortis stop.
[B] voiceless (semi-voiced) media lenis (M. 79, T. 228).

/b/ [b] bilabial voiced lenis stop.
[ƀ] bilabial voiced fricative, resembling Spanish b in haber 'to have' (X. 57, X. 86).

/f/ [f] labiodental voiceless fricative (only in loanwords; suf 'water' in Minorsky 421 may be su̜˙v or su̜˙V).

/v/ [v] labiodental voiced fricative (<*/-b-/, */-b/, and in loanwords).
[u̯] bilabiovelar sonant with only slight lip rounding and no friction (as the English /w/), cf. 7.2.

/m/ [m] bilabial nasal sonant.

/y/ [y] palatal sonant, almost semi-vowel, but (in contrast to [i̯]) with a slight friction, i.e., tending to be an affricate (the voiced correspondent of German [x́] in ich 'I'). T. 241 äyri̯ 'crooked' (< *ägrē), for example, is not = äiri̯, that is, is no diphthong. As soon as [y] loses (or almost loses) its fricative character, we write [i̯]. Cf. M. 89 yi̯ˡl 'year,' but bи̯i̯il 'this year'; cf. 7.2. Also note such cases as M. 18 'hat' bi̯˙ri̯àk, X. 18 bi̯ri̯äk (<bȏrk), in contrast to M. 31 hàlyäk´ 'sieve' (< älgǟk).

[ʸ] slightly pronounced [y], hardly distinguishable from [ǵ]; see above.

/r/ [r] dentoalveolar (single-flap) sonant.

[ṛ] cf. /g/ above.

[ʳ] slightly pronounced [r].

/l/ [l] dentoalveolar lateral sonant. Always the front ("European") [l], never the velarized [ł] as in the Russian byl 'he was' or as in the English bill. (Perhaps in this case also Khalaj has preserved PTu. /l/ without allophones [l] : [ł], in contrast to CTu. and C. But an Iranian influence cannot be excluded.)

/š/ [š] alveopalatal voiceless fricative as in English sh.

/ž/ [ž] alveopalatal voiced fricative as French j in jour (a rare sound, occurring only in loanwords).

/s/ [s] dentoalveolar voiceless fricative (as s in son).

/z/ [z] dentoalveolar voiced fricative (as z in zoom).

[Z] voiced (semi-voiced) media lenis (T. 207, M. 14), occurring rather frequently in auslaut.

[ᶻ] slightly pronounced [z] (M. 65).

[đ] voiced dental fricative as English th in this; perhaps only an individual variant of [z] (T. 55, T. 121).

/h/ [h] glottal voiceless spirant (breathed glottal fricative with very slight friction).

7.2 Semi-vowels and similar phenomena. In this section we distinguish the following categories:

(a) [y], the slight friction of which prevents it from being regarded a genuine semi-vowel.

(b) Frictionless glide-sounds [i̯] (palatal, [u̯] (labial). They always occur between vowels, [i̯] (in sandhi position) sometimes alternating with [y] (in absolute position, i.e., after open juncture; e.g., X. 89 bú̯i̯il 'this year' (but yi̯·l 'year'); also in M. 16 bé̯i̯in 'today'; T. 186 hau̯u̯z 'basin,' T. 282 sǫu̯u̯q 'hard,' etc.

(c) Diphthongs (mostly as the second parts of falling diphthongs) [$^{\underset{\wedge}{i}}$], [$^{\underset{\wedge}{u}}$], [$^{\underset{\wedge}{ü}}$]; e.g., T. 159 hā^{ai} 'moon,' T. 17 bà$^{\underset{\wedge}{i}}$ 'son-in-law' (← Az.), M. 6 lǫ$^{\underset{\wedge}{u}}$ 'lip' (← local P. < older P. lab), M. 30 hö$^{\underset{\wedge}{ü}}$ 'house.' Less frequently we find such cases as T. 308 $^{\underset{\wedge}{u}}$ǫ·n 'ten,' M. 85 k$^{\underset{\wedge}{i}}$ę$^{\underset{\wedge}{i}}$ 'chest,' where [$^{\underset{\wedge}{u}}$], [$^{\underset{\wedge}{i}}$] occur as the first part of diphthongs. (Diachronically [$^{\underset{\wedge}{i}}$] normally = the /y/ of ATu. and other Tu. dialects, /y/ also being pronounced in these dialects as [$^{\underset{\wedge}{i}}$]; [$^{\underset{\wedge}{u}}$], [$^{\underset{\wedge}{ü}}$] are derived from ATu. /b/.) These diphthongs are independent vowel glides in the sense of Jones 1949.57 (paragraph 219). One has the impression that these sounds have no sonant (vocalic) but consonantal character, though pronounced even more slightly than those of category (b). One may say that they are neither consonants nor vowels.

(d) [$^{\underset{\cdot}{a}}$], [$^{\underset{\cdot}{i}}$], [$^{\underset{\cdot}{u}}$], etc., (placed high with diacritical signs marking the vowel quality). These sounds also occur, just as those of category (c), as the second part of "diphthongs," but with a merely vocalic character. These are, so to speak, less genuine diphthongs than products of a certain pitch of long (two morae) vowels, as in ā^ə, ū^u, etc. Whereas /ā/ has a level intonation, /ā^a/ consists of a long vowel plus an immediately following ^a. ā in /ā^a/ is two to three times longer than a. This is a falling intonation with a long first and a short second part, whereas ^i in diphthongs does not participate in intonation, since it is no vowel. Besides falling pitch we also find falling-rising pitch.

(e) High-placed reduced vowels, which, of course, are no semi-vowels. Though we transcribe them just as in category (d), they are easily distinguishable from (d): they occur only after consonants and are not the second part of vowels, as [^u] in M. 27 ha·^id^ular 'they said,' cf. 8.1.

In summary, then, we can say of the previous categories that (a) is no genuine semi-vowel because of the slight friction; (b) and (c) may be called semi-vowels [(c) less than (b)]; (d) is a part-vowel of a long total-vowel (a vocalic affricate, so to speak); (e) is a pure and genuine vowel.

8
PHONOLOGY, VOWELS

8.1 <u>Quality of vowels</u>. The vowel system of Khalaj is phonetically complicated (though less so phonologically). The following square may serve as a help toward phonetic orientation (the chart is, of course, only provisional, subject to the changes which further study of Khalaj may dictate).

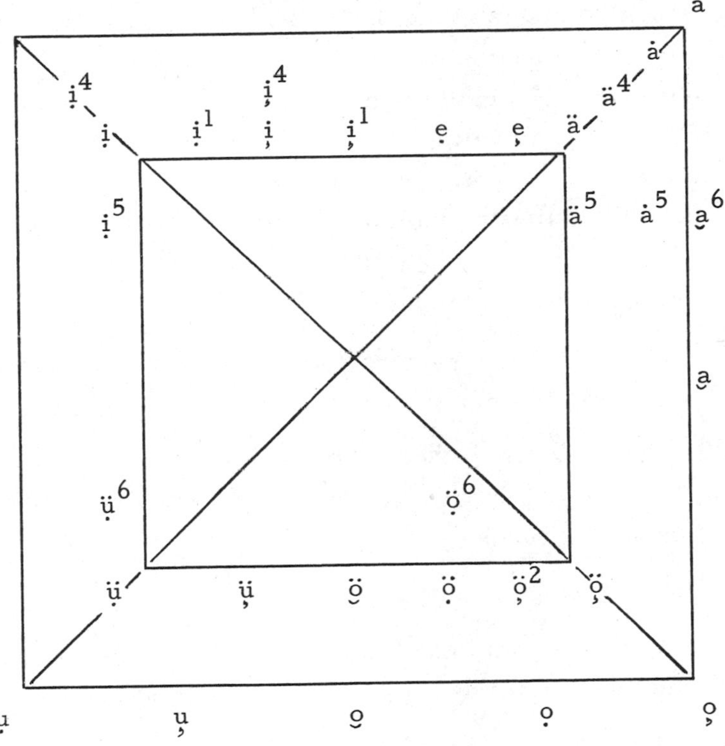

In order to avoid complicated signs for sounds occurring rarely (and normally only as variants of other sounds representing the "norm"), we prefer to employ the following system in this study: we mark the distinction between high and low vowels as <u>ị</u> (high) and <u>i̧</u> (low), the dot always marking a close, the cedilla, an open pronunciation. Slight deviations from such "normal" sounds as <u>ị</u> and <u>i̧</u> are marked by the following high-placed figures:

1: slightly lower (more open)
2: slightly higher (closer)
3: slightly more front
4: slightly more back
5: slightly labialized (rounded)
6: slightly delabialized (unrounded).

For example, <u>ị</u>^{1} means a sound intermediary between <u>ị</u> and <u>i̧</u>. (It is obvious that <u>i̧</u>^{2} would be the same; one may employ <u>ị</u>^{1} for a somewhat closer vowel, <u>i̧</u>^{2} for a more open quality; but this distinction would be hardly perceptible.)

We find the following vowel phonemes and allophones in Khalaj:

/a/ [a] very low back unrounded.

[a̮^{6}] very low back, very slightly rounded, i.e., a slightly delabialized variant of [a̮]

[a̮] very low back slightly rounded

/o/ [o̧] low back rounded

[ọ] low-mid back rounded

[o̮] between low-mid and high-mid back rounded (in the middle between [ọ] and [u̧]). But see note at end of 8.1.

/u/ [u̧] high-mid back rounded

[ụ] high back rounded. But see note at end of 8.1.

/ä/ [ȧ] slightly front variant of [a].

[ȧ5] = [ȧ] slightly rounded

[ä4] more front/lower than [ȧ], more back/higher than [ä]

[ä] low front unrounded. The distinction between [ä], [ȧ5], and [ä] is not always clear. When repeated, the same word may sometimes have the [ȧ] sound, sometimes the [ä]. The same suffix may be pronounced with [ȧ], [ȧ5], [ä]. Therefore a simple transcription [ä] seems to be sufficient.

[ä5] = [ä] slightly rounded

[ȩ̣] low-mid front unrounded

/ö/ [ọ̧̈] low front rounded

[ọ̧̈2] low front rounded, slightly low, more mid (i. e., higher)

[ọ̈] low-mid front rounded

[ọ̈6] = [ọ̈] slightly delabialized

[ö̥] between low-mid and high-mid front rounded. But see note at end of 8. 1.

/ü/ [ụ̧̈] high-mid front rounded

[ụ̈] high front rounded

[ụ̈6] = [ụ̈] slightly delabialized. This vowel was found in Xält-a̯ba̯d as the normal variant of /ü/, but we transcribe it simply as [ụ̈]. There are, by the way, even more delabialized (half-rounded, so to speak) variants of /ü/ (resembling y in Swedish lys 'light') and of /ö/ in, for example, Mehr-e Zämin, that is, in the material not yet published.

[ị5] high front, very slightly rounded, phonetically a variant of [ị] but phonologically an allophone of /ü/

/i/ [ị] high front unrounded

[ị^1] = [ị], slightly lower

[i̦] high-mid front unrounded. But see note at end of 8.1.

[i̦^{1}] = [i̦] slightly lower, almost [ẹ]

[ẹ] between low-mid and high-mid front unrounded

[ị^4] = [ị], slightly more back, in the vicinity of [q], [ġ]

[ï] high back unrounded, often in the vicinity of [q], [ġ]. It sometimes alternates with [ụ] (cf. X. 57 qā̜^{a}dụn ȧbȧ 'mother-in-law,' the normal Kh. form, ~ qā̜^{a}dïn ȧbȧ). In this case we may regard [ï] as an allophone of /u/, delabialized in a special position. But after [q], [ġ] [ï] is an allophone of /i/, just as [i̦^{4}], [ị^4]. So we may say that PTu. /ï/ is no longer a phoneme in Kh. but that sounds which are [ï] or are similar to [ï] are either allophones of /u/ or of /i/.

We seldom find the nasalized variants ĩ̦ (T. 64), ã̦ (T. 243) < iŋ, aŋ. We finally find reduced vowels in "reducing position," i.e., when the vowel has neither the main stress nor an accessory stress (which normally is on the first syllable). We find reduced vowels [^{u}], [^{i}], [^{ü}] either in the middle syllables of trisyllabic words — M. 27 hạ˙^{i}d^{u}lạ^{6}r 'they said' (< hā̀ydī̈lā́r), M. 32 ị̄˙tt^{i}lä^{1}r 'they did' (< ềttïlā̈́r) — or in the last syllables of disyllabic words, the first part of which has the stress: X. 16 bụ́^{ü}i̦˙n 'today' < bố-kǖn.

Note. The following short vowels are only allophones of long vowel phonemes, hence are, from the phonematic point of view, "long vowels":

ọ̈ as in X. kọ̈z 'eye (T. kọ̈^{2}z, but cf. T. kọ̈t 'anus,' etc.), X. kọ̈n- 'to burn.' This [ọ̈] is an allophone of /ō̈/ (*kō̈z), cf. 13.11.2.

o̧ as in M. q̧o̧l 'arm,' T. čo̧la̧q 'weak' (but T. to̧qqu̧z 'nine,' etc.), T. yo̧rġā̧n 'blanket,' T. yo̧qqa̧r 'above,' M. qo̧n 'sheep.' This [o̧] is an allophone of /ō/ (*qōl), cf. 13.11.2.

u̧ as in T. bu̧ru̧n 'nose' (but cf. T. qu̧d^{u}ru̧q 'tail,' etc.), T. yu̧n^{k} 'wool,' T. yu̧m^{u}ša̧q 'soft,' T. Çu̧lā̧q (M. qu̧la̧q). This [u̧] is an allophone of /ū/ (*būran, etc.), cf. 13.11.2. But cf. M. ha̧vu̧l 'good' (X. ha̧vu̧l), where [u̧] is but an assimilative variant of [u̧], belonging to /u/.

Furthermore, [i̧] is a phoneme different from [ị] in the following cases:

(1) In the southern dialects, where /i/, /ü/ have become [ị] (e.g., *küün 'day' > M. kịn), whereas */ö/, */ȫ/ have become [i̧], [i̧^{1}] (e.g., kȫz 'eye' > M. ki̧^{1}z), cf. 10.

(2) In those dialects (e.g., X. and T.) which have preserved an old opposition PTu. */e/ : */i/ in auslaut. Here */e/ >[i̧], but */i/ >[ị]. Cf. 9.6: *äkkī 'two' > àkkị, but *yättē 'seven' >yättị, etc.

8.2 Quantity of vowels.

(A) Phonetically Khalaj has the following quantities of vowels:

(a) long vowels with moved pitch (ā̧^{a} ...)
(b) long vowels with level pitch (ā̧ ...)
(c) half-long vowels (a̧˙ ...)
(d) short vowels (a̧ ...)
(e) reduced vowels (^{u} ...).

Furthermore Khalaj has

(f) long diphthongs with moved pitch (ū̧^{o} ...)
(g) short diphthongs with level pitch (ụ^{o} ...).

(B) Phonematically this system can be reduced to the following pattern:

(a) long vowels with moved pitch = (a) and (f) above (symbol: /â/...)

I shall call them "moved long vowels."

(b) long vowels with level pitch = (b), (c), and (g) above (symbol: /ā/ . . .). I shall call them "level long vowels." Some vowels of (d) above are in this category, cf. 8. 1, not

(c) short vowels = (d) and (e) above (symbol: /a/ . . .).

The phonetic difference between (a), (f), (g) and (b) in section A above may be described as follows:

Aa and Af consist of a first part which is two-three times longer than the second part. The second part is pronounced deeper than the first (with falling intonation, sometimes with falling-rising

Ag has no perceptible falling intonation, both parts being equall (or almost equally) long; but the first part is stressed. Ab is a two-morae vowel, i. e., longer than Ad, without falling intonation (and Ac has one and a half morae).

It must be said, however, that in Khalaj a tendency toward shortening vowels exists. Practically, we find the following varian

(a) Ad ~ Ae, e. g., ụ̱ ~ ̱ᵘ̦, cf. above. Vowels in "reducing position" often are reduced; this, however, concerns only low vowels cf. 8. 1 above.

(b) Ab or Ag ~ Ac ~ Ad, e. g., ụ̄ ~ ụ˙ ~ ụ. Shortening to half-long vowels mainly occurs in unstressed syllables, e. g., T. 43 qạ˙ rụn (< *qārïn). But it sometimes even occurs in stressed syllables, e. g., 'arm, sleeve' = T. 223 qụ°˙l ~ X. 68 qọ˙l ~ M. 68 qọl. In such cases it is often only the quality of vowels which indicates an old long (level) vowel: an original *qol would have become *qọl, and *qul would have become *qụl in Khalaj, whereas qọl represents an old *qōl and in the phonologic sense represents a separate phoneme. In Khalaj there is a tendency (just as in German) to open short vowels and to close long vowels (quš 'bird' > Ģụš, but bûz 'ice' > bụ̄ᵘ˙z). For other examples of this type cf. 8. 1, note. One may say that some short vowels belong to the same category as Ab, Ac, Ag. However, this grouping does not always work, since a̧, for example, has no low variant indicating an old a̱. The phonemic distinction exists only in ō̱/o̱, ū̱/u̱, ȫ̱/ö̱, but not in ā̱/a̱, etc. Especially a long ǟ̱ does not exist in the three dialects we investigated, cf. 13.11.5.

Thus the situation is rather complicated. For the diachronic development, see 13. Phonologically we may say that /ā/ ... is represented by [ā] ... (Ab), [a˙] ... (Ac), [u°] ... (Ag) and even sometimes by short vowels (Ad): [o̜], [ö̜], [ṷ]. The following is a simple enumeration of some cases of Ab, Ac, Ag, Ad, insofar as they are relevant for phonology (I give but one example):

Ab: /ā/ ... [ā̜] T. 208 ā̜š 'soup,' [ī̜] T. 73 ī̜t 'dog,' [ō̜] T. 135 hō̜ġraqᶜ 'sickle.'

Ac: /a˙/... [a̜˙] T. 288 ha̜˙ġa̜ 'behind,' [ȧ˙] T. 52 ȧ˙l 'hand,' [o̜˙] T. 23 bo̜˙š 'head,' X. 68 qo̜˙l 'arm,' [ṷ˙] T. 146 sṷ˙v 'water,' [i̥˙] M. 82 ti̥˙l 'tongue,' [ö̜˙] X. 50 kö̜˙nmäk 'to burn.'

Ag: /u°/... [ṷ°] T. 223 qṷ°l 'arm,' [i̥ᵉ] M. 50 ki̥ᵉndi̥ 'it burnt.'

For Ad see 8.1, note. Although phonemes of this type may occur even in a short form, they never can be reduced (in contrast to the genuine short vowels of type Ad).

8.3 Moved long vowels. Furthermore, we find the phoneme "moved long vowel", symbol /â/ .... Here we find the following variants: Aa or Af ∼ Ab ∼ Ac ∼ Ad ∼ Ag, e.g., [ṷ̄ᵘ] ∼ [ṷ̄] ∼ [ṷ˙] ∼ [ṷ] ∼ [ṷ°]. This phoneme, too, never can occur in a reduced form. Short variants are employed less frequently than in /ā/ .... They occur almost exclusively in unstressed syllables (in the first syllable of disyllabic words), in contrast to /ā/ .... But in unstressed syllables an original /â/ ... may also be shortened, e. g., T. 252 balla 'small' < *bâla (T. bāla). Since this feature is important only to diachrony, we shall treat it later. The following list, however, gives some examples.

Aa: /â/ ... [ā̰^{a}] T. 268 ā̰^{a}č 'hungry,' [ụ̄^{u}·] T. 60 bụ̄^{u}·t 'thigh,' [ọ̄̈^{ö}·] T. 157 kọ̄̈^{ö}·k 'blue,' [ȫ̰^{ö}] T. 133 gȫ̰^{ö}l 'lake,' [ụ̄̈^{ü}·] T. 209 sụ̄̈^{ü}·t 'milk,' [ị̄^{i}·] M. 61 sị̄^{i}·t 'milk.'

Af: /ū^{o}/ ... [ị̄^{e}·] T. 218 ị̄^{e}·m 'trousers,' [į̣̄^{e}ʾ] X. 41 į̣̄^{e}ʾšį̣k 'door,' [į̣̄^{e}·] T. 163 kį̣̄^{e}·čä 'night,' [ụ̄̈^{ö}·] T. 294 kụ̄̈^{ö}·k 'blue,' [ȫ̰^{ö}ʾ] X. 51 kȫ̰^{ö}ʾk 'blue,' [ụ̄^{o}·] T. 154 hụ̄^{o}·t 'fire,' [ų̣̄^{o}·] X. 35 hų̣̄^{o}·t 'fire, [ụ̄^{u}ʾ] T. 111 Ģụ̄^{u}ʾt 'wolf.'

Ab: /ā/ ... [ị̄] T. 299 bị̄ 'one' (< *bîr), T. 61 tị̄z 'knee' (< *tîz), M. 87 hị̄nȧk 'let us mount' (< *ûn-), [ụ̄] T. 318 yụ̄z 'a hundred' (< yûz ?, but perhaps < *yūz, then belonging to 8. 2).

Ac: /a· / ... [ị·] T. 246 hị· rkȧk 'male,' T. 32 tị· š 'tooth,' M. 110 yị· z 'a hundred' (cf. above), [ụ·] T. 216 pụ· ta 'shrub,' [a̰·] T. 68 ya̰· ġ 'fat' (but T. 275 yā̰^{a}ġlų̣x 'fat,' adjective), [o̰·] X. 42 yo̰· llą̣^{6}maq 'to send.'

Ad: /a/ ... forms such as T. 252 balla < bâla 'small,' T. 257 qų̣rrų̣Ġ < qûrïġ 'dry,' which phonologically belong to short vowels /a/ ....

Ag: /u^{o}/ ... [ọ̈^{ö}·] T. 220 bọ̈^{ö}·k 'hat,' [ų̣^{o}ʾ] T. 286 tų̣^{o}ʾla 'full,' [ụ^{o}·] M. 83 tụ^{o}·ra̰· q 'dried milk' (T. 214 tụ̄^{o}·ra̰q), and in a sense [ị̑ę̣] T. 286 bȧdị̑ę̣tmä 'angry.'

A special case arises with *ôn 'ten': T. 308 ^{u}ǫ̣· n, M. 100 ^{u}ǫ̣· n, X. 100 ǫ̣· n, ^{o}ǭ̣n, unstressed T. 309 ǫ̣n bị̄, X. 101 ǫ̣n, M. 101

o̤²˙n. As one can see, stressed /â/ ... normally falls into the categories of Aa and Af. Cases of Ab (/ā/ ...) are dealt with in this chapter only for diachronic reasons; synchronically they may be /ā/ ... (although we cannot be sure because of the scarcity of our material). Even synchronically words with such vowels often become special cases: bī̤ has lost an -r (which may exist in such cases as bī̤ri 'one of them'?). This word normally occurs in an extremely unstressed position, e.g., as an indefinite article. Another case: ī̤ in hī̤nȧk is unstressed, but perhaps in stressed position we would find ī̤ⁱ˙ (e.g., in hī̤ⁱ˙n 'mount'). T. 68 ya̤˙ġ 'fat' seems to be an individual variant, since we find yā̤ᵃġlṳx, etc. Cases of Ac (/a˙/ ...) normally occur only in unstressed syllables (pṳ˙ta 'shrub,' etc.); half-long vowels may be regarded as belonging partially to /ā/ ...; in other cases they are only variants of /â/ ... (apart from ya̤˙ġ, also yo̤˙lla̤⁶maq 'to send' < yṳ̄ᵒ˙l 'way'?). Also /uᵒ/ sometimes seems to be only a variant of /â/ ..., e.g., M. 83 tṳᵒ˙ra̤q ~ T. 214 tṳ̄ᵒ˙raq 'dried milk': perhaps ṳ̄ᵒ˙ has been shortened because of its unstressed position; should it always be pronounced shortened (as in KhM.), it would be /ā/ ..., but if in KhM. variants such as tṳ̄ᵒ˙ra̤˙q should exist, it would be /â/ ...; I cannot resolve this question. The situation is similar for tṳᵒ˙la 'full'; ie̤ in bȧdie̤tmä 'angry' (~ M. 32 ī̤ᵉ˙ttⁱ˙läˡr 'they did'; bȧdie̤tmä actually means 'ill-doing') is with certainty a variant of [ī̤ᵉ˙], hence /â/ .... ö̤ᵒ̈˙ in bö̤ᵒ˙k 'hat' may phonologically be regarded as /ā/ ...; here /â/ ... > /a/ ... may be caused by the dropping of -r- (ATu. bȫrk). However, we do not find ṳ̈ᵒ̈˙ (as expected in the analogy in qṳᵒ˙l 'arm'); we find ö̤ᵒ̈˙, which resembles the normal development of /ȫ/, e.g., in kō̤̈ᵒ˙k 'blue.' Hence we may regard ö̤ᵒ̈˙ as /ȫ/ (generally as /â/ ...) even in this case.

8.4 Summary. We may summarize as follows: We have to distinguish /â/ ..., /ā/ ..., /a/ .... In unstressed position all these vowels tend to be shortened; /ā/ ... especially tends to be shortened to /aˑ/ ... even in stressed position. Besides /â/ ... = [ā̯^{a}], [ụ̄ˑ^{o}], etc., we find [a̯ˑ], [ụˑ^{o}], etc., in unstressed position. Besides /ā/ ... = [ā̯], [ụˑ^{o}], etc., we find [a̯ˑ], [o̯] not only in unstressed but even in stressed position. Besides /a/ ... we find reduced vowels in an (extremely) unstressed position. Thus there is this tendency: /â/ ... > /ā/ ... >/a/...; but the old quantitative system is still preserved.

Some of the variants given above are dialectal; others may be individual. These matters cannot be decided until we undertake other expeditions.

Diagrams showing the difference between moved and unmoved long vowels will be given in a subsequent volume.

9

SOME MAIN FEATURES OF THE DIACHRONIC DEVELOPMENT

In this chapter I shall deal with the diachronic development of Khalaj. Since a complete description before the publication of the entire material is impossible, I shall restrict myself to an explanation of the most important facts. As I dealt with this subject rather extensively in 1968, I will refer to this article in all cases where the last expedition has brought no new results.

9. 1. Comparison with Azerbaijani. Let us consider at the outset some points of minor relevance: Kh. has not undergone the marked changes which Az, its neighbor in central Persia, has undergone. It has preserved k: T. 158 kṳ̈n 'day' (Az. gün); t-: T. 31 tịl 'tongue' (Az. dil); y- before i, ï: T. 164 yịl 'year' (Az. il); -G-, -G: T. 75 sịčgā̤n 'mouse' (Az. sičan); T. 276 hā̤^{a}čṳx 'bitter' (Az. aǰi) [my indication in 1968. 101 that ATu. -q and -ġ and -ġ- have become g- is false: -q normally is -q, -qʿ, -^{q}x, -x; -ġ is Kh. -ġ, -Ġ, -x; -ġ- is -ġ-]; -b has been preserved even in ATu. sûb 'water' (Az. su): T. 146, M. 78 sụ˙v (but X. 78 sṳ̄).

9. 2 Iranian influence. We find a strong influence of P. in the lexical system, cf. 3. 2. But we also find an influence of the P. sound system. For example, Atu. â, ā, a have become labialized: ā̤^{a}, ā̤∼ a̤˙, a̤ (âč 'hungry' > T. 268 ā̤^{a}č; āš 'soup' >T. 208 ā̤š; and bāš 'head' >M. 15 ba̤˙š; at 'horse' >T. 71 ha̤t). ATu. ǟ, ä have become ȧ˙ ∼ ȧ∼ ä^{4}∼ ä, e. g., *ǟl 'hand' >T. 52 ȧ˙l; ät 'flesh' >T. 67 ȧt. But ȧ (with the variants indicated) is typically P. Also the rather open ṵ, sometimes o̤, is char-

acteristic of P. (q̄ōl 'arm' >M. 68 qǫl). The change of ï > ị (ï, ị^{4}, ị^{4} to be found in the neighborhood of q, ġ only) may be due to P. influence, e.g., ïït 'dog' >T. 73 ịt (but q̈ïrq 'forty' > X. 104 q̈ïrq, M. 104 qị^{4}rq, T. 312 qị^{4}rq, etc.). However, even the system of vowels is not totally Iranized. The preservation of three quantities, the sounds ö̧, ü̧ at least in the northern dialects (contrary to my assumption of ȯ, u̇ in 1968.82-3, 103), the distinction between ǫ and ų, etc.: all these characteristics are quite un-Iranian. An Iranian influence in the system of consonants does not seem to exist, except for the frequent change q- > Ģ-, e.g., quš 'bird' > T. 103, M. 72, X. 72 Ģųš 'sparrow.

9.3 Long vowels. Contrary to my skeptical explanation in 1968.101-2, (moved and level) long vowels have been preserved in Khalaj. Since this subject is of special importance and can be adequately treated only at length, I shall discuss it in Chapter 13

9.4 Uniformity of */k/. PTu. */k/ has not been split into a front and a back allophone ([k] and [q] in the other Tu. languages) but has, on the whole, been preserved as a uniform sound, cf. Chapter 7: only *ki has become k'i (*kï has not). There is no relevant difference between the remaining sounds, as, say, in T. 203 käčä 'felt' and T. 43 qạ˙rụn 'bellow,' the last word being written kạ˙rụn, as well. That in the last case /k/ is pronounced (very slightly) more to the back is but a natural assimilation found even in European languages which do not use [q].

9.5 Ancient Turkic ń. ATu. -ń(-) has not become y, as in most Tu. dialects, but n. We find *qâńāq 'cream' >T. 210, M.X. 61 qā^{a}naq; *qâńō 'which?' > M. 60 qā^{a}nị, X. 60 qā^{a}nị; *qōń 'sheep' >T. 78 Ģụ^{o}n, M. 70 qǫn, X. 70 qǫ˙n; *kȫń- 'to burn' >M. 50 kị^{e}ndị, X. 50 kö̧˙nmäk. I shall pursue this topic further in Chapter

9.6 Proto-Turkic *-ē, *-ë̄. To a Tu. -ï, -i corresponds often (but not always!) the Yakut -a, -ä (after o, ö of the first syllable: -o, -ö). It is interesting to see that we find a correspondence to this situation in Khalaj. As I shall show in 13.11.5, 14.3.3 and 14.4.2 ATu. had not eight vowels (in three quantities) but ten, eventually even twelve (that is, thirty-six, counting quantities). We have to assume */e/ (pronounced between /ä/ and /i/) and /ë/ (between /a/ and /ï/). The only Tu. language which has preserved both */e/ and */ë/ is Chuvash: e.g., sas 'voice' < PTu. *säs, but sik- 'to jump' < PTu. *sek-; C. xur 'goose' < PTu. *qâz, but sïpă 'handle' (in other Tu. languages mostly sap, K. sāp) < PTu. *sëp (whereas PTu. */ï/ has become C. /ĕ/). It seems likely that /e/, /ë/ existed in non-initial syllables, too. And I suppose that Y. has preserved a reflex of PTu.-/ē/, -/ë̄/ in the cases mentioned above. Here is a short list:

T.	Y.	KhM.	KhX.	KhT.
yigrimi 'twenty'	sürbä	yị̄^{i}·rmị	yịgịrmị̦	yịịịrmị̦
yädi 'seven'	sättä	yättị	yättị̦	yättị̦
(but iki 'two'	äkki ~ ikki	ȧkkị	ȧkkị	ȧkkụ̈)
böri 'wolf'	börö	bị̄^{e}·rị^{1}	bị̄^{e}·rị̦^{1}	bị̄^{e}·rị̦
altï 'six'	alta	a̯lta̯	a̯lta̯	a̯lta̯

(Most of the other Tu. languages have -i, -ï, although sometimes such forms as yigirmä can be found; also *kâmä ~ *kâmi 'ship' < *kâmē, etc.) This means that KhM. has lost the difference between -/ï/ and -/ē/ (e.g., ȧkkị = yättị), but KhX. has preserved the opposition: PTu. *-/ï/ > /ị/, PTu. *-/ē/ > /ị̦/ (ȧkkị, yättị̦), and the distinction is extremely remarkable in KhT. where *-/ï/ > /ụ̈/ (ȧkkụ̈, yättị̦) and all Kh. dialects have changed PTu. *-/ë̄/

>/a̮/: a̮lta̮ 'six' (but PTu. *tōlï 'hail' >tụ°lọ, etc.). This concordance of two Tu. language groups spoken in such distant areas seems to show that we must assume *-/ē/, *-/ḕ/ even in non-initial syllables of PTu.

Incidentally, the opposition of PTu. *-/ī/ : *-/ē/ has been preserved in Brahmi script, cf. A. von Gabain, Türkische Turfan-Texte VIII, Berlin, 1954: 90 iki 'two,' but 103 yte 'seven' and ygirme (yerme, ygirmë, ygermi) 'twenty.' Therefore it seems probable that even ATu. still had preserved *-/ē/, *-/ḕ/. We may find a similar phenomenon in New Uighur, cf. PhTF. 539, 541-2, 547.

9.7 Ancient Turkic d. Tu. -d(-) has been preserved in Khalaj. Up to this point in Turcology we accepted a simple scheme: in the west Tu. area (with the exception of Chuvash) we considered -d(-) as having become y (e.g., ATu. adaq 'foot' > Osman ayak); only in the far east Tu. area did we consider -d(-) as having been preserved in some form or other (Y. atax, Tuv. adaq, Khakass azax). But now this simple scheme has been destroyed: in Khalaj, spoken about 2500 miles from Tuvinian (the "next neighbor" which has preserved d) we find d: T. 59 ha̮da̮q, M. 22 ha̮da̮G = ATu. adaq. Our texts, in fact, include a number of words with -d(-): ATu. qudruq 'tail' = T. 92 qụdᵘrụq, M., X. 67 qụrdụq; ATu. küdän 'wedding' = T. 16, X. 54 kụ̈dȧn, M. 54 kịdȧn; ATu. küdägü 'bridegroom' = M. 46 kịdȧiị; ATu. qâdïn 'brother-in-law' = T. 19, M. 57 qāᵊdụn, X. 57 qāᵊdïn; ATu. sīdök 'urine' = T. 69 sịdȧk; ATu. qudġu 'fly' = T. 109 qụdᵘġụ, M. 74 qụdġị[4]. In the texts not published in this book we find still further examples (KhT.): bọda̮mịšlȧr 'they colored,' similarly KhX. (ATu. bodo-); bụ°d 'figure,' similarly KhX. (ATu. bōd: K. bōd, T. boy); ọdġa̮n- 'to wake up' (ATu. odġan-); kȧD- 'to clothe' (ATu. kä̈d-: K. kä̈d, käd-, kät-, T. gäy-, Y. kät-). In other cases we also find ụdụ-

'to sleep' (ATu. ûdu-, ûdï-); hạdrị, hạdrụ 'separate' (ATu. adrï); yịd 'smell' (ATu. ŷid); yịd- 'to send' (ATu. îd-). These fifteen examples would seem to confirm our theory, as does the fact that we never found an instance of -y(-) (T. 19 qa^{i}narvadụ 'sister-in-law' is a loanword from Az. g̱ayïnarvadï; the genuine Khalaj term is qā^{a}dụn kịssị). In this respect Khalaj is, so to speak, an archaic enclave in a progressive territory.

9.8 Khalaj h- < Proto-Turkic *p-. But Khalaj has a feature which seems to be even more archaic, cf. Doerfer 1968.105-6. It has preserved h-, going back to PTu. *p-, cf. ATu. oyma 'felt stocking, felt boot' = Mo. hoyimasun = Manchu fomon, older *pomon, *poman; i.e., correctly: PTu. *poyma → Mo. *poyma (later within Mo. itself *poyma+sun, with the singular suffix) → Manchu *poyiman > *poman > *pomon > fomon. PTu. *p- has been preserved, in the form of h-, in other Tu. languages, too; cf. Räsänen in Uralaltaische Jahrbücher 33.146-8, 1961. But these are only sporadic cases, such as Az., New Uighur, Karakalpak höl, Uzbek hol, cf. Doerfer 1968.105-6 (Kh. họ̄^{ö}·l, hị̄^{e}·l); some authors therefore have not been convinced of the existence of Tu. *h- < *p-.

I myself cited two examples which seem to contradict an original existence of Tu. *h- = Mo. h- (which must go back to *p-, cf. Doerfer JSFOu, against Sir Gerard Clauson's views): Az. hör- 'to weave' and Kh. hâr 'man' seemingly do not fit Mo. örmege 'mantle' (derived from ȍr- 'to weave'), ere 'man.' But this assumption was false. Cf. TM I.103: örmege, ere simply are loanwords not from early Bolgar (these would have become Mo. *hörmege, *here), but from early CTu.; here *p- already had become zero, whereas -e in auslaut still had been preserved; hence Mo. örmege ← early CTu. *ȍrmǟkä < PTu. *pȍrmǟkä and Mo. ere < early CTu. *ärä ← PTu. *pärä are quite regular. In other cases we find a correspondence; Tu. h- = Mo. h-: Uzbek hokiz, New Uighur höküz 'ox' = Mo. hüker (Evenki hukur) 'bull'; Az. hürk- 'to be frightened' = Mo. hürgü-; Az. him (< *hïm) 'sign, token' = Mo. *him (Evenki *him); these are loanwords from early Bolgar *pọkärẓ, *pürk-, *pïm.

But one cannot do much with this knowledge, since examples with h- are found only sporadically in Tu.: we do not possess more than about a dozen certain examples, and we often find exceptions (e.g., Az. hör- 'to weave,' but New Uighur ör-, Uzbek or-; Az. has öküz 'ox,' etc.). The only Tu. language which has fully preserved h- < *f-<*p- is Khalaj. As I have shown in 1968, there are four proofs that Khalaj has preserved a genuine PTu. opposition *p- (> h-) : zero:

(1) Examples with h- are consistent and numerous, as these further examples indicate (cf. the vocabulary, Chapter 14); hạdạq 'foot,' hạt 'horse,' hạğạč 'tree,' hụ̈dụ̈m 'grape,' họ̄ğrax 'sickle,' hụ̄ᵒt 'fire,' hȧv 'house,' hạ̄ᵊčụx 'bitter,' etc. Compare all examples with an anlaut vowel in the vocabulary.

(2) No secondary h- can be found, with the exception only of T. 130 harra, M. 24 hạrrạ 'saw' ← P. ärré (without h- also in local P. dialects). However the h- form is not found throughout the whole territory of Khalaj: X. 24, e.g., has ȧrrä (and so have other Kh. dialects, a fact I did not know in 1968). This form seems to be a typical case of "hypercorrectness." There are many other P. loanwords with initial vowel (but I found no other example with the addition of h- in Khalaj); cf. afsạr 'halter,' ạ˙lụ 'plum,' ạ˙smạ˙n 'heaven,' ạstȧr 'lining,' etc. (Incidentally, cf. Kipchak-Uzbek harra 'saw,' Abdullaev 100; here the h- is secondary.)

(3) We find a regular retention of h- in derived forms: both hụ̄ᵒt 'fire' (T. 154) and hụ̄ᵒčạq 'hearth' (T. 195), a derivation of hụ̄ᵒt, have h-; similarly hȧr 'man' and hị˙rkȧk 'male'; on the other hand we find ạltạ 'six,' ạltmịš 'sixty,' etc.

(4) The examples with and without h- are about equal in number so that we have a quantitatively well-balanced opposition. We

cannot say that h- has been added afterwards, according to some phonetic law, because we find many examples without h-. We furthermore cannot say that the opposition h- : zero is the consequence of a mixture of dialects, for in the numerals, for instance, we find ǖš 'three,' but hǫttųz 'thirty,' a phenomenon which would not seem to be caused by a mixture of dialects. We also cannot say that zero >h- is typically Kh. whereas the examples with zero are loanwords from another Tu. dialect. Admittedly, we find some examples which à la rigueur could be Az., e.g., ųząq 'long' (local Az. uzax), ärik 'plum' (local Az. ärig; should be ärik; see Azizbekov 1965.156). But there are numerous examples which are genuinely Kh., which certainly are not Az., and which in all probability are not the result of the influence of any other Tu. dialect, e.g., ȧ˙rįn 'lip,' ąlųmlą 'apple,' ī˙ᵉm 'trousers,' altą 'six,' etc. Hence both h- and zero occur in genuine Kh. words. The statistics of h- : zero in genuine Tu. words is, according to the vocabulary, 26 : 34.

Khalaj preservation of h- means that Khalaj is in this respect the most archaic Tu. language, even more archaic than seventh-century RTu., which lost h- very early (or, at least, did not retain it in script).

9.9 Archaic features of Khalaj morphology. Khalaj has also preserved some archaic features in morphology. It has, for example, preserved the ATu. ablative in .dA (unpublished material of Mänṣur-ąbąd, Xärrąb): hȧvįdȧ (KhM.) 'from the house' (= RTu. äbindä, later äbindin, äbindän); on the other hand, the locative ends in .čA (an old prolative-terminalis which has become an equative in many Tu. languages, but in ATu. still bêlčǟ 'up to the hips,' etc.): X. 86 ǖčą 'in the sleep,' (unpublished material) yāᵊnįčą 'at his side,' etc. (Khalaj, however, has lost the pronominal -n-.) X. 89 kȧšgųlį įįl 'last year' is an interesting case: here kȧšgųlį < *käčgüli<*käčügli (i >ü in closed non-first syllables) < käč-igli (or rather *käčěglī). This is the RTu. participle in -glī, preserved in no other Tu. dialect, according to Räsänen 1957. 123 and to PhTF. Some dialects, e.g., those of Mehr-e Zämin and Čąhäk, have preserved the ATu. necessitative in -GULUK as a future form. For other archaic features cf. Doerfer 1968. 100 (dative in .KA, future in .GA).

9. 10 The numeral system of Khalaj. In the numerals of Khalaj we find traces of a peculiar trigintesimal system, to be found, I think, in no other language of the world. Cf. X. 106 'sixty' ȧkk^{i}-ǫttụz (literally 'two-thirty'), 'seventy' ȧkk^{i}-ǫttụz-ǫ·n (literally 'two-thirty-ten'); Wolfram Hesche has, since the compiling of the word lists, encountered the following expressions in Xärrąb: äkki ottuzugirmi (80), üčottuz (90), bäšottuz (150), these literally being 'two-thirty-twenty,' 'three-thirty,' 'five-thirty' respectively. Compare, however, Osman üç otuzunda kocakarı 'a very old woman' (literally 'a woman in her three thirties'), Dede Korkut, ed. Muharrem Ergin, Ankara, 1955, 74 üç otuz 'ninety' (literally 'three thirties').

I mentioned in 1968 the interesting form učümün 'third' (Minorsky 1940. 420) found in Kondurud. Similar forms occur in the unpublished material of Xorąk-ąbąd: üčminči, törtminči 'third, fourth' (ịčmịnčị, tịrtmịnčị? Mäzrä^{c}ä-ye Nou), birminči 'first.'

9. 11 Archaic features in the vocabulary of Khalaj. The vocabulary of Khalaj is also archaic. The following words occur in ATu. or Middle Tu. but occur infrequently or not at all in modern dialects (see Doerfer 1968. 106-7): T. 238 dąġ 'not' (K. 165 dāġ, Arghu, not found in any other Tu. dialect); X. 20 är < ärür 'is' (ATu. är- 'to be,' in the most modern dialects shortened >

e-, i-); T. 16 küdän 'wedding' (K. küdän); T. 218 ïᵉm 'trousers' (Türkische Turfan-Texte VII and K. öm, erroneously üm, Kipchak Houtsma em, erroneously im, Old Osman em, erroneously im; preserved only in C. yĕm, Yellow Uighur yem); T. 289 hürün, M. 39 hirin 'white' (ATu. ürüŋ 'bright'); T. 115 a⁶lumla 'apple' (K. almïla, in all other dialects alma, elma); X. 86 ū 'sleep' (preserved in Y. ū, but in most of the dialects replaced by derivations from ûdï- 'to sleep' or other forms); T. 109 quḍᵘġu 'fly' (K. 373 qudġu). In the unpublished material we find baluq 'village' (ATu. balïq: Mänṣur-abad, Čahäk, Mehr-e Zämin), va- 'to bind' (ATu. bâ-, in the modern dialects mostly the derived form bâ-ġ+la-: Mänṣur-abad, Čahäk).

10
DIALECT DIFFERENCES

Although our texts are rather scarce, they show clearly some dialect differences. These are of two kinds:

(1) The western dialects (KhX., KhT., etc.) have undergone a stronger P. influence than have the eastern dialects (particularly the southeastern dialects), which have preserved to a greater extent the Tu. character. The following are some examples taken from the lists of KhM. and KhX.: 6 M. 'lip' ȧ˙ ri̯n (ATu. ǟrin) = X. lȧb, lo̯^{u} (← P. läb, local P. lo̯^{u} respectively, cf. Aš. Keya̯ 1335. 159); 12 'waist' M. bī̯^{e}l (ATu. bêl) = X. kȧmȧrbȧnd (← P. kämärbänd); 13 'bowels' M. bo̯ġa̯rsu̯q (ATu. bağirsôq) = X. ru̯˙ da̯ (← P. rudé); 20 'bitter' M. hā̯^{a}ču̯^{q}x (ATu. âčiġ) = X. zȧ˙ r (← P. zähr 'poison'); 21 'tree' M. ha̯ġa̯č (ATu. aġač, yïġač) = X. di̯räxt (← P. deräxt); 37 'hearth' M. hū̯^{o}ča̯q (ATu. ôčâq) = X. ka̯la̯k (← regional P., cf. Keya̯ 139 käläk); 53 'oar' M. ki̯ryäk (ATu. kür-gäk) = X. pa̯˙ ro̯ (← P. pa̯ru); 55 'dove' M. gȧ^{5}u̯ȧ^{r}či̯n (ATu. kȫ-körčgün) = X. kȧftȧr (← local P., cf. Keya̯ 137 käfder); 67 'tail' M. qu̯rdu̯q (ATu. qudruq) = X. do̯m (← P. dom); 74 'fly' M. qu̯dġi̯^{4} = X. ma̯ga̯s (← P. mägäs); 107 'seventy' M. yätmi̯š (ATu. yȃtmiš) = X. hȧfta̯˙ d (← P. häfta̯d); 108 'eighty' M. sa^{i}san (ATu. säkiz-ôn) = X. hȧšta̯˙ d (← P. hägta̯d); 109 'ninety' M. to̯^{q}xsan (ATu. toquz-ôn) = X. nȧvȧd (← P. nävävd). In nos. 12, 20, 21, 67, 107, 108 we often find original Tu. as well as P. forms, but the Tu. words always have been elicited from informants only through our suggesting the form as a possible variant (the Tu. forms evidently are still known, but the P. forms are more usual in everyday speech). In the other cases (Nos. 6, 13, 37, 53, 55, 74, 109)

informants have expressly stated that only P. forms exist, the Tu. forms being expressly denied.

(2) The northern dialects have preserved ancient *ö̱, *ü̱ (> ö̱, ü̱), whereas the southern dialects have changed these sounds > i̱, i̱. Actually we find many transitions from ü̱ > ü̱^{6} > ü̱^{66} (an even more delabialized ü̱) > i̱^{5} > i̱. See Chapter 5 for further discussion of this point. Of course we can give a complete analysis only after all the material has been gathered and evaluated. Sometimes we find delabializations in words of a dialect which normally has preserved ö̱, ü̱; e.g., X. 36 hı̣̄·^{e}l 'wet' (= M. 36) "should be" hȫ̱·^{ö}l (as it is in T. 256), since KhX. normally preserves ö̱ (thus X. 94 = T. 302 tȫ̱·^{ö}rt 'four,' but M. 94 tı̣̄·^{e}rt < ATu. tö̂rt). These instances may be crossings of various dialects.

(3) We also find other dialect differences. In KhT., for example, we find a strong tendency to change i, ˈi in all non-first syllables > ü̱, u̱; e.g., T. 21 kı̣šı̣̃ babasu̱ 'father-in-law' = X. 57 kı̣šı̣ babasˈi, and so always in the possessive suffix (T. 62 ha̱da̱qı̣̃ a̱^{6}sDo̱, 221 ha̱da̱q qā̱^{a}bo̱, etc.); T. 314 altmu̱š 'sixty' = M. 106 a̱^{1}tmı̣š, X. 106 a̱ltmı̣š; T. 276 hā̱^{a}ču̱x 'bitter' = M. 20 hā̱^{a}ču̱^{q}x, but X. 20 hā̱^{a}čı̣^{q}x, T. 300 ȧkkü̱ 'two' = M. X. 92 ȧkkı̣, etc. Another instance occurs in Mouǰa̱n and Sorxädé, where instead of ı̣̄·^{e} (e.g., bı̣̄·^{e}l 'waist') we find ē̱·^{e} (bē̱·^{e}l), etc. We shall deal more fully with these dialect differences existing in Khalaj after we evaluate the entire material.

11
KHALAJ = NEW ARGHU

Minorsky (1940. 417-37) and Köprülü (Islâm Ansiklopedisi 5. 114-6, headword "Halaç"), who have tried to investigate the past of the Khalaj, have adequately treated such topics as the early notes about the Khalaj in Persian sources. Part of their investigation, however, must be regarded with some mistrust. The alleged connection, for instance, of the Iranian Khalaj with the "Khiljī" (or Khaljī), who played a role in twelfth/thirteenth century India, is not wholly tenable. This apparent connection arises from a certain similarity of tribal names. But similarity of Altaic tribal names does not prove the premise. Names such as Kiräyt (= Mo. Kereyit), Nayman (= Mo. Naiman) and even Qïtay exist as Nogay tribal names, but a significant historical connection of the Nogay tribe Qïtay with the Qïtay (even with the Qara-Qïtay) of ATu. sources cannot be proved. If a connection did exist at all, it may have been so marginal that it did not alter the original character of the language of the people. The Khiljī, then, may have had a slight contact with the Khalaj, may even have adopted their name, but may not have sustained any considerable linguistic or cultural influence. Of course, this latter supposition is purely academic; I do not affirm, nor even suppose, that even marginal contact existed. The Bulgars of today, for instance, have the same name as a Turkic tribe on the Volga river, but there exists not a single Bolgar Tu. loanword in their language. We must not, then, overestimate the importance of names, educing from them absurd historical liaisons. Just such an absurdity would occur were one to claim, for instance, that in 1813 a Scandinavian tribe and a Baltic tribe defeated a German tribe and conquered their capital. Yet thus might the Russian and the Prussian victory over France under Napoleon be described were one to play the historical name-game, for Russian (Rus´) is a Scandinavian name, Róþsmenn or similar, cf. Vasmer 1955. 551-2; Prussian is a Baltic name, i. e., the name of a nation speaking a language belonging to the Baltic branch of the Indo-European family of languages (Prūsis, cf. Vasmer 1955. 451); French (France) is a German name (the same as Francons, Franconia, cf. Vasmer 1955. 551). Surely there have been historical contacts, but these were long ago; and whereas the influence of the Scandinavians on the Russians and that of the Francons on the French has existed, though it be slight, a linguistic influence of the Baltic Prussians on the Prussians of Berlin has not existed at all. Neither has linguistic influence of the Turkic Bolgars on the Slavic Bulgars existed. Why must the case of the Khalaj be different? A similar case in point is that of the Xalač, mentioned by al-Kāšġarī as living on the banks of the Amu-Darya. To assume that al-Kāšġarī's Xalač = the Afghano-Indian Xalǰī = the Persian Khalaj would be extravagant (although some historical contact will not be denied, contact not relevant to the languages

Let us look to another source about the past of the Khalaj: origin-legends. It is well known that the Yakut have preserved the memory of their formerly more southern fatherland in legends. But legends dating from antiquity do not exist among the Khalaj; these people seem to have forgotten the remote past and to have preserved in their memory and traditions only more recent events.

Linguistics, then, must provide the needed clues. Indeed, linguistics is the only means of illuminating the shadows of Khalaj antiquity. Although these clues, of course, are scanty, the number of things which they reveal is somewhat surprising.

(1) As I have shown in 8. 5 above and in 1968. 103-4, 107, ATu. -ń(-) has not become -y(-) in Khalaj (as in most of the Tu.

dialects) but -n̲(-). We find *qā̰^{a}naq* 'cream' (< *qâńāq*); *qā̰^{a}nị* 'which?' (< *qâńō*); *Çụ^{o}n* 'sheep' (< *qōń*); *kị^{e}n-*, *kö̰˙n-* 'to burn' (< *kōń-*). Now al-Kāšġarī reports that the Arghu, Turkicized Sogdians living between Isfiǧāb (or Ṭarāz) and Balāsāġūn (cf. W. Barthold, *12 Vorlesungen über die Geschichte der Türken Mittelasiens*, Berlin, 1935. 82), have no *y* but *n* in the following cases: *qanaq* 'cream,' *qanū* 'which?,' *qōn* 'sheep,' *kön-* 'to burn.' These are precisely the words given above. This striking correspondence may be a clue that the Khalaj of today are descendants of the old Arghu. But one correspondence is, of course, not sufficient evidence. There is, however, other evidence.

(2) Let us cite here a negative instance. According to K. III 218, the Khalaj changed *q-* > *x-* (whereas the Arghu did not, cf. above *qanaq*, *qanū*, *qōn*); al-Kāšġarī cites *xïzïm* 'my daughter' instead of *qïzïm*; *xandā* 'where?' instead of *qandā*; Khalaj of Persia has *qī^{i}z* and *qā̰^{a}nị*, which is derived from the same root as *qandā* (**qâ+*).

(3) According to K. III 140, the Uighur Tu. vowel *ï/i/u/ü* has become *u/ü* in Arghu. Instead of Tu. *bardïm* 'I went,' Oghuz *bardam*, the Arghu say *bardum* and *käldüm* 'I came.' We find the same evolution in Khalaj. Here are some examples from our unpublished material of KhM. (a dialect which has preserved only *u*, since every *ü* > *ị*): *va̰rdụm* 'I went,' *va̰rdụn* 'thou wentest,' *va̰rdị* 'he went,' *va̰rdụqụn* 'we went,' etc. And consider these other examples (in which even KhX. often has *u*, although it normally tends to preserve *ï*, cf. 10.3): T. 19 *qā̰^{a}dụn* 'brother-in-law' (ATu. *qādïn*), M. 57 *qā̰^{a}dụn*, *qā̰^{a}dịn*, *qā̰^{a}din*, X. 57 *qā̰^{a}dụn*, *qā̰^{a}dïn*; T. 43, M. 62 *qa̰˙rụn* 'bellow' (ATu. *qārïn*) = X. 62 *qa̰˙rïn*; X. 46 *kȧlụn* 'bride' (ATu. *kälin*) = T. 15 *kȧlịn*; T. 291 *sā̰^{a}rụx* 'yellow' (ATu. *sârïġ*) = X. 73 *sā̰^{a}ro̰^{g}*; T. 44, X. 48 *kụndụk* 'navel' (ATu. *kindik*) = M. 48 *kịndịk^{c}*, etc. But it must be noted that *u/ü* often occur in open syllables (cf. 10.3), as in T. *babasụ* < *babāsï* 'his father,' *ȧkkụ* < *äkkī* 'two,' or in originally open syllables, as

in T. 115, M. 4 a⁶lụmlạ, X. 4 a⁶lọmlạ < alïmla < almïlā 'apple' (so K.). Furthermore, we often find i instead of u/ü, e.g., in the Uighur suffix +lïġ/+lig/+luġ/+lüg as in T. 263 ḣanlịG 'broad' (ATu. Uighur ênlig). The situation seems complicated, but, at any rate, a change of ï/i > u/ü does exist.

(4) According to K. III 153 for 'not' the Arghu say dāġ or dāġ ol, and the Arghu are the only Tu. nation to possess this word. Indeed, in all Tu. languages of today we find *ärmäz 'is not' or *tägül (Osman değil), and other forms. There is only one Tu. nation which has dāġ: the Khalaj. Cf. T. 238 hạvụl da⁶ġ 'is not good,' M. 19 ha⁶vụl daġ, X. 19 hạvụl daġ. And in Minorsky 422 we even find daġïläm 'I am not' (< dāġ ol). (For the etymology of dāġ ol and tägül cf. Doerfer 1968.107.) I think that the Khalaj use of dāġ is the most striking proof that Khalaj = Arghu, more precisely = New Arghu.

(5) This last piece of evidence is not so certain. According to K. the Arghu had -đ- instead of the -z- of other Tu. nations, e.g., ködäč 'cup' (= közäč, közöč elsewhere); even qađiq 'hollow trunk' may be derived from qazï- (or, less probably, qaz-) 'to hollow out.' Now we find T. 121 hụđụm 'grape' (also T. 55 đụmrụq ~ zụmrụq 'wrist'). This form, however, may be an individual variant; cf., on the other hand, T. 260, X. 28 ụzāq 'long' with a pure -z-, no -đ-.

KHALAJ, AN INDEPENDENT TURKIC LANGUAGE GROUP

The usual classification of the Tu. languages is this:

(1) Chuvash or Bolgar group
(2) Southwestern Tu. or Oghuz group
(3) Northwestern Tu. or Kipchak (Kypchak) group
(4) Southeastern Tu. or Uighur group
(5) Northwestern Tu. or South-Siberian group
(6) Yakut

Some scholars, however, have modified this scheme. Benzing, for example, puts Yakut (6) into group 5, PhTF 4. In the classification introducing PhTF (pp. vii, viii) group 3 has been split up into central Tu. (Kazakh, Karakalpak, Nogay, Kipchak-Uzbek, Kirghiz) and western Tu. (Karaim, Bashkir, etc.). Some authors (Menges, Poppe) have separated (more or less rigidly) Chuvash from all other Tu. languages. I do not think this separation is justified, for C. is a genuine Tu. language, cf. my remarks in <u>Indogermanische Forschungen</u> 71.116, 1966. C. has exactly the same numerals as all the other Tu. languages, wheras Mo. and Tungus have completely different numerals (with the exception of '4,' '1,000,' '10,000,' which may be borrowed). Menges 1968.60-1 gives a classification which deviates in some points from his classification in PhTF 6. He combines Uighur and Oghuz into one group and separates Oyrot (Altay Tu.) from the other south-Siberian languages (this separation is justified in a way, as Oyrot may be regarded as providing a transition between Kirghiz and south-Siberian; the combining of Uighur and Oghuz, however, sharply deviates from common practice.) Poppe 1965.33-53 agrees with our classification given above (though he employs other terms: 2 is called Turkmen; 4, Chaghatai; 5, Tuva-Khakass). However, the majority of modern Tu. scholars ascribe to this "classical" six-group classification.

Can we put Khalaj into one of these six groups ? Clearly we cannot classify it with Bolgar: of the relatively old Bolgar rhotacism and lambdacism (found as early as in the Bolgar loanwords in Hungarian, presumably from the eighth century) we find no trace in Khalaj. When Tu. is divided into Bolgar and CTu., Khalaj belongs obviously to CTu. (CTu. **tî̇z* 'knee' = KhT. 61 *tịz*, but C. *čĕr*, etc.). It seems obvious, furthermore, that we cannot put Khalaj into one of the groups 2-4. Here we find an old development *-d-* > *-đ-* > *-y-*, as attested to in al-Kāšġarī (eleventh century), e.g., *ađïġ* 'bear' = *ayïġ* in Oghuz and Kipchak. In the Uighur group *-đ-* > *-y-* is a bit younger, but is found in the spoken languages at least since the thirteenth century, as some hypercorrect forms prove; e.g., Ananjasz Zajączkowski, *Najstarsza wersja turecka Ḫusräv u Šīrīn Quṭba* III, Warszawa, 1961,3: *ađaq* 'cup' instead of the correct *ayaq* shows that *đ* must be pronounced *y*. Hence we may also conclude that *ađaq* 'foot' was only a historic transcription, just as English *wine* [wa·^{i}n] which was pronounced [wi:n^{e}] in the middle ages. Now Khalaj has preserved *-d-*; hence it does not belong to groups 2-4 (and we can find many other features clearly separating Kh. from 2-4). Can Khalaj be ranked with group 5 or 6? Let us consider the scheme given by Poppe 1965.34 (where C. has been disregarded):

atax	adaq/azaq	ayaq 'foot'		
tïa	taġ	tau/tu	taġ/daġ 'mountain'	
-ï	-ïġ	-ï	-ïq	-ï
Yakut	Tuva-Khakass	Kypchak	Chaghatai	Turkmen

Now Khalaj has hạdạq 'foot' (ATu. adaq), tā̤^{a}ġ 'mountain' (ATu. tâġ), sā̤^{a}rụ̧x 'yellow' (ATu. sârïġ, also Kh. hànlị̧$^{\dot{G}}$ 'broad,' etc.), and it thereby corresponds to the "Tuva-Khakass" (or south-Siberian) group. Must Khalaj, therefore, be regarded as a south-Siberian dialect?

Before resolving this problem we have to consider two points:

(1) The investigator who devised this scheme before knowing Khalaj could judge only on the material known to him. Thus we cannot blame him if his scheme turns out to be incorrect. On the other hand, it is clear that an accepted explanation, just because it has been accepted, need not and must not be considered correct *a priori* for all time.

(2) The argument that Khalaj and Tuvinian are spoken at places so distant that a connection is thereby improbable would be to oversimplify the case: English is spoken, for instance, in England, North America, and Australia, places which are even more distant from each other than Khalaj and Tuvinian are and which are separated by even more languages (pass from England through Asia to Australia!); but English remains one language, nevertheless.

I think, however, that Khalaj cannot be classified with any other Tu. group, for some special features separate it from all other branches of Tu.:

(1) The development of PTu. ń. See V.M. Nadeljaev, "Čtenie orchono-enisejskogo znaka ꜩ i ėtimologija imeni Ton'ukuk Tjurkologičeskie issledovanija, Moskva and Leningrad, 1963. 197-213, and Doerfer 1968. 103-4: Khalaj is the only Tu. language to have n (for PTu. ń) in all positions. Yakut has preserved this sound as a nasalized y (transcribed ɉ), the other dialects having mostly y, the Oghuz group having sometimes yVn: T. köy- 'to burn < kȫń-; goyun 'sheep' < qōń. (Some of Nadeljaev's conclusions, by the way, are false; Tuvinian, for example, has not preserved ń.) Let us consider now four words where Khalaj has n < ATu. ń:

ATu.	Kh.	Y.	Tuv.	Khakass
qōń 'sheep'	Ģụ°n	_____	xoy	xoy
qâńāq 'cream	qā^a naq	xaɉax	_____	xayax
qâńō (which'	qā^a nị	_____	qaÿi	xay
kȫń- 'to burn'	kọ̈·n-	kȫɉör-	_____	köy-

Yellow Uighur	T.	Nogay
qoy	goyun	qoy
qayaq	(gaymaq)	(qaymaq)
qay	xaysï	qaysï
_____	köy-	_____

The normal correspondent of ń is y in Tuv., cf. F.G. Isxakov and A.A. Pal'mbax, Grammatika tuvinskogo jazyka 84, Moskva, 1961: simply xoy, not xoɉ. In the eastern dialect ɉ also appears, but not always representing old *ń. The authors cite these examples: iɉi 'two' (<*iyi <*ägi < äki); Duruɉā 'crane' (<*turńa);

ijä 'mother' (Khakass ičä, inä, Tuv. iyä, perhaps a baby's word); ïɉaš́ 'tree' (< *yïġač). Hence in this respect Khalaj is quite isolated.

(2) The existence in PTu. not only of /a/ and /ï/, /ä/ and /i/ but also of the intermediary phonemes /ë/ and /e/. The development of these vowels is traced below in three groups: A, anlaut; B, inlaut; C, auslaut (CTu. means here all Tu. languages with the exception of C., Y., Tuv. and Kh.; we do not regard quantities in the tables):

	PTu.	C.	Y.	Tuv.	CTu.	Kh.
A	a-	u	a	a	a	a̯ < a
	ë-	ï (~ u)	ï (~ a)	a	a	a̯ < a
	ï-	yĕ, yï	ï	ï	ï	ị < ï
	ä-	a	ä	ä	ä	ȧ < ä
	e-	i	ä	ä	ä	ȧ < ä
	i-	ĕ	i	i	i	ị < i
B	-a-	u	a	a	a	a̯ < a
	-ë-	ï (~ u)	ï (~ a)	ï (~ a)	a	a̯ < a
	-ï-	ĕ	ï	ï	ï	ị < ï
	-ä-	a	ä	ä	ä	ȧ < ä
	-e-	i	ä	ä	ä	ȧ < ä
	-i-	i (î >ĕ)	i	i	i	ị < i
C	-a	a	a	a	a	a, a̯ < a
	-ë	ă	a	ï	ï	a̯ < a < ë
	-ï	ĕ	ï	ï	ï	ị ~ ụ̧ < ï
	-ä	a	ä	ä	ä	ȧ < ä
	-e	ĕ	ä	i	i	ị̧ < e
	-i	ĕ	i	i	i	ị ~ ụ̈ < i

And here is an example for every item (ATu. adāq 'foot,' āy- 'to say,' ï̄t 'dog,' ät 'flesh,' äkkī 'two,' ič- 'to drink'; qarā 'black,' sāp 'handle,' qîz 'girl,' käč- 'to pass,' kǟl- 'to come,' kišī 'person'; qarā 'black,' altï̄ 'six,' qārï̄ 'old,' kêčä̅ 'night,' yêt(t)ē 'seven,' äk(k)ī 'two'):

C. ura, ïyt-, yïtă, aš < at + šĕ (possessive suffix), ikkĕ, ĕ
xura, sïpă, xĕr, kaś-, kil-, ___(tilĕ 'fox' < tilkü, etc.)
xura, ultă, ___(possessive suffix + ĕ), ___(keśśä 'felt'), śiččĕ, ikkĕ

Y. atax, ïy-, ït, ät, äkki (~ ikki), is-
xara, up<ïp, kï̄s, käs-, käl-, kisi
xara, alta, kirïy- 'to grow old,' kiäsä, sättä, äkki ~ ikki

Tuv. adaq, ayït-, ït, ät, iyi (< igi < ägi), iš-
qara, sïp, qïs, käš-, käl-, kiži
qara, aldï, kirï-, ___ (dägä < täkä 'he-goat'), čädi, iyi

T. ayaq, ayt-, it (but cf. ï̄z 'trace'), ät, iki (< äki), ič-
gara, sap, gï̄z, gäč-, gäl-, kiši
gara, altï, garrï, gī̌jä, yädi, iki

Kh. ha̤da̤q, ha̤ˑy-, ı̤̄t, ȧt, ȧkki̤, i̤č- (unpublished material)
Ga̤ra, ___ (va̤r- 'to go' = C. pïr-), qı̤̄ˑiz, kȧš-, kȧl-, kiši̤
Ga̤ra, a̤lta̤, qa̤rri̤ (~ babasṳ 'his father'), kı̤̄ˑeča, yätti̤, ȧkki̤ (~ ȧkkṳ̈).

We can see that in respect to the vowel development traced above, Kh. is clearly distinguished from all other Tu. dialects: although it resembles Y. and Tuv. in the preservation of -d-, it has ë-, e-, -ë-, -e- >a, ä, just as CTu. has; but unlike CTu. it has preserved -ë, -e as -a̤, -i̤, in this respect resembling only Y. (but not Tuv., which has -ï, i, just as CTu. has). This situation is peculiar to Kh. alone.

(3) The preservation of *h-*. Kh. is the only Tu. language which has preserved *h-* systematically, *h-* occurring only sporadically in Az., T., Kumyk, Uzbek, New Uighur, and Karakalpak. For Kipchak-Uzbek cf. Abdullaev 100; for some further sporadic occurrences cf. PhTF 780 "h = cons. prothèse." But in all these languages *h* is preserved only in isolated words. The south-Siberian dialects have no trace of this phenomenon.

(4) The ablative in .*dĀ*. Khalaj is the only Tu. language which has preserved the RTu. ablative in .*dĀ*. In all other Tu. languages this form functions only as a locative (in Y. as a partitive, but the ablative of Y. is .*tAn*, which, by the way, is found in Kh., too, as .*dAn*). The participle *kȧšgụ̈lị* < *käčĕglī* is characteristic, cf. above.

(5) The unique word *da̤ġ* 'not' < *dāġ*, not found in any other Tu. dialect, cf. 9.11.

(6) Original Tu. quantities. As we shall see later, Kh. is the only Tu. language which has preserved all three original Tu. quantities, cf. especially 13.12.4 below.

The preceding considerations may be sufficient to show that Khalaj represents a separate, a seventh branch of the Tu. family of languages. Admittedly, some of its features may be found in other Tu. languages, but neither with such systematic regularity nor in the particular Kh. ensemble.

13
THE PROBLEM OF QUANTITY

13.1 *Introduction.* The problem of quantity is one of the most sophisticated in Tu. linguistics. It has even been asserted that Tu. originally possessed no long vowels at all (Ščerbak 1967, influenced by some sceptical, but not absolutely negative, remarks of Doerfer, "Langvokale im Urmongolischen?" *Journal de la Société Finno-ougrienne* 65.16-7, 1964). I do not wish to present here the endless details in the many articles of the many authors who have written about this subject. The reader may find bibliographies for a detailed treatment of this topic in the two most recent works about the quantity of Tu. vowels: Biišev 1963 and Ščerbak 1967.

I think a detailed refutation of the older theories is unnecessary for two reasons: the older investigators did not adequately consider the many "exceptions" in vowel quantity, nor did they know Khalaj.

13.2 *Former investigations and the "exceptions."* Generally K., T. and Y. have the same quantity of vowels, e.g., K. *āč* 'hungry' = T. *āč* = Y. *ās̀*; K. *ač*- 'to open' = T. *ač*- = Y. *as*-.

But there are many "exceptions." Here are some of them: K. *āš* 'food' = T. *aš*, Y. *as*; K. *qōl* 'arm' = T. *g̨ol*, Y. *xol*; K. *är* 'man' = T. *ǟr*, Y. *är*; K. *il*- 'to attach' = T., Y. *īl*-; K. qal- 'to remain' = T. *g̨āl*-, Y. *xāl*-, etc. K. often has alternances, even in the headwords of his vocabulary, as in *qōd*-∼ *qod*- 'to place'; and we find even more alternances in the text samples, e.g., *üč* 'three' (headword)∼ *ǖč* (sample). Let us see what attempts to explain such alternances have been made so far.

Ligeti 1938. 184-5 explains: "Il est à remarquer que chez Kāšġarī le nombre des mots dans lesquels une longue alterne avec une brève est assez élevé, preuve péremptoire de ce qu'au XIe siècle le processus de réduction des voyelles longues était déjà en plein cours et que dans le dialecte qui aux yeux de Kāšġarī avait le plus de prestige, le xaqani, il était très avancé." And he says further (192-3) that in the Tu. dialects we find the following categories: "1° dans un certain groupe de mots la longue se maintient dans toutes les langues sans exception, 2° dans un autre groupe, les formes à vocalisme long alternent avec celles à vocalisme bref d'une langue à l'autre, parfois même à l'intérieur d'une même langue, 3° enfin dans certains mots la réduction de la longue s'est produite même dans les langues les plus conservatrices à cet égard, comme le yakoute (üs 'trois'...). Du reste l'ouvrage de Kāšġarī prouve jusqu'à l'évidence que la réduction des voyelles longues est une tendance très ancienne. Ainsi l'état de choses moderne n'a rien qui puisse surprendre: à part quelques langues fidèles à l'ancien système de vocalisme long, la réduction est à mi-chemin dans un certain nombre de dialectes, tandis que dans la plupart des langues modernes elle est entièrement révolue."

Now let me present three objections to Ligeti's explanation.

(1) An objection to his style, to his mode of expression. Ligeti likes strongly affirmative terms; it is characteristic of him that he accuses the author of "criticisme coutumier" (Acta Orientalia Hungarica 21.120, 1968). I do not think that the transcription of vowels in al-Kāšġarī's dictionary can be called "une preuve péremptoire" (a peremptory proof) that Karakhanid had a tendency to shorten vowels in monosyllabic (and other) words. Ligeti has regarded only his own theory without considering other possibilities. And "peremptory proofs" are rather rare in science.

(2) An objection to Ligeti's assertion that in one and the same language we find ǖč ∼ üč, and that, furthermore, in the same old source some long vowels have been reduced, others preserved. Arguments such as these are not particularly convincing. Why did Ligeti not regard the possibility of half-long vowels (ü·č), which might have been written sometimes one way, sometimes another? Surely in the face of such strange conditions as described above, one should try every possible explanation.

(3) An objection to Ligeti's "reduction" theory. Ligeti says that a tendency toward reduction explains the instances where K.'s long vowels have become shortened in later T., Y. sources. But Ligeti has not taken into account the fact that K. often has a short vowel in places where the younger sources T., Y. have a long vowel (cf. above, K. il-, T., Y. īl- 'to attach'). If K. was so "advanced" in reducing long vowels, why has he preserved these long vowels in so many cases where even the "conservative" languages T. and Y. have short vowels? Some kind of contradiction is inherent in Ligeti's argument.

In summary, I think that Ligeti's thesis has been largely provisional in its character.

Räsänen 1949.68 has noted eleven cases of incongruence between Y. and T.; for instance, Y. ōl 'that' = T. ol; buol- 'to become' = bol-; är 'man' = ǟr, etc. (I shall mark these cases with the name "Räsänen" in the list given below.) Räsänen writes, "Merkwürdigerweise kommen diese Schwankungen nur vor einem urspr. r und ŕ sowie vor l vor." This explanation, namely, that the special nature of r, ŕ (>z) and l may have caused the incongruences between Y. and T., does not account for the incongruences between T. and Y. which occur with consonants other than -r, -z, -l; e.g., T. āy 'moon' = Y. ˙iy; g̡an- 'to become satisfied' = xan- ∼ xān-; g̡oyun 'bosom' = xōy; g̡uč- 'to embrace' = kūs-; mün- 'to mount' = mīn-, etc. Cf. 13.7.

Meyer Dissertation 81 gives a list of twenty-six cases where K. has a long vowel whereas T. (and, less frequently, Y.) has a short vowel. (These cases will be marked with the name "Meyer" in our list below.) Meyer does not attempt to explain the cause of such incongruences.

Biišev 1963 explains all Tu. long vowels by an original vowel + i̯ (*ai̯ > ā, etc.). Ščerbak 1967.37 questioned this explanation and with good reason. This theory is obviously erroneous, for the very old early Bolgar loanwords in Mo., e.g., Mo. boro (K., Gagauz bōz 'grey'), show no trace of *i̯ whatever. There is no proof (nor even hint) that Biišev's thesis is correct, either in Tu. itself or in Tu. loanwords in other languages. And Biišev did not address himself to the "exceptions" at all.

Ščerbak 1967 ignores the exceptions also; he gives neither a list of them (such as Y. mīn- 'to mount' = T. mün-), nor an explanation of their origin. But the exceptions must be explained before a theory can become credible; at least an attempt at explanation must be made.

13.3 Disyllabic words in al-Kāšġarī. And, indeed, there are many "exceptions," that is, incongruences among vowel quantities in the various Tu. languages! In the following investigation we can treat only sketchily such disyllabic roots as T. bȫri 'wolf' (Kh. bį̄ᵉri̯) = Y. börö, K. börī. It is well known that T. normally has long vowels in disyllabic roots, whereas Y. and K. have short vowels (Kh. corresponding with T.). Here are some other cases: T. (gur-)bāġa 'frog' = Y. baġa, K. baqā; T. āla 'colored' = Y. ala, K. alā, etc.; see the long list in Biišev 1963.47-51. (Unfortunately the author largely forgot to note Y. and K. forms, giving only T. forms with long vowels.) As the vowels of the first syllables in these forms are unstressed, we can surmise that they have been shortened secondarily. (As we shall see later, such secondary shortening holds true for Y., whereas this explanation must be somewhat modified to fit K.). Al-Kāšgarī's material in III 237-8, I 410, I 406-10 (word types CV̄CV̄, CV̄CV̄C, CV̄CVC) cannot convince us of the contrary. These disyllabic words with long vowels in the first syllables are for the most part either (a) derivations from monosyllabic roots (*sǖčig* 'sweet' < **sǖt* + *sig*, literally 'milky,' *bēr-im* 'debt' from *bēr-* 'to give,' etc.); or (b) onomatopoetics (*ǖhī* 'owl'); or (c) foreign words, where long vowels seemingly have been preserved in this position because they belong to another layer of the language; e.g., words beginning with *l-* (an anlaut unfamiliar to Tu. phonology), *lāġūn* 'a kind of vessel,' *lāčin* 'falcon'; the Žuan-žuan word *qātūn* (TM III No. 1159), *čātir* 'tent' ← P. (TM III No. 1042), *čātir* 'salmiac' ← P. *nušādir*, etc. Of twenty-nine words we find only six which cannot be put into one of these categories: *kǖpik* 'roughly sewed' (but *küpī-* 'to sew roughly'), *kȫšik* 'curtain' (but *kȫšī-* 'to cover'), *kȫlik* 'shadow' (but T. *köläġä*!), *bēšik* 'cradle' (T. *bīšik*), *sōġon* 'onion' (T. *soġon*!), *sīġun* 'deer' (T. *sūġun*). Six is an extremely low number, considering the many cases where the long vowel of the first syllable (preserved in T.) has been shortened. And these examples of K. seem the more dubious, as in two cases K. has a long vowel (*sōġon*, *kȫlik*) where T. has a short one (*soġon*, *köläġä*). Thus K. does not seem to be too useful to our investigation. However, we shall see (in 13.7) that another Karakhanid source (QB) will help us solve this particular problem of quantity.

13.4 *Monosyllabic words in al-Kāšġarī compared with Türkmän, etc.* But even in the monosyllabic roots we find exceptions in the correspondences of K. : T. : Y. (we shall take note of Khalaj, too, and occasionally of other languages). In the following survey I shall enumerate all words of K. for which we find correspondences at least in T. Let us see how many exceptions we find, in order to derive some statistics and thereby see whether the problem of the exceptions is quantitatively relevant or whether it can be legitimately disregarded. In the survey I have employed the following code:

(A) K. long vowel — T. short vowel
(B) K. short vowel — T. long vowel
(C) K. long ~ short vowel — T. long vowel
(D) K. long ~ short vowel — T. short vowel
(E) Y. deviation from K. (sometimes with correspondence tc
(F) Y. deviation from T. (sometimes with correspondence tc
(G) Statistically insignificant.

In the category "statistically insignificant" we put monosyllabic roots ending in a vowel, such as bā- 'to bind': such words must be long, for roots of the type CV do not exist in Tu. Furthermore čïq- 'to come out' < tašïq- is insignificant since it is only secondarily monosyllabic. Foreign words are put into this category, als

	K.	English	T.	Other languages
	āč	hungry	āč	Y. ās, Gagauz āč, Kh. ā̬ᵊč
	ač	to open	ač-	Y. as-
	āġ	to mount	āġ-	
	āq	white	āq	
	aq-	to flow	aq-	C. yux-, Kh. aqǤa̬ˑr 'rivulet'
	āl	cunning	āl	
	al-	to take	al-	Y. ïl-, WOD. āl-, C
	and	oath	ant	
EF	ār-	to get tired	ār-	Y. ïr- ~ ï̄r-, C. ïrxa Kh. harqā̬n 'tired'

B	art	back	ārt	Gagauz ārt
	art-	to increase	art-	Y. ˙irt- 'to pile up' [and <u>orduk</u> 'more' as a loanword ?]
	ās, āz	ermine	ās	[perhaps Y. <u>ās</u> 'white horse,' since ermines are white in winter; cf. German Fuchs 'fox' used for fox-red horses]
A	ās-	to hang up	as-	
AE	āš	food	aš	Y. as, QB āš, Kh. ā̯š
	āš-	to surpass	āš-	Y. ās-
	āt	name	āt	Y. āt, Gagauz āt, Kh. (unpublished material) ā̯^{ə}t
	at	horse	at	Y. at, Kh. ha̯t
	at-	to throw	at-	Y. ˙it-, WOD. āt-
	āw	hunting	āv	
EF	āy	moon	āy	Y. ˙iy, Kh. hā̯^{ai}
	ay	ah!	ay	
	ay-	to say	ayt-	Y. ˙iy-, Kh. ha̯·^{i}-, ha̯^{i}-
	āz	little, few	āz	Gagauz āz
	āz-	to go astray	āz-	
G	bā-	to bind	bā-ġ+la-	Y. bāy-
	baq-	to look	baq-	
A	bāl	honey	bal	(Meyer)
	bār	existing	bār	Y. bār
	bar-	to go	bar-	Y. bar-, C. p̈ir-, Kh. b̄a̯r-, WOD. vār-
	bars	leopard	bars	Y. bar ← Mo.
	bas-	to press	bas-	WOD. bās-
AE	bāš	head	baš	Y. bas, QB bāš, WOD. bāš, Kh. bo̯·š, ba̯·š
	bāš	wound	bāš	Y. bās
	bat-	to sink	bat-	Y. bat-, Kh. ba̯t-
	bāy	rich	bāy	Y. bāy

A	bǟg (and bēg 'husband')	prince	bäg	Y. bī, Kh. bȧg
	bäk, bärk	fast, solid	bärk	Y. bärt, Kh. bȧk
	bēl	waist	bīl	Y. bīl, Kh. bị̄^{e}·l
AF	bēr-	to give	bär-	Y. biär- (Räsänen), W vēr-, T. according to Ligeti bǟr-
	bēš	five	bǟš	Y. biäs, WOD. bēš, Kh. bị̄^{e}š
	bēz	gland	mǟz	
	bič-	to cut	bič-	Y. bis-
	bil-	to know	bil-	Y. bil-
DEF	bīr, bir	one	bir	Y. bīr (Räsänen), Kh. T. on-bīr 'eleven,' etc
	bit	louse	bit	Y. bit, PhTF 442 Noga Kipchak-Uzbek, 540 Ne Uighur bīt, C. pïytă
	biz	we	biz	(but cf. sīz!)
A	bōd	stature	boy	KhT. bụ^{o}d (unpublished material)
	boġ-	to strangle	boġ-	Y. buoy-
A	bōq	excrements	boq	(Meyer)
D	bōš, boš	empty	boš	(Meyer)
A	bōz	grey	boz	Gagauz bōz
	buz- (in the text erroneously boz-)	to destroy	boz-	WOD. bōz-
	bök-	to surfeit	bök-	
B	börk	hat	bȫrük	Kh. bọ^{ö}·k, bị· ri̯ȧk, bịri̯
	bȫz	linen	bīz	
G	bū	this	bū	Y. bu, WOD. bū
G	bū	steam	būġ	
A	būd-	to freeze to death	buy-	
	buq-	to crisp	buq-	

D	būr-, bur-	to smell	burun 'nose'	Kh. bụrụn, Y. murun
	būt	thigh	būt	Y. būt, Kh. bụ̄^{u}·t
	būz	ice	būz	Y. būs, Kh. bụ̄^{u}·z 'cold'
	bür-	to crisp	bür-	Y. bür-
	büt-	to stop	bit-	Y. büt-
BF	čaq	just this	čaq 'measure' (but čāġ 'time')	Y. sax 'time'
	čaq-	to beat	čaq-	Y. sax-
	čāl	grey	čāl	
	čal-	to beat	čal-	WOD. čāl-, Kh. ča̱l-
	čap-	to beat	čap-	
	čat-	to unify, to join	čat-	Kh. ča̱t-
	čǟk	kind of textile fabric	čǟk	
	čäk-	to pull	čäk-	
	čïġ	a kind of reed	čïġ	
G	čïq-	to come out	čïq-	(< tašïq-)
D	čīn, čïn	true, correct	čïn	
B	čïp	thin branch	čïbïq	
C	čēl, čel (in the text erroneously çil)	stripe	čīl	(< čēl, cf. 13.11.5)
A	čīt	kind of fabric	čit	
A	čōġ	bag	čov 'lappet'	
	čōġ	glowing fire	čōġ	
A	čōq	bad (Oghuz)	čoq 'company'	Osman çok 'much, many'
A	čōr	obscene woman	čor 'dirt'	
	čök-	to kneel	čök-	Y. söx-
	čöp	cookie	čöp	
D	čȫp, čöp	splinter	čöp	(Meyer)
	čuņ	big	čuņ 'deep'	
	čüm-	to dive	čüm-	

	äg-	to bend	ˈäg-	
	äk-	to sew	ˈäk-	
EF	ēl	land, peaceful	ˉil	Y. il
	äm	medicine	äm	Y. äm
	ēn	breadth	ˉin	Y. iän, Kh. hȧnlį$^{\dot{G}}$ 'broad'
	äņ-	to go astray	äņ-	
BF	är	man	ǟr	Y. är (Räsänen, Kh. hȧ
	ēr-	to frighten	ˉir-	WOD. ēr- (T. 'to get tired')
	ärk	might	ˈärk	
	ät	flesh	ät	Y. ät, Kh. ȧt
AF	ēt-	to do	ät-	Y. ˉit- 'to load a rifle,' Brahmi ät-, Kh. ˉịẹt-, cf. T. äd-il- 'to be don
	(according to the position et-)			
B	ew-, äw-	to hurry	ǟv-	
	äz-	to scratch out	äz- 'to crumple'	
	xān	ruler	xān	Y. xān
	ˉiš, ˉiš	work	ˉiš	
	ˈit	dog	it	Y. ˈit, Kh. ˉịt, PhTF 28 Qashqai, 540 New Uigh ˉit, C. yïtă
	ič	inside	ič	Y. is
	ič	to drink	ič-	Y. is-
	ˉig	sickness	ˉigli 'sick'	
BE	il-	to attach	ˉil-	Y. ˉil-
	it-	to push	it-	
	qač-	to flee	g̬ač-	WOD. g̬āš-
A	qād	snow storm	g̬ay	(Meyer)
D	qāq, qaq	dried fruit	qaq 'dry'	(Meyer)
	qaq-	to beat	qaq-	
BE	qal-	to remain	g̬āl-	Y. xāl-, WOD. g̬āl-
	qān	blood	g̬ān	Y. xān, C. yun

EF	qān-	to get satisfied	g̬ān-	Y. xān-, xan-, WOD. g̬āndïr-
	qāp	sack	g̬āp	Kh. ha̱da̱q qā̱ᵃbo̱ 'shoe'
	qap-	to get hold	g̬ap-	Y. xap-
	qār	snow	g̬ār	Y. xār, Gagauz kār, Kh. G̬ā̱ᵊr
C	qār-, qar-	to mix	g̬ār-	
	qāš	stone	g̬āš	
	qāš	eyebrow	g̬āš	Y. xās, Kh. G̬ā̱ᵃš
	qat	layer	g̬at	Y. xat
	qat-	to add	g̬at-	Y. k̇itar-, Kh. qa̱t-
A	qāw	flint	g̬ov	Y. k̇ia
	qay-	to glide, slide	g̬ay-	
	qāz	goose	g̬āz	Y. xās, Gagauz kāz, C. xur
	qaz-	to dig out	g̬az-	Y. xas-, WOD. g̬āzdïr-
	kēč	late	gīč	Y. kiäsä, Kh. kịᵉčä 'night'
	käč	to pass	gäč-	Y. käs-, WOD. gǟš-
D	käd-, kād-, kät-	to put on clothes	gäy-	Y. kät-, Brahmi käd-, KhT. käD- (unpublished material)
B	ked-, ket-	to go	git-	Crimean Tatar kät-, Crimean Osman ket-, Brahmi ket-, ked-, WOD. gēt-. Cf. T. gid-iš- 'to go together'
	käl-	to come	gäl-	Y. käl-, WOD. gǟl-, Kh. kål-
G	känd, känt	town	känt	Sogdian loanword
	kär-	to stretch	gär-	
	kärt-	to cut	kärt-	Y. kärt-
	käs-	to cut	käs-	Kh. käs-är 'axe,' WOD. kǟs-
B	käw-	to chew	gǟvüšä-	

	käz	to rove	gäz-	
	qïl	hair	g̬ïl	Y. kïl
CE	qï̄n, qïn	sheath	g̬ï̄n	Y. kï̄n
	qïr	mountain step	g̬̬ïr	
B	qïr	grey	g̬ï̄r	
	qïr-	to dig out	g̬ïr-	
	qïrq	forty	qïrq	Kh. qïrq and similar
B	qïs-	to shorten	g̬ï̄sg̬a 'shŏrt'	Y. kïsay-, Kh. qïsqȧ (Meyer)
	qïš	winter	g̬ïš	Y. kïs
	qïy-	to cut off	g̬̬ïy-	Y. kïy- 'to break'
BE	qïz	girl	g̬̬ï̄z	Y. kï̄s, WOD. g̬ï̄z, Kh. qị̈̄ⁱz
	kim	who	kim	Y. kim
BE	keņ (in the text erroneously kiņ̆)	broad	gīņ	Y. kiäņ, Kh. kị̄ᵉņᵏ
	kēp (in the text erroneously kip)	pattern	gǟp	Y. kiäp
BE	kir-	to enter	gīr-	Y. kīr-
	qoč	ram	g̬oč	
EF	quč- (in the text erroneously koç-)	to embrace	g̬uč-	Y. kūs-. Cf. T. gǔjaq 'embrace'
DE	qōd-, qod-, qoy-	to put	g̬oy-	Y. xot-, WOD. g̬ōyve- < gōdū bêr- (Osm̂an koyuver-) 'to free'
D	qōq-, qoq-	to stink	qoqa-	
AE	qōl	arm	g̬ol	Y. xol (Meyer), Kh. qụᵒl, qo̧l, qo̧·l
	qōl	plain	g̬̬ōl	
	qōm	camel's saddle	g̬ōm	
A	qōn, qōy	sheep	g̬oyun	(Meyer), Kh. G̬ụᵒn, qo̧n, qo̧·n
AE	qōn-	to settle	g̬on-	Y. xon-
	qop-	to jump	g̬op-	
A	qōr	yeast of yoghurt	gor 'sea-soning'	

	qorq-	to fear	gorq-	WOD. gōrxu 'fear'
AE	qōš	pair	goš	Y. xos
EF	qoš-	to add	goš-	Y. kuosar-
AF	qōy	bosom, embrace	goyun	Y. xōy, xōyn
	köč	move	göč	Y. kös
	köč-	to move	göč-	Y. kös-
	kȫk	blue, heaven	gȫk	Y. küöx, H. kọ̈̄ᵒk, kị̄ᵉ·k
	kök	origin, base	kök	Kh. kọ̈k 'thick' ← Az.
	kȫl	lake	kȫl	Y. küöl, Kh. gọ̈̄ᵒl ← P.?
	köm	to dig in	göm-	Y. köm-
	kȫn	leather	gȫn	
	kön-	to straighten	göni 'straight'	Y. kön-, könö
	köp	much	köp	
	kör-	to look	gör-	Y. kör-, WOD. gȫr-
EF	kön-, köy-	to burn	köy-	Y. kȫǰör- and similar forms 'to cook,' Kh. kịᵉn-, kọ̈· n-
	qul	slave	gul	Y. kulut
	qum	sand	gum	Y. kumax
C	qōm	wave	gōm	But K. qom- (in the text erroneously kum-) 'to wave'
	qun-	to peel off	gunuš-	
	qur-	to gather	gur-	
B	qurt	worm, wolf	gūrt	Kh. Gụ̄ᵘt
	qus-	to vomit	gus-	
	quš	bird	guš	Y. kus, Kh. Guš
	qut	blessing	gut	Y. kut
D	qūz, quz	shadowy place	guzay	
	kǖč	force	güyč	Y. kǖs
	kǖd-	to wait	güt- (Biišev 40)	Y. küt-
	kül	ash	kül	Y. kül, Kh. kụ̈l
	kül-	to laugh	gül-	Y. kül-

	kün	day	gün	Y. kün, Kh. kụn, kịn, kị̄n, WOD. gǖn, Volga Bolgar كوان küọn?
	kür	hero	gür 'thick' < 'strong'	Y. kür
BF	küz	autumn	güyz	Y. küs (Räsänen)
	män	I	män	Y. min, WOD. bǟn
	mäņ	mole	mäņ	Y. mäņ
	miņ	a thousand	müņ	Kh. mịn, mịņ^{k}
EF	mün-	to mount a horse	mün-	Y. mīn-
G	nǟ	what	nä	But T. nǟlär (plural)
DE	ōq, oq	arrow	oq	Y. ox
EF	ol	that	ol	Y. uol, ōl, ol (Räsänen)
AF	ōn	ten	ōn (on-bīr 'eleven')	Y. uon, Kh. ụ̄ọn and similar, WOD. ōn
	oņ	easy, right	oņ	
AE	ōr-	to cut, sickle	or-	Y. or-, Kh. họ̄ġraq 'sickle'
	ot	medicine	ot 'grass'	Y. ot
	ōy	valley	ōy	
	ōy-	to excavate	ōy-	
A	ōz-	to surpass	oz-	
EF	ȫč	vengeance	ȫč	Y. ös
A	ǖd	time	öylä 'afternoon'	
A	ȫg-	to praise	öv-	
	ȫl	wet	ȫl	Y. üöl, Kh. họ̄^{ö}l, hị̄^{e}l
	öl-	to die	öl-	Y. öl-, WOD. ȫl-
BE	ǖn- (in the text erroneously ön-)	to come out	ȫn-	Y. ǖn-, Kh. hị̄n- 'to mount,' Brahmi ün-
	öņ	before	öņ	
	öp-	to kiss	öp-	
	ȫr-	to grow	ȫr-	

EF	ȫr-	to weave	ȫr-	Y. ör- (Räsänen)
	ört	flame	ört	
	ürt-	to cover	ört-	
	ȫt	bile	ȫt	
	öt-	to pass	öt-	Y. öt-
	ȫz	self	ȫz	Y. üös
	bïš- (in the text erroneously piş-)	to cook	bïš-	Y. bus-
	bus- (in the text erroneously pus-)	to lie in wait	bus-	
G	sā-	to count	sāy-	
	sač	hair	sač	Y. as, Kh. sa̯č
	sač-	to scatter	sač-	Y. ïs-
A	sāġ	right	saġ	(Meyer)
	saġ-	to milk	saġ-	Y. ïa-
	sāl	raft	sāl	Y. āl
	sal-	to throw	sal-	
AE	sāp	handle	sap	Y. up < *i̯p (Meyer). Kh. Wena̯reǰ šâp 'thread' (unpublished material)
	sap-	to wrap	sap-	
	sar-	to become furious	sar-	
	sarq-	to drip	sarq-	
	sat-	to sell	sat-	
A	sāy	sandbank	say	
	sän	thou	sän	Y. än, WOD. sǟn
	säw-	to like	söy-	Y. iäy-
G	sī̈-	to break	sī̈-n-dïr-	
	sïġ-	to fit	sïġ-	
A	sī̈q	little, few	sïq 'thick, frequent' (lucus a non lucendo)	

	ṡiq-	to press	ṡiq-	
	ṡirt	mountain ridge	ṡirt	
CF	ṡīs, ṡiš	lance	čiš	Y. sis 'spine' [dubious: s̲- should become zero]
D	ṡīz-, ṡiz-	to soak into	ṡiz-	
D	sīd-, sid-	to urinate	siy-	Kh. sịdȧk, sị˙däk 'urine
	silk-	to shake	silk-	Y. ilk-
	siŋ̦-	to soak	siŋ̦-	Y. iŋ̦-
A	sīz	ye	siz	Y. ähigi (but K. biz) (Meyer)
	soġ-	to get	sov- 'to spend'	
	suq- (in the text erroneously sok-)	to stick into	soq-	Y. uk-
	sōl	left	sōl	
	soŋ̦	afterwards	soŋ̦	
B	sor- according to the position sōr-)	to suck	sōr-	
B	sor-	to ask	sōra-	WOD sōr-
	soy-	to skin	soy-	
	sȫg-	to curse	sȫg-	
	sök-	to divide	sök-	
AE	sȫz	word	söz	Y. ös, QB sȫz (Meyer), T. ac̦cording to Ligeti 191 sȫz
A	sūw	water	suv	Y. ū, Kh. sụ˙v. T. suu̯ or sūu̯?
EF	sür-	to drive on	sür-	Y. ǖr-, Kh. sụr-, sịr- (Räsänen)
	sürt-	to rub	sürt-	
	süs-	to throw away	süs- 'to beat'	
	sǖt	milk	süyt	Y. ǖt, Kh. sụ̄ᵘ˙t, sīⁱ˙t
	süz-	to sieve, filter	süz-	
	tāġ	mountain	dāġ	Y. t̆ia, Kh. tā̦ᵃġ

	taq-	to follow	daq-	
	tam-	to drip	dam-	
B	taņ	wonderful	tāņ	
	tap-	to find	tap-	Y. tap-, Tuv. tĭp-
	tār	narrow	dār	Y. tār, Kh. tā̯^{ə}r
	tār	float	dār 'gallows'	
A	tār-	to spread	dara-	Y. tarā-
	tart-	to pull, draw	dart-	Y. tart-
	tas	bad	tas 'hardly'	
	tāš	stone	dāš	Y. tās, Kh. tā̯^{ə}š
AE	tāš	outside	daš	Y. tas (Meyer)
AE	tāy	colt	tay	Y. tĭy (Meyer), ATu. tāń
B	tay-	to glide, slide	tāy-	
G	tē-	to say	diy-	Y. diä-, WOD. dē-
	täg-	to touch	däg-	Y. tiäy-
A	tǟg (in the text erroneously tek)	like	däk	
	täņ	equal	däņ	Y. täņ
	täp-	to kick	däp-	Y. täp-
	tär	sweat	där	
	tēr-	to gather	tīr-	Y. tīr- 'to draw.' But Az. där-, Brahmi täril-
G	tärs	odd, cross	tärs	Iranian loanword
	täz-	to run away	täz-	
	tĭq-	to fill	dĭq-	Y. tĭk-
DE	tī̆l, tĭl	tongue	dil	Y. tĭl, Kh. tị˙l and similar (Meyer)
EF	tĭn	breath	tĭn	Y. tī̆n (T. Biišev 45)
BE	tĭn-	to breathe	dī̆n-	Y. tī̆n-
	tīš	tooth	dīš	Y. tīs, Kh. tị˙š
	tik-	to stick	dik-	Y. tik-
C	tīn, tin	bridle	dīn	

	tiņ	steep (towering up)	diņ 'minaret'	
	tīz	knee	dīz	Kh. tīz
AE	tōd-	to get satisfied	doy-	Y. tot- (cf. toq 'satisfied
A	tūġ- (in the text erroneously toǧ-)	to be born	doġ-	Cf. Uzbek, New Uighur tuġ-
	toq	satisfied, full	doq	Kh. tọx, tọq
	tōn	clothes	dōn	Kh. tụ̄^{o}n (Y. suon?)
	toņ	frost	doņ	Y. toņ
	toņ-	to freeze	doņ-	Y. toņ-
D	tōp, top	ball, round	top	(Meyer)
AE	tōr	net	tor	Y. tor, Mo. toġor, tour
AE	tōy	camp	toy 'festival'	Y. toy 'many'
AF	tōy	clay	toyun	Y. tuoy, ATu. tōń
	tōz	dust	tōz	Gagauz toz
A	tȫg-	to beat	döv-	
	tök-	to pour	dök-	
A	tȫl	young animal	döl 'sperm'	(Meyer)
	tȫn-	to turn	dȫn-	WOD. dȫn-
	tȫr	seat of honor	tȫr	
CE	tȫrt, tört	four	dȫrt	Y. tüört, Kh. tọ̄̈^{o}rt, tị^{e}rt
	tȫš	chest	dȫš	Y. tüös, Kh. tọ̄̈^{o}š
A	tȫz-	to suffer from cold	döz-	
	tūġ	standard	tūġ	Chinese loanword? TM 622
A	tūl	widow	dul	(Meyer)
DE	tūr-, tur-	to stand	dur-	Y. tur-
	turq	length	durq	
EF	tūš	similar, opposite	dūš	Y. tus
	tut-	to hold	tut-	Y. tut-

	tuy-	to feel	duy-	
	tūz	salt	dūz	Y. tūs, Kh. tụ̄^{u}z
G	tǖ	down	tüy	Y. tǖ, Kh. tụ̈̄^{ü}k
	tüg-	to join	düv-	
BE	tün	night	düyn 'yesterday' but tün (Biišev 45 dün) 'night'	Y. tǖn
	tǖp	bottom	düyp	
BE	tür-	to fold	düyr-	Y. tǖr-
	türk	mature and strong	türk 'Turkic'	
	türt-	to besmear	dürt-	
G	tüš	place of rest	düšäk 'bed.' [In most Tu. languages döšäk, töšäk from töšä- 'to spread.' Or töšäk > düšäk by analogy of düš- 'to lie down'?]	
	tǖš	dream	düyš	Y. tǖl?
	tüš-	to fall, lie down	düš-	Y. tüs-, WOD. dǖš-
DE	tǖz, tüz	level	düz	Y. tüs (Meyer)
	ūč	corner, end	ūč	
	uč-	to fly	uč-	
AE	ūl	base	ulï 'big'	Y. ulū < uluġ < ūllaġ, literally 'having a firm base'
	ūn	flour	ūn	
EF	ur-	to beat	ur-	Y. ūr- 'to put,' WOD. vūr-
	ut-	to win, gain	ut-	
	ūz	master	ūz	Y. ūs, from ū- 'to be able'
	üč	three	üč	Y. üs, Kh. ụ̈̄š, ị̄č, WOD. ǖš, New Uighur PhTF 540 ǖč

C	ǖn, ün	voice	üyn	
BF	ür-	to bark	üyr-	Y. ür- (Räsänen)
	ürk-	to be frightened	ürk-	Y. ürt- (aorist ürgär)
B	üš-	to gather	üyš-	
	üt-	to singe	üt-	Y. üt-
	üz-	to cut into pieces	üz-	
G	yā	bow	yāy	Y. sā
D	yād-, yad-	to spread	yay-	
	yāġ	fat	yāġ	Y. sïa, Kh. ya̮ˑ ġ, yā̮ᵊġlųx
	yaġ-	to rain	yaġ-	
	yaq-	to burn	yaq-	
	yāl	mane	yāl	Y. sāl
	yal-	to flame	yalïn 'flame'	Y. sal-
	yān	crupper	yān 'side'	
	yan-	to burn	yan-	
	yaņ	model, pattern	yaņ 'echo'? (cf. K. yaņqū)	Y. saņ 'character'
	yap-	to cover	yap-	Y. sïp-
B	yar-	to split up	yār-	Y. ï̄r- [why y̲- >zero?
	yār	board	yār	Y. sï̄r
	yās	death	yās 'funeral'	
CE	yaš but yāš 'tear' (the same word)	wet	yāš	Y. sās, Kh. yā̮ᵊšųl 'gr
	yaš-	to hide	yaš	
	yāt	foreigner	yāt	
	yat-	to lie	yat-	Y. sït-, Kh. yā̮t-, WOD. yāt-
B	yay-	to shake	yāy-	
	yāz	spring	yāz	Y. sās

EF	yaz-	to go astray	yaz-	Y. sïs- 'to be near,' sï̄s- 'to fail,' QB yāzuq 'sin'
B	yaz-	to tie up	yāz-	
	yaz-	to write	yaz-	WOD. yāz-
G	yē-	to eat	iy-	Y. siä-, WOD. yī-
A	yēg	best	yäg	
AE	yēl	wind	yäl	Y. säl (Meyer), QB yēl, Kh. yẹ·l
	yänč-	to bite off	yänč-	
	yeŋ	sleeve	yäŋ	
AE	yēr	earth	yär	Y. sir (Meyer)
EF	yēr-	to hate	īr-	Y. sir-
	yet-	to reach	yät-	Y. sit-
B	yät-	to guide, lead	īt-	Y. siät-
	yïġ-	to gather, join	yïġ-	
	yïq-	to destroy	yïq-	
	yïl	year	yïl	Y. sïl, Kh. yịl, yị·l
	yïp	thread	yüp	
	yïrt-	to rend to pieces	yïrt-	
	yīg	raw, uncooked	īg 'pure-bred, unmixed'	
	yīn	body	īn	
	yit-	to get lost	yit-	
AE	yōd-	to destroy	yoy-	Y. sot-
	yoq	dirt, grease	yoq	
	yōq	not existing	yōq	Y. suox, WOD. yōq, Kh. yụ̄ºq (unpublished material)
	yōl	way	yōl	Y. suol, Kh. yo̯·lla- 'to send'
	yol-	to pluck	yol-	
	yort-	to gallop	yort-	
G	yū-	to wash	yuv-	Y. sūy-

	yum-	to lock	yum-	
	yuṇ	wool	yüṇ	Y. suṇ, Gagauz ǖn, K. yuṇ[k]
BE	yurt	nomadic territory	yūrt	Y. sūrt
	yūt-	to gulp	yuvut-	
	yük	burden	yük-	Y. sük- 'to burden' (?)
AF	yǖz	face	yüz	Y. sǖs 'front,' QB yǖz (Räsänen)
	yüz-	to skin	yüz-	

13.5 Statistical data. We have found 406 examples, 15 of which are insignificant. From the examples we can derive the following statistics of correspondence between K. and T. (the correspondence of K. and T. to Y. and other Tu. languages will be investigated later):

A. Coincidences

K. long vowel = T. long vowel	90 examples
K. short vowel = T. short vowel	188 examples

B. Deviations

K. long vowel = T. short vowel	54 examples
K. short vowel = T. long vowel	32 examples
K. long ∼ short vowel = T. long vowel	9 examples
K. long ∼ short vowel = T. short vowel	18 examples

There are, then, 278 coincidences and 113 deviations. It is obvious that, should we consider the deviations in other Tu. languages, we would get a far greater figure (cf., e.g., K., Y. ït 'dog' = T. it, but Kh., Qashqai, New Uighur īt). But even the deviations between K. and T. are so numerous that they are relevant and need detailed explanation.

Let us consider now a statistic of probability. How many monosyllabic roots (ending in a consonant) would be possible theoretically (without consideration of quantity)? According to the usual count (i. e., not counting PTu. *e̲, *ë̲, which are traceable only through C., which has a rather limited archaically inherited vocabulary), we get the following sounds:

In anlaut 7 phonemes:	vocalic anlaut, b, k/q, t, s, č, y;
In inlaut 8 phonemes:	the 8 vowels a, ä, ï, i, o, ö, u, ü;
In auslaut 17 phonemes:	b, k/q, t, s, č, y, p, g/ġ, d, z, š, l, r, m, n, ŋ, ń

The theoretically possible roots would be 7 x 8 x 17 = 952. Counting short and long vowels separately would double this figure, i. e., would make it 1904 roots. But actually this figure is much too high! Many possibilities are not utilized (e. g., no roots exist of the types *bab, *bup, *büń, etc.; ń, in general, is rare, etc.). To be sure, this figure will increase when auslaut clusters (such as ärk 'power,' yūrt 'nomadic territory') are added. But these cases are relatively rare. We can count no more than about 800 monosyllabic PTu. roots. Of these, 113 would be a rather large portion.

13.6 The graphic element in al-Kāšġarī's transcription. Now let us consider the deviations of K. : T. Before attempting an explanation, however, we must consider that K. has a remarkably graphic element, which cannot be utilized for linguistic (phonemic) purposes. After all, al-Kāšġarī was no modern phonetician, and what he has written down is no article in the transcription of the Association Phonétique Internationale!

In the list given above I have utilized only the headwords in K., leaving aside the words in the samples. This procedure was absolutely necessary for reasons of method. Ligeti (and, after him, Biišev) considered the words in the samples, too, e.g., Ligeti 192 "K ǖč, üč 'trois'" (whereas the headword is only *üč*). This procedure has some serious disadvantages. One gets the impression that al-Kāšġarī tried to give a precise transcription only when dealing with the headwords and only there is he *relatively* reliable (but even in the headwords we find such errors as *il-* instead of *īl-* 'to attach' or such variants as *būr-* ~*bur-* 'to smell'). But in the text we often find deviations from correctly noted headwords. For example, *qār* 'snow' has a short vowel in K. II 204-13 (text sample), and a correctly noted *ač-* 'to open,' though elsewhere short, occurs with a long vowel in I 358-20, etc. If we considered all the samples, almost every vowel given by K. would be *anceps*! (And they would be saved from this fate only when occurring in the headword alone or in a very restricted number of samples, where, according to the law of probability, the danger of both quantities occurring would not be so great.) Such a situation would amount to chaos! Admittedly, "correct" variants normally prevail in the samples; *qïz* 'girl,' for example, has a short vowel as a headword (I 326). But it occurs only in a very restricted number of examples with a short vowel (I 236-15, 442-1, III 120-6 *qïz*, I 326-10, III 218-21 *qïzïm*; on the whole, *qïz* 6 times). But we find *qīz* in I 7-15, 291-10, 312-21, 382-8, 412-21, 474-5, II 94-25, 96-16, 109-23, 272-1, 276-8, 277-12, 340-8, III 137-25, 203-4, 259-14, 260-16, 289-17, 301-21, 328-20, 371-20, 380-18; furthermore we find *qīzïm* in III 218-21, *qīzïn* in I 280-13, 299-11, II 182-25, *qīzqā* in II 304-14, *qīzlār* in II 220-11, i.e., *qīz* 36 times. These figures seem to indicate that one should consider the samples. But statistics are not always so comfortable: they sometimes fail for the simple reason that the number of cases is too limited (with two or three cases one cannot make up a set of statistics).

Many surprising ("false") quantities may be explained by means of prosody (cf. 13. 7). But the many variants are, in the last analysis, a *terra incognita*. We shall therefore take into account only the headwords, a consideration of samples being precipitous at the present time.

Another problem — a graphic one — arises. K. seems to prefer not to write long vowels (plene transcription) in words closed by clusters (or better, before two consonant signs). Therefore he generally writes *art* 'behind' (T. *ārt*), *börk* 'hat' (T. *b̄örük*), *qurt* 'wolf, worm' (T. *ġūrt*), *keŋ* 'broad' (T. *giŋ*), *taŋ* 'wonderful' (T. *tāŋ*), *yurt* 'nomadic territory' (T. *yūrt*). Seldom do we find variants: *tȫrt* ~ *tört* 'four' (T. *dȫrt*), *bērt* ~ *bärt* 'taxes' (from *bēr-* 'to give'). In *keŋ*, *taŋ* the merely graphic character is rather obvious (/ŋ/ is one sound, but is transcribed with two signs in the Arabic script: *ng*, just as in English 'to sing' [sɪŋ]). This explanation is provisional, of course; cf. also 13. 7.

But there are other graphic elements in K. One sometimes feels that what K. indicates with plene versus defective transcription is not so much longness or shortness of vowels but rather a mixture of quantity on the one hand and a distinction between open and closed syllables on the other. (Non-reduced) vowels in open non-first syllables, for example, normally are written as plene, e. g., *išlǟ-* 'to work' (in this paragraph I transcribe literally: *ǟ* means plene transcription, etc.), but as soon as the syllable is closed we find *išläl-*, *išlän-*, *išläš-*, *išlät-* (passive, reflexive, cooperative, causative), cf. 13. 11. The merely graphic character of al-Kāšǧarī's transcription is particularly evident in such cases as *ban-* 'to be bound,' from *bā-* 'to bind' (but aorist *bānïr*); *san-* 'to be counted,' from *sā-* 'to count'; *sïn-* 'to break' (intransitive), from *sï̄-* 'to break'; *tun-* 'to be covered,' from *tū-* 'to cover'; *yel* (~*yēl-*) 'to be eaten,' from *yē-* 'to eat'; *yun-* 'to wash (oneself),' from *yū-* 'to wash (another person).' In these cases one would expect *bān-*, *sān-*, etc., and in the modern languages we do find long vowels, e.g., T. *sī̈n-*. Here the transcriptions *ban-*, *san-*, etc., seem to indicate closed syllables rather than actual shortness.

Another proof for the graphic character of K.'s transcription is category C: *tīn* ~ *tin* 'bridle' (T. *dīn*), i.e., the many variants in closed syllables, furthermore the fact that sometimes vowels are written as short where they should be long according to "position"; e.g., 'to suck' (T. *sōr-*) is written *sor-*, but in a context where we merely find verbs of the type C$\bar{V}$C, i.e., it must be read long: *sōr-*. The other verbs are *kēčtī* 'was late,' *būrdī̈* 'smelled,' *bērdī* 'gave,' *tārdī̈* 'spread,' etc.

A last proof of the graphic character of K.'s short vowels is the fact that headwords which have a short vowel (but which should have a long one according to T., Y.) often have a long vowel in the text samples. Although this situation must be interpreted cautiously, still the vowel quantity of the text samples is sometimes genuinely significant. As we have seen, the long vowel of the form *qī̈z*, which appears thirty-six times in the text samples, must be correct, despite the headword *qïz*, since the short vowel form appears in only five text samples.

Now this graphic tendency gives us the key for an explanation (provisional) of category B, i.e., of the many cases where K. has short vowels whereas T. (and Y.) have long ones, e.g., K. *čïp* 'thin branch' = T. *čī̈bïq*, *il-* 'to attach' = *īl-*, *qal-* 'to remain' = *g̱āl-*, etc. The vowels are written as short because they are in a closed syllable. This explanation may also apply to category C, i.e., to the cases where K. has variants: long ~ short vowel, and where T. (and Y.) have a long vowel, e.g., K. *čēl* ~ *čel* 'stripe' = T. *čīl*, *tīn* ~ *tin* 'bridle' = T. *dīn*, etc.

Let us repeat this provisional explanation: unexpected short vowels in K. may be explained by his graphic tendency to mark closed syllables by a defective transcription. Long vowels in closed syllables are in some words written as plene (because of their long quantity), in some words they are written as defective (because of their position in a closed syllable), in some words they are written as plene ~ defective (because of their double character).

But now what about A and D, i. e., the cases where K. has a long vowel (plene transcription) which in T. is short (A), or where K. has variants long ~ short (plene ~ defective) which in T. are short (D)? According to data in Räsänen 1949. 68 (cf. above), one could expect K. to have long vowels before r, l, z, š, more often than T. has. But this expectation is false: there are many examples where other consonants follow in the categories A, D; e. g., K. ās- 'to hang up' = T. as-; bǟg 'prince' = bäg; bōd 'stature' = boy; bōq 'excrements' = boq, etc. Similarly K. čï̄n, čïn 'correct' = T. čïn; K. čȫp, čöp 'splinter' = čöp, etc. Here we may accept as a provisional explanation Ligeti's thesis that K. long vowels are corrcct and precisely reflect the PTu. quantity.

Summarizing the two provisional explanations of incongruence of vowel quantity between K. and T., we may formulate the following: If K. has a long vowel, PTu. must have had a long vowel. If K. has a short vowel but T. (and/or Y.) have a long vowel, the short vowel in K. is merely graphic, T. (and/or Y.) attesting to the PTu. long vowel. More briefly, if any one of the three sources K., T., Y. has a long vowel, its occurrence reflects a PTu. long vowel.

13. 7 Vowel quantity in Karakhanid. Perhaps this explanation seems convincing at first, but when one examines it closer, its

incompleteness becomes apparent. Two questions arise:

(1) Why have many vowels in K. remained long in T. (e.g. qār 'snow' = g̱ār; qāš 'eyebrow' = g̱āš), whereas so many others have become short, e.g. K. āš 'food' = aš; bāl 'honey' = bal; qōl 'arm' = g̱ol, etc. How can we explain category A? Ligeti's explanation that a tendency to shorten vowels, dating from the eleventh century, succeeded in some cases, in other cases failed, does not satisfy: we ask why in some cases the tendency succeeded, why in other cases it failed. We see no cogent reason for the difference.

(2) Why (cf. 13.3 above), despite all tendencies toward graphic transcription in K., do we find a majority of cases where the "long vowel" (plene transcription) is correct in monosyllabic roots: K. āč 'hungry' = T. āč; āġ- 'to mount' = āġ-, etc., and why in disyllabic roots do we sometimes find— contrary to the graphic convention (K. börī 'wolf' = T. bȫri) — a "long vowel" (cf. 13.3: K. sīġun 'deer' = T. sūġun, etc.). Can this latter phenomenon be explained by a merely graphic tendency?

Let us consider first the (easier) second question. The problem may stem not so much from a general Turkic but from a special Karakhanid character, i.e., al-Kāšġarī's spellings may reflect a special Karakhanid stage of development.

To investigate this Karakhanid stage of development, let us consider Tekin's superb article (1967). Tekin's starting point was the meter in QB, which is mutaqārib (⏑ - - / ⏑ - - / ⏑ - - / ⏑ -). He found that only such syllables were prosodically treated as long which were closed by a consonant (long syllables by position) or which contained open syllables with a long vowel (be the word of Turkic or of foreign origin). For instance, one may find ātïm 'my name' (but never ātïm 'my horse'; this must be atïm). Thus the PTu. long vowels are reflected not only in K., but also in QB. However, one must consider the following points:

(1) Tu. long vowels are, to be sure, anceps, e.g., besides ātïŋ 'thy name' and ātï 'his name,' atïŋ and atï respectively may also be found.

(2) Whereas long first syllables in disyllabic roots seldom occur in K., they occur somewhat more frequently in QB. Here I shall enumerate all such cases found in Tekin 1967: āčïġ 'bitter' (from āčï- 'to be bitter,' K. ačïġ, ačï-, T. ājï); āġū 'poison' (K. aġū, T. āvï); bārū 'since' (T. bāri); īdī 'completely' (which is, I think, contrary to Tekin's assumption, no derivation from īd- 'to let go'; īd- has in the RTu. inscriptions a back d, i.e., we must read ïd-, whereas īdī is written with a front d in the RTu. inscriptions, i.e., it is īdī); īsiz 'bad' (K. isiz); qādïn 'in-law' (K. qadïn, T. ġāyïn); ötā- 'to pay' (K. ötā-, T. ōdä-); qūrï- 'to dry' (K. qurï-, T. ġūrï 'dry'). We also find some disyllabic derived words with a long first vowel where K. normally has a short vowel: qïn+a- 'to punish' (K. qïna-); kēč+ā 'evening' (K. kečā); kē.din 'after' (K. ___); sāqïn- 'to think' (K. saqïn-); sāqïnč 'sorrow' (K. saqïnč); sāqïš 'counting' (K. ___); sūčig 'sweet' (also K. sūčig), tātïġ 'taste' (also K. tātïġ); tōzün (Tekin erroneously tūzün) 'gentle' (K. tözün); yāzuq 'guilt' (K. yazuq).

(3) Some instances are somewhat doubtful: ālig 'fifty': in the modern languages we find mostly ällig or a similar form, with two l's; in the languages closest to Karakhanid, that is, in Uzbek and New Uighur, we find ällik. I think we have to read ällig in QB, too; that is, the first syllable is only positionally long (is closed by the first l of ällig). A similar case is Tekin's "īki" 'two': we have ikki in Uzbek and New Uighur; in QB, too, we must read ikki or ekki; "ēki" in the Yenisey inscriptions does not necessarily mean a long vowel, that is, the "long" mark does not mark a quantity but denotes instead the qualitative character of the closed e: äki, äkki has become eki (or even ekki) in the Yenisey inscriptions, as a kind of assimilation. However, ēkki may be correct, since we find īgi in Shor (Biišev 1963. 53).

(4) QB has some instances of long vowels where T., Y. (or one of them) have short vowels. QB coincides always with K. (and Kh.) in these instances: āš 'food (K. āš, Kh. a̭š — T. aš, Y. as); bāš 'head, chief' (K. bāš, Kh. ba̭·š — T. baš, Y. bas); bōl- 'to become' (T. bol, but Y. buol-); kȫz 'eye' (Kh. kö̭z — T. göz, Y. kös. K., by the way, normally has kȫz in the text samples); yǖz 'face' (K. yǖz, Y. sǖs — T. yüz). In 13.4 and 13.5 we have enumerated 113 deviations between K. and T. In QB we find the following further examples: bōl- = T. bol- (but Y. buol-, Räsänen); kȫz = T. göz, Y. kös. We now have found 115 "exceptions."

I think QB gives us a much better explanation of the development in Karakhanid than does our provisional thesis in 13.6. But now let us consider three items of a more general character.

(1) We have assumed (rather naively) that the terms "long vowel," "short vowel" express the only existing and possible quantities. But such an assumption is false and simplistic. In Low German, for example, four kinds of quantity exist, cf. Essen 1953.112-6: we find short, half-long, long, and over-long vowels, e.g., snak 'talk!' short vowel; ri·t'n 'to tear,' half-long vowel with following tenuis; ri:dn 'to ride,' long vowel with following media; hu::s '(in the) house,' mü::s 'mice,' over-long vowel with a particular substitutional lengthening (words which go back to older *hūzə, *mǖzə).

(2) Furthermore we have assumed (again rather naively) that this one possibility exists: that a long vowel immediately becomes a short vowel, e.g., that K., QB must have had āt 'name,' that modern New Uighur must have at (Uzbek a̭t), and that there has been no transition at all. But in the real development of languages there are always transitions. Latin -a (e.g., in rosa 'rose') has not immediately become zero in French ([ro:z]) but we have to assume (and we know several points by

the reports of grammarians) that *rosa* at first became something like *ro:ză* (with a slightly reduced vowel, as in Portuguese) > *ro:zə* (as in German *Rose*) > *ro:z^{ə}* (as in the over-reduced Kalmuck vowels) > *ro:z.*

(3) And finally we assumed (once again naively) that language is a static thing, with no variations, no social classifications (layers), no situational variants in speech. (De Saussure would say that we did not consider *la parole* but only *la langue.*)

Correction of these three linguistic misconceptions allows one to give an explanation of Karakhanid vowel quantity which is more satisfactory than that provided by any previously existing theory.

I think we have to assume that in the Karakhanid period the PTu. long vowels already had become half-long (points 1 and 2). These half-long vowels may in swift colloquial speech often have become short or almost-short vowels (allegro forms, point 3). This shortening may have been true especially of unstressed vowels (i. e., first vowels in disyllabic roots or even in stems). Unstressed vowels normally are shorter than stressed vowels in other languages, e. g., bār (ba:r) 'existing' > Karakhanid ba˙r, but āġū 'poison' > almost aġū, only in very distinct speech a˙ġū. (We shall speak later on about the vowel of the second syllables.) There may have been a sharp distinction between slow and swift speech (lento forms and allegro forms); and especially in everyday speech (which always is the progressive form of speech, in contrast to the more conservative upper style of the "standard" language) allegro forms (with half-long or even short vowels) may have prevailed. It is generally recognized that such a difference exists in many languages and often leads to a change in the system of a language. See, for example, the opinion of N. Poppe, *Khalkha-mongolische Grammatik* 17, Wiesbaden, 1951: "In drei- und mehrsilbigen Wörtern, besonders in schneller Rede, fällt das _v_ der einen oder der anderen Silbe sogar oft aus." Unstressed vowels in particular are often shortened, cf. for English Jones 1949. 217: "The 'long' vowels ... are shorter in unstressed syllables than in stressed syllables," that is, the swifter speech is the greater is the chance of shortening, especially in unstressed syllables. Here is an example characteristic of my mothe tongue. In German we have the following pronunciations of haben 'to have':

(a) [hābä́n] only in over-distinct speech, to correct a misunderstanding, e.g., "Ich sagte nicht [zī hābä́n], sondern [dū hābä́st]."

(b) [hābən] in careful speech

(c) [hābn̥], mostly pronounced

(d) [hābm̥] in everyday colloquial speech

(e) [hā^{b}m] or even

(f) [hām] as allegro forms in swift and careless (or vulgar) speech, which may even become

(g) [ha˙m].

In Karakhanid we may have had a similar situation: in stressed syllables bār (= ba:r) 'existing' (very careful speech, lento form) ~ba˙r (colloquial speech, allegro form); in unstressed syllables a˙ġū 'poison' (careful speech, lento form) ~aġū or aġu˙ (colloquial speech, allegro form). (An exception may have existed for anlaut, cf. 13.11, 'name,' e.g., a^{a}t ~a˙t.)

With this assumption we can explain the many puzzling facts of Karakhanid transcription:

(a) It explains the variants in K., such as tīn ~tin 'bridle,' ǖn ~ün 'voice,' qōd- ~qod- 'to place,' etc. We have to assume ti˙n, ü˙n, qo˙d-. And these half-long vowels sometimes were written as plene (as long vowels), sometimes as defective.

(b) It explains why defective writing was used instead of plene writing in such cases as il- 'to attach' (T. īl-), q̇iz 'girl' (T. g̱īz), etc.: i˙l- may be written il- since it is not merely long, etc.

(c) It explains variable writings in the text samples of K. such as q̇iz ~ q̇īz 'girl' (cf. above 13.6), and it explains variable (anceps) meters in QB such as ātïṇ ~ atïṇ 'thy name.' It is obvious that a half-long vowel is quite naturally anceps.

(d) It explains why expecially before auslaut clusters we find mostly defective writing: such consistent defectiveness cannot be attributed to something purely graphic (cf. 13.6); it must occur primarily because the tendency toward vowel shortening before double consonants is even greater than elsewhere, e.g., *yûrt 'nomadic territory' (T. yūrt) > yu˙rt > yurt (allegro form). See Essen 1953.95, "Je mehr Laute dem akzentuierten Vokal folgten, desto kürzer wurde er." The same holds true for išlät- against išlǟ-, etc., cf. 13.6.

(e) It explains why long vowels in the first (unstressed) syllables of disyllabic words were normally "short": even in stressed syllables we have half-long vowels in allegro forms (ba˙r); unstressed syllables tend to be shortened still more, i.e., even the lento form a˙ġū 'poison' must become an allegro form aġū. Therefore we find in K. such forms as qadïn 'in-law,' börī 'wolf,' balā 'young animal,' tolū 'full,' tolī 'hail,' etc. (T. g̱āyïn, bȫri, bāla, dōlï, dolï — but Kh. tu̥°lo̥).

(f) It likewise explains why in some cases we find long vowels in the first syllables of disyllabic words, such as K. bēšik 'cradle,' sīġun 'deer' (T. bīšik, sūġun; for K. kȫlik 'shadow,' sōġon 'onion,' cf. 13.11), etc., cf. above. It is characteristic that QB has preserved many more long vowels in this position: its poetic language makes it tend more to lento forms. Some QB forms with long vowels where K. has short vowels are āčïġ 'bitter' (K. ačïġ, T. āǰï), āġū 'poison' (K. aġū, T. āvï), etc., cf. above.

Now let us consider quantity in non-first syllables of Karakhanid words. Seemingly, we have to distinguish between long and short vowels (written respectively as plene and defective). But it is curious that where Karakhanid has "long" vowels, T. sometimes has long vowels (e.g., the comparative suffix +rĀK, QB, Tekin 1967.169, which has the same form in T.) and sometimes has short vowels (e.g., the plural suffix +LĀr = +LAr in T.). I think that we must make a distinction here. We must consider that some suffixes even in QB never have long vowels (namely all suffixes with the fourfold variant ï/i/u/ü, e.g., the passive suffix). For an explanation of this situation cf. 13.11.

I have investigated another Karakhanid source, Yüknekī 1951, which has the same mutaqārib meter as QB. In this source I found the same situation, e.g., 453 aǰunqa bu sōküš (!) mälāmät ničin 'what is this cursing at the world for?' (hendiadyoin), 470 sözüm munda qālur (!) barur bu özüm 'my word will remain here, I myself will go away,' 472 tükātür ʿümürni bu yāzïm (!) küzüm 'this spring and autumn will finish my life,' 476 qalï barsa ōzüm sözüm qalsa tep 'saying, "When I myself go away, this my word shall remain,"' etc. It would be interesting to investigate this (rather short) source completely. We even find here many long vowels in words where vowel quantity is not establishable in modern languages, such as 257 bu bōdun 'this people,' etc. It would be useful to investigate all the other Middle Tu. sources (including Khorezm Tu., Chaghatay, etc.), in order to see at what time the long vowels disappeared definitively. But since this question is without importance for the investigation of PTu. quantity, I shall not deal with it here. For Yüknekī cf. Talât Tekin, Journal de la Société Finno-ougrienne 68:5, 1967.

13.8 Vowel quantity in Yakut. At the beginning of 13.7 I asked two two questions: how can we explain quantity in Karakhanid (this question has been answered) and how can we explain that some long vowels in K. have corresponding long vowels in T., (qār 'snow' = g̬ār), whereas other long vowels in K. have corresponding short vowels in T. (āš 'food' = aš).

Can we answer this second question by utilizing Yakut? I doubt that we can. We must consider that a long vowel in K. often has a corresponding short vowel not only in T. but also in Y. Here is a list of such cases:

K.	T.	Y.
āš 'food'	aš	as
bāš 'head'	baš	bas
qōd-, qod- 'to put'	goy-	xot-
qōl 'arm'	g̬ol	xol
qōn- 'to settle'	g̬on-	xon-
qōš 'pair'	g̬oš	xos
ōq, oq 'arrow	oq	ox
ōr- 'to sickle'	or-	or-
sāp 'handle'	sap	*ïp >up
sȫz 'word'	söz	ös
tāš 'outside'	daš	tas
tāy 'colt'	tay	tïy
tōr 'net'	tor	tor
tōy 'meeting'	toy	toy
tǖz, tüz 'level'	düz	tüs
yēl 'wind'	yäl	säl
yēr 'earth'	yär	sir
yōd- 'to destroy'	yoy-	sot-

It is clear that in these cases Y. does not explain more than T. But let us enumerate all deviations between T. and Y., comparing also the K. forms (if such can be found):

K.	T.	Y.
ār- 'to get tired'	ār-	ï̄r-, ïr-
āy 'moon'	āy	ïy
bēr- 'to give'	bär-	biär-
bīr 'one'	bir (∼on-bīr)	bīr
čaq 'just that'	čaq 'measure' (∼ čāġ 'time')	sax 'time'
ēl 'land, peaceful'	īl	il
ä̈r 'man'	ā̈r	är
ēt- 'to do'	ät- (∼äd-il-)	īt-
qān- 'to get satisfied'	g̨ān-	xān-, xan-
qïs- 'to shorten'	g̨ï̄sg̨a 'short'	kïsay-
quč- 'to embrace'	g̨uč-	kūs-
qoš- 'to pair'	g̨oš-	kuosar-
qōy 'embrace'	g̨oyun	xōy, xōyn
köy-, kön- 'to burn'	köy-	kȫǰör- and similar forms
küz 'autumn'	güyz	küs
mün- 'to ride'	mün-	mīn-
ol 'that'	ol	uol, ōl, ol
ōn 'ten'	ōn ∼ on-bīr	uon
ȫč 'vengeance'	ȫč	ös
ȫr- 'to weave'	ȫr-	ör-
sï̄s, sï̄š 'lance'	čī̌š	sis 'spine'
sür- 'to drive on'	sür-	ǖr-
tïn 'breath'	tïn	tï̄n
tōy 'clay'	toyun	tuoy
tūš 'opposite'	dūš	tus
tün 'night'	tün	tǖn
ur- 'to beat'	ur-	ūr-

ür- 'to bark'	üyr-	ǖr-
yaz- 'to go astray'	yaz-	sï̄s- (and sïs- 'to be near')
yēr- 'to hate	īr-	sir-
yǖz 'face'	yüz	sǖs

We furthermore have the following examples not found in K. as a headword:

T.	Y.
bol- 'to become' (Biišev bōl-)	buol- (Räsänen)
g̬iz- 'to get red'	kï̄s-
māl 'cattle	māl, mal
yüz 'a hundred'	sǖs (Räsänen)

And we have the following examples not found in T. but only in K.:

K.	Y.
iš 'smoke'	īs
sun- 'to extend'	ūn-
tār 'pie'	tar 'curd' (Meyer)
yūt 'death by frost'	sut

Here let us continue our statistics of deviation. As noted in 13.5 and 13.7, we found 115 deviations in K. : T. (cases where K. and T. have different vowel quantities). In this chapter we have found these further deviations (where Y. has vowel quantities other than those of K. and/or T.): Y. ï̄r-, ïr- 'to get tired' = K., T. ār-; ïy 'moon' = K., T. āy; il 'peaceful' = K. ēl, T. īl; xān-, xan- 'to get satisfied' = K. qān-, T. gān-; kūs- 'to embrace' = K. quč-, T. g̬uč-; kuosar- 'to pair' = K. qoš-, T. g̬oš-; kȫǰör- 'to cook' = K., T. köy- 'to burn'; mīn- 'to ride' = K., T. mün-; uol, ōl, ol 'that' = K., T. ol; ös 'vengeance' = K., T. ȫč; ȫr- 'to weave' = K., T. ȫr-; ǖr- 'to drive on' = K., T. sür-; tīn 'breath' = K., T. tïn; tus 'opposite' = K. tūš, T. dūš; ūr- 'to put' = K., T. ur- 'to beat'; sï̄s- 'to go astray, fail' = K., T. yaz- (but QB yāzuq 'sin'); sir- 'to hate' = K. yēr, T. ī̈r-. We have now found 17 more deviations, the number now being 132.

How can we explain these deviations?

(a) Y. sis 'spine' is dubious; cf. the vocabulary in 13.4: we should expect *is or another form without s-.

(b) Some words may be loanwords from Mo.: il (Mo. el, ėl); māl ~ mal (Mo. mal); ös (Mo. ös, öš); sut (Mo. ǰud); sax (Mo. čag). (But for sut cf. 13.11: it may be derived from *yūt.)

(c) The transcription K. iš̌ 'smoke,' sun- 'to extend' may be explained as in 13.7, that is, as merely graphic (actually half-long) vowels.

(d) kïsay- 'to shorten' is short because long vowels of the first syllables of disyllabic words quite regularly are shortened in Y. (bȫri 'wolf' > börö, etc.).

(e) In some cases the vowel must have been shortened secondarily in Y.: ïr- ~ ï̄r- 'to get tired' (ïr- dialectal variant?); ïy 'moon' (probably *ï̄y > ïy because of the similarity of ï̄ and y); ä̈r 'man' (with a short vowel in many Tu. languages, already Brahmi ä̈r; cf., however, 13.11.5); xān- ~ xan- 'to get satisfied'; küs 'autumn'; ör- 'to weave'; tus 'opposite'; ür- 'to bark'; sïs- 'to be near' ~ sï̄s- 'to fail'; sir- 'to hate'; tar 'curd.' In most of these cases the vowel must have been shortened, because K. and T. agree (ï̄r- ~ ïr-, ïy, xān- ~ xan-, ör-, tus, sir-) or because at least T. has a long vowel (ä̈r, küs, ür-; K. küz, ür- may be only graphic for kü˙z, ü˙r-, cf. above) or because at least QB has a long vowel (sï̄s- ~ sïs-; cf. QB yāzuq 'sin'; similarly Y. tar = K. tār). However, the reason for this sporadic shortening is quite unclear: is it dialectal influences? or analogies? (e.g., küs 'autumn' in analogy to kïs 'winter'?) Whatever the reason may be, these exceptions do not solve the problem of PTu. quantity. They seem to be merely Y. developments.

(f) In other cases the vowel must have been secondarily shortened in T.: bär- 'to give' (~b$\bar{\bar{a}}$r-, however, only according to Ligeti); bir 'one' (but cf. on-bīr 'eleven,' bīr-bīr 'each'); ät- 'to do' (but -d- in äd-il- 'to be done' is proof of an older long vowel); goš- 'to pair' (cf. K. qōš 'pair'); goyun 'embrace'; on-bīr 'eleven' (cf. ōn 'ten'); tin 'breath' (but dīn- 'breathe'; tin must be a loanword because of t-); toyun 'clay' (I have the impression that T. has a tendency to shorten long vowels before y; cf. goyun, also qaymaq 'cream' <*qâńaq); tün 'night' (but düyn 'yesterday'; tün must be a loanword because of t-); bol- 'to become' (~bōl-, but only according to Ligeti); giz- 'to become red'; yüz 'a hundred.' These vowels must be shortened because we find variants either in T. itself (bär- ~b$\bar{\bar{a}}$r-, bir ~ bīr, tin ~dīn-, on-bīr ~ōn, tün ~düyn, bol- ~bōl-), or because a special tendency exists (before -y-), or because -d- proves a formerly long vowel (ät- ~äd-il-), or because K. and Y. agree (goš- = K. qōš, Y. kuosar-). But even giz-, yüz seem to belong here. As for guč-, cf. gujaq 'embrace,' apparently <older *qūčaq (-č- becomes -ǰ- only before long vowels), but secondarily shortened. There are some clear cases of secondary shortening in T., e.g., yädi 'seven' (K. yeti, yetti); ät- (cf. äd-il- < *$\bar{\bar{a}}$d-il- < *$\bar{\bar{a}}$t-il-); git- 'to go' (cf. gid-iš 'march'); guč- 'to embrace' (cf. gujaq 'embrace'). These words must contain a shortened vowel (which originally was long) according to an established phonetic law: -t-, -p-, -k-/-q-, -č- become -d-, -b-, -g-/-ġ-, -ǰ- only after long vowels. A further example is ärtä 'early' (< *$\bar{\bar{a}}$rtä, cf. īr 'early' < *ēr); ärkäk 'male' (< * $\bar{\bar{a}}$rkäk, cf. $\bar{\bar{a}}$r, but cf. also 13.11.5); buġa 'bull' < būqa, cf. 13.11.8. See also T. tay 'colt' < ATu. tāń: according to the phonetic laws we should expect *dāyin (cf. 12); tay must be a loanword from another Tu. language.

(g) However, there are some cases which are hardly explicable: mün- 'to mount' (perhaps mü'n- in K., thus Y. mīn-

representing the older form); ol 'that' (perhaps Y. ōl being an affective lengthening, or *ōl having been shortened because of its being mostly proclitic), sür- (perhaps sü˙r- in K., thus Y. representing an older *sǖr-); ur- (perhaps u˙r- in K., thus Y. representing the older form). Since in all these cases K. shows a defective transcription which, after all, may represent an older long vowel (cf. 13.7), it is possible that Y. has the more archaic form, whereas the T. form is shortened, i.e., category G would be = category F. But even in these cases we do not know why the long vowels have become short in T. In some cases allegro forms may have been the reason, e.g., bōl- > bol- (which often is an enclitic modal verb or copula); ur-, sür- also occur often in an enclitic position. It is noteworthy that all the "exceptions" of G are verbs (only ol is a pronoun, but cf. above). Whatever the cause of this phenomenon may be, the number of exceptions remains rather small; and these exceptions do not solve the problem of PTu. quantity, for they seem to be merely Türkmän.

There is, however, one striking fact: Tu. *ô, *ö̂ in Y. usually become uo, üö, but we find Y. xōy(n) 'embrace' [not *kuoy(n)], kȫjör- 'to cook' [not *küöjör-], ōl 'that' (~uol ~ol). These cases are inexplicable on the basis of the older theories. Our solution will be given in 13.11.2 (a solution of the Y. "exceptions" in general).

13.9 Sporadic long vowels in many Turkic languages. Let us look for other languages to solve the problem of PTu. quantity. Are the Oghuz (Türkmän) dialects in the Khorezmian region of Uzbekistan useful for our purpose (see Abdullaev 1967)? We must say at the outset that this is not a dialect of Uzbek (which is an eastern Tu. language) but simply a dialect of Türkmän. This dialect has preserved some archaic features (e.g., qattï 'solid,' with q-, whereas the T. written language has gatï); on the other hand, it has undergone some (slight) Uzbek influence. Perhaps it would be best to call it "Khorezmian Türkmän." The vocalic quantities of this dialect are rather complicated. Sometimes it has preserved old lengths, e.g., (Abdullaev 93) dūz 'salt' (T. dūz, Y. tūs, K. tūz), (48) dāš 'stone' (T. dāš, Y. tās, K. tāš); sometimes it has lost the original length, e.g., (171) don 'clothing' (T. dōn, K. tōn), (176) döš 'chest' (T. dȫš, Y. tüös, K. tȫš). Tu. short vowels normally are short, e.g. (48) at 'horse' (K., T., Y. at, Kh. ha̯t); but sometimes one finds long vowels where no other Tu. dialect has such, e.g., (45) īč 'inside' (T., K. ič, Y. is), (47) qīr 'hill' (T. g̨ïr, K. qïr), (48) sāč 'hair' (T., K. sač, Y. as, Kh. sa̯č). Sometimes we find short vowels where K. and/or WOD. (but not T.) have a long vowel, e.g., (35) üč 'three' (T. üč, Y. üs, but WOD. ǖš), (53) baš 'head' (T. baš, Y. bas, but WOD. bāš); cf. furthermore (35) gün 'day,' (40) män 'I,' sän 'thou,' gäl- 'to come,' (48) ör- 'to weave,' qoy- 'to put,' yat- 'to lie,' (53) göz 'eye,' (67) göy- 'to burn,' (93) dĭl 'tongue,' dur- 'to stand,' (111) ölĭ 'dead,' (176) top 'ball,' tay 'colt,' doy- 'to become full.' But sometimes we find long vowels in this case: (47) qūǰaq 'embrace' (T. g̨uč- 'to embrace,' K. quč-, but Y. kūs-, and T. g̨uǰaq 'embrace' proves an older *qūč-); (48) qōy 'sheep' (T. g̨oyun, K. qōn, qōy); qōš 'pair' (T. g̨oš, Y. xos, K. qōš); āš 'food' (T. aš, T. as, K. āš); (52) sāp 'handle' (T. sap., Y. up, K. sāp).

However, these vocalic quantities seem to be of no value, because on p. 52 Abdullaev indicates that the opposition of long and short vowels in this dialect mainly serves *for the distinction of homonyms*. Here we find three cases:

(a) The quantities correspond to T., Y., e.g., (47) uč- 'to fly' — ūč 'end' (T. uč-, ūč); (48) at 'horse' — āt 'name' (T. at, āt); (52) al- 'to take' — āl 'red' (T. al-, āl).

(b) Single T. roots with various meanings have been split up: (48) qoš- 'to add' — qōš 'pair' (T. goš-, goša); (52) sap 'end' — sāp 'handle' (T. both sap); gök 'blue' — gȫk 'heaven' (T. both gȫk); aq 'white' — āq 'cataract' (T. both āq); geč 'evening' — gēč 'late' (T. both gīč).

(c) T. genuine homonyms have been split up: (45) īč 'inside' — ič- 'to drink' (T. ič, ič-); (48) qāš 'eyebrow' — qāš 'incrustation' (T. both gāš); ala 'colored' — āla 'not cleaned rice' (T. āla 'colored'; perhaps āla 'not cleaned rice' is the same word); ara 'middle' — āra 'make up' (T. āra 'middle'); dar 'narrow' — dār 'gallows' (T. both dār); (52) qan- 'to become satisfied' — qān 'blood' (T. gān-, gān); qara 'black' — qāra 'silhouette' (T. both qara, the last word <Mo. qaraġan).

I do not know whether Abdullaev's phonetic transcription is correct. Faulty apperception is always possible, cf. Essen 1953. 148 or (as a special example) the problem of Tu. stress in Räsänen 1949. 32-42; the various authors apperceived the Tu. stress very differently from each other. And Abdullaev's mateial seems to be the more unreliable as it often contradicts what the same author has said in his book Xorezmskie govory uzbekskogo jazyka, Taškent, 1960. Here are some examples: Abdullaev 1960. 21 āla 'colored' (but 1967. 48 ala); 1960. 21 āra 'between' (but 1967. 48 ara); 1960. 30 būt 'leg' (but 1967. 52 but); 1960. 90 ūč 'end' (but 1967. 53 uč; however, 47 ūč); 1960. 71 ōǰ 'vengeance' (but 1967. 122 höč/öč; however, 48 ȫč); 1960. 48 īn 'cave' (but 1967. 122 ĭn/hĭn). But even if Abdullaev's transcription were correct, it is obvious that such cases as īč 'inside' (<ič), ala 'colored' (<āla) are secondary, only developed in order to avoid ambiguity (homonyms), i. e., the quantities in this case are secondary and hence are irrelevant. And as we have seen above, even apart from homonyms the quantities sometimes are "false": don 'clothing' instead of dōn; döš 'chest' instead of dōš (words *dōn, *dōš with other meanings do not seem to exist). Hence we cannot do much with these quantities. Sometimes we find even a total reversion of what should be correct, e.g., 48 aš- 'to surpass' — āš 'meal' (T. āš- and aš); especially clear in 52 but 'leg' — būt 'idol' (T., Y., K. būt 'leg' but T. but 'idol ← P. but!). Thus I think we may leave this dialect aside.

There are still other Tu. sources (used by Ligeti 1938) which we shall leave aside because they are equivocal (just as Khorezmian Türkmän is); it would take too much time and paper fully to show the equivocality.

Sometimes (but only sometimes) C. is helpful, e.g., in kăvak 'blue' < *koak (cf. A.S. Kanjukova, Čuvašskaja dialektologija, Čeboksary, 1965. 82, Sundyr dialect koak ~ kăak ~ kaak; Cheremis still has üä, ua instead of C. ăva; e.g., in Cheremis śüäś ~ suas, soas = C. čavaš; cf. M. Räsänen, Die tschuwassischen Lehnwörter im Tscheremissischen, Helsinki, 1920. 65) < *köäk (cf. Hungarian kék) < *kȏk. But C. is not very useful; e.g., Ščerbak's contention (based on Kanjukova; see Ščerbak 1967. 36, note 15) that C. has preserved long *ō in dialects is false: śu^{o}k 'not,' pu^{o}l- 'to be,' tu^{o}l- 'to become full,' etc. Cf. Kanjukova 57: in the central upper dialect u^{o} does exist, but it stands for literary u (dialectal o) in all quantities, not only in śu^{o}k < yôq, but also in tu^{o}psa 'finding' < tap-, u^{o}ra 'foot' < adaq, etc.

Tuvinian is rather important. Here we find the following situation, illustrated by examples:

	K.	T.	Y.	Tuv.
'horse'	at	at	at	aʾt
'name'	āt	āt	āt	at

Note that where K., T., Y. have a long vowel, Tuv. has a simple short vowel; where K., T., Y. have a short vowel, Tuv. has a "laryngeal" vowel with a special kind of acute intonation resembling the Danish stød; for a phonetic description see A. A. Pal´mbax "Dolgie i poludolgie glasnye tuvinskogo jazyka,' Issledovanija po sravnitel´noj grammatike tjurkskix jazykov I. 179-81, Moskva, 1955. This laryngal vowel is said to be half long. We find lists of such examples in the following works: Ščerbak 1963. 27-8 (the same as in 1967. 47); Pal´mbax, Grammatika tuvinskogo jazyka, Moskva, 1961. 23-6; F. G. Isxakov, Tuvinskij jazyk, Moskva and Leningrad, 1957. 31-3; Pal´mbax, Tuvinsko-russkij slovar´, Moskva, 1955. 620-1 (see also the vocabularies themselves). However, even these instances are not without problems: (a) we sometimes find variants: čäʾp ~ čäp 'cord,' čaʾrt ~ čart 'hard,' üʾp ~ üp 'trophy,' etc.; (b) Mo. words sometimes have laryngal vowels (čöʾp 'well'), but for the most part they do not (why not? one sees no cogent reason); (c) Pal´mbax's notations often do not agree, e. g., in Issledovanija ïʾt 'dog,' in Slovar´ ït (here are some further words with laryngal vowels in Issledovanija, simple vowels in Slovar´: qaʾdïq 'porridge,' buʾduq 'branch' = T. pūdaq, which should be buduq, qaʾš 'how much,' qïʾš 'winter,' oʾq 'cartridge,' quʾš 'bird,' iʾrt 'ram,' böʾrt 'hat' = T. bȫrük!, aʾġar 'flows,' aʾdïġ 'shoot,' käʾš 'skin,' čäʾdär 'arrives'). On the whole, even this material is too scarce and too ambiguous to allow a satisfactory evaluation.

We furthermore find long vowels in Gagauz, cf. N. K. Dmitriev, "Dolgie glasnye v gagauzskom jazyke," Issledovanija po sravnitel´noj grammatike tjurkskix jazykov I. 203-7, Moskva, 1955. and L. A. Pokrovskaja, Grammatika gagauzskogo jazyka, Moskva, 1964. 29. Here we find two categories:

A. Gagauz agrees with T.

āč 'hunger' = T. āč

ārt 'behind' = ārt

dōru 'red-brown' = dōr

kār 'snow' = g̭ār

kōr 'coal' = g̭ōr

ǖšen- 'to be lazy' = üyšän-

yārïn 'tomorrow' = yārï̄n

sāya 'fresh butter' (< *sārï yāġ 'yellow fat'? , length of contraction?)

āz 'few' = āz

āra- 'to search' = āra-

āt 'name' = āt

kāz 'goose' = g̭āz

tōz 'dust' = tōz

B. Gagauz differs from T.

ārï 'bee' = arï

ǖn 'wool' = yüņ (K. yuņ, Y. suņ)

bōz 'grey' = boz (but K. bōz)

On the whole, Gagauz has preserved only a few words with a long vowel (the numerals, for instance, never contain long vowels: *bir*, *dört*, *beš* = T. *bīr*, *dȫrt*, *bǟš*). On the other hand, Gagauz has some long vowels where T. has not. But such variances occur too sporadically.

The same holds true for Kirghiz, which, according to K. K. Judaxin, *Kirgizsko-russkij slovar´*, Moskva, 1965, has preserved some long vowels, e. g., *ārï* 'bee' (cf. Gagauz!); *bārï* 'all' (but *bar* 'exists,' the root of *bārï*); *kȫrük* 'bellows.' But normally we find short vowels (*at* 'name' = *at* 'horse,' *aš* 'food,' *bol*- 'to become,' *qar* 'snow,' etc.). These few words may have come from T., eventually from Khorezmian T., via "Kipchak-Uzbek."

We find some traces of long vowels in Az. of Nukha, cf. PhTF 284, but only in the sequence *ā-ï* (secondary?): sārï 'yellow,' *āǰï* 'bitter,' *g̭ārï* 'old' (?), *ārï* 'bee,' *yāzï* 'script' (?), *yāġï* 'enemy' (?); cf. also Qashqai *vār* 'existing,' *īt* 'dog,' forms which occur quite sporadically. We furthermore find long vowels in the following languages, but their occurrence is either sporadic or badly attested to, cf. PhTF: Balkar (348), Kumyk (394), Kazakh, Karakalpak, Nogay, Kipchak-Uzbek (442), Uzbek (493), New Uighur (540), Khakass (667), Soyon, especially Karagass (646). Sometimes we find valuable facts even here, e.g., *īt* 'dog' occurring in New Uighur, (= C. *ÿită*!); also *bīt* 'louse' = Nogay, Kipchak-Uzbek (and C. *p̈iytă*!). But for a reconstruction of PTu. these forms are not so relevant, as we shall see.

Compare also J. Németh, *Die Türken von Vidin*, Budapest, 1965.30-1 (long vowels in the sequence *ā-ï*, such as *qād̈ïn* 'wife'; furthermore in *qāz-* 'to dig,' *ya˙s* 'grief'; hence only with the vowel *a*). And see Räsänen 1949.64-8. According to this latter source we find a substitutional lengthening of the vowel of the first open syllable before the reduced vowel of the second syllable in Kazan-Tatar, Bashkir, Chuvash, Osman dialects, Karachay, Koibal, Kirghiz, Kazakh, above all in the sequence *ā-ï*; cf. Nukha, Vidin. Concerning the long vowels in New Uighur Räsänen writes: "Die Längen in der SO-Gruppe, besonders bei von Le Coq, sind mir grossenteils unbegreiflich." He furthermore mentions Kazan-Tatar of Nižegorod (cf. O. Böhtlingk, *Über die Sprache der Jakuten*, St. Petersburg, 1851.135): "Der jakutischen Länge entspricht im nishegorod'schen Tatarisch nicht selten eine Länge; aber wohl eben so häufig auch eine Kürze. Der umgekehrte Fall, dass einer jakutischen Kürze eine nishegorod'sche Länge gegenübersteht, gehört auch nicht zu den Seltenheiten" (however, the examples of Y. short vowel = Nižegorod long vowel are useful: they always reflect CTu. /ā/ ... or /â/ ...). Räsänen further enumerates a Karachay dialect, Khorezmian T., "Kipchak-Uzbek" in Afghanistan, New Uighur of Kāšġar and Turfan, Koibal, Karagass, Soyon, Salbin, Kandov,

Tūra, Kūrdak, Tobol, Tümen, Kirghiz, Kazan-Tatar (Weil), Kumyk (= Ligeti 1938. 180); all these long vowels are, however, as Ligeti remarks, "longues sporadiques" (and, let us add, not always incontestable in their quantity).

13.10 <u>Quantity in western Osman (Anatolian) dialects</u>. The western Osman dialect described by Korkmaz 1953, utilized by Biišev 1963. 34-46, is very important. Here we find the following categories:

(A) WOD. correspondence with K., T., Y.

bēš 'five' = K. bēš, T. bǟš, Y. biäš (Kh. bị̄^{e}·š)
bȫl-mä 'separating wall' = T. bȫl- 'to part, to separate'
dē- 'to say' = K. tē-, T. diy-, Y. diä-
ēr- 'to arrive' = K. ēr- 'to get frightened,' T. īr- 'to get tired, bored' [cf. German <u>mir reicht's</u>, literally 'it is arriving to me' = 'no more of this,' 'I am sick and bored of it']
yōq 'is not' = K., T. yōq, Y. suox (Kh. yū̥^{o}·q in unpublished material)
kēvdir- '?' [said to be connected with Y. <u>kiäp</u> 'pattern' (= K. <u>kēp</u>, T. <u>gǟp</u>); <u>kēvdir</u> is a misprint. According to Z. Korkmaz, <u>Güney-Batı Anadolu Ağızları</u>, Ankara, 1956. 21, this is <u>kēydir-</u> 'to put on clothes,' cf. 13.8 K. <u>kǟd</u>-].
ōn 'ten' = K., T. ōn, Y. uon (Kh. ^{o}·ǭn and similar forms)
dāl- 'to faint' = T. dāl-, Y. tāl-
dȫn- 'to turn' = K. tȫn-, T. dȫn-
yī- 'to eat' = K. yē-, T. iy-, Y. siä-

(B) WOD. correspondence with only one of the languages K., T., Y.

ōl- 'to become' = Y. buol-, but T. bol- (secondary!)
vēr- 'to give' = K. bēr-, T. bǟr-, Y. biär-
bū 'this' = K., T. bū, Y. bu (Y. secondary)

gēt- 'to go' = T. git- [gid-iš- proves the originally long vowel], but K. ked-, ket-

g̬āl- 'to remain' = T. g̬āl-, Y. xāl-, but K. qal- (graphic, = qa·l-)

g̬āndïr- 'to satisfy' = T. g̬ān-, K. gān-, Y. xān-, xan-

g̬ïz 'girl' = T. g̬īz, Y. kīs, but K. qïz (graphic, = qï·z, cf. Kh. qị̄ⁱz

g̬ōy- in g̬ōyve- 'to free' = K. qōd-, qod-, T. g̬oy-, Y. xot-

vūr- 'to beat' = Y. ūr-, but K., T. ur-

sōr- 'to ask' = K. sor-, T. sōra-

Normally we find a long vowel either in T. or in Y., so here the vowel must have been originally long, too.

(C) WOD. correspondence with none of the languages K., T., Y.

āl- 'to take' = K., T. al-, Y. ïl-

ālt 'beneath' = T. alt

āt- 'to throw' = K., T. at-, Y. ït- (C ïvat-, ït-, ut-)

ǟv 'house' = T. öy

bās- 'to press' = K., T. bas-

bǟn 'I' = K., T. män, Y. min

bōz- 'to destroy' = K. buz-, T. boz-

vār- 'to go' = K., T., Y. bar-

yāz- 'to write' = K., T. yaz- (but Az. Nukha yāzï 'script')

yāt- 'to lie' = K., T. yat-, Y. sït- (Kh. yạ̄t-)

gǟš- 'to pass' = K. käč-, T. gäč-, Y. käs-

gǟl- 'to come' = K., Y. käl-, T. gäl- (Kh. kȧl-)

gȫz 'eye' (in gȫzlät- 'to order, to guard') = T. göz, Y. kös (Kh. kọ̈z, QB kȫz)

kǟs- 'to cut' = K. T. käs-

gȫr- 'to look' = K., Y. kör-, T. gör-

gǖn 'day' = K., Y. kün, T. gün (Kh. kụ̈n, Volga Bolgar کوان küọ̈n, but Kh. Wenạreǰ kị̄n, unpublished material)

ȫl- 'to die' = K., T., Y. öl- (C. vil-)

g̬āz- 'to dig' (in g̬āzdïr-) = K. qaz-, T. g̬āz-, Y. xas-
g̬āš- 'to fly' = K. qač-, T. g̬ač-
g̬ōrx- 'to fear' (in g̬ōrxu 'fear') = K. qorq-, T. g̬orq-
sǟn 'thou' = K., T. sän, Y. ǟn
dǟl- 'to bore' = K., Y. täl-, Az. däl- (T. däš-)
dǖš- 'to fall' = K. tüš-, T. düš-, Y. tüs-
ǖš 'three' = K., T. üč, Y. üs (C. viśĕ, Kh. ụ̈̄s, ị̄č, New Uighur
    PhTF 540 ǖč)
čāl- 'to beat' = K., T. čal- (Kh. ča̯l-)

The quantity of these long vowels seems at first to be incorrect and the material accordingly worthless. However, the C. forms seem to certify the original length of vowels in the correspondences of *āt-* and *gǖn*. Furthermore QB proves that *gȫz* must be correct (and perhaps *gȫr-*, too, which may be derived from the same root). The Az. dialect confirms *yāz-* as correct (we temporarily leave Khalaj aside). This material is, as we shall see later on, extremely valuable, but only after the facts and forms of Khalaj are taken into account. By itself it is *no key* to the exploration of PTu. quantity. Without knowing Khalaj one may be inclined simply to explain that WOD. has preserved original long vowels which have been lost in all other Tu. dialects. It seems curious that it has preserved them in so many cases (categories A and B : C = 20 : 25), but we cannot refute this thesis *a priori.*

Before solving the problem of PTu. quantity, I would like to complete my statistics. In 13.8 we found 132 "exceptions" or "deviations,' i.e., cases where K., T., Y. and QB do not coincide. It would be easy to augment this figure by including Khalaj forms, such as Kh. *hā̯ᵃm* 'cunt' = K. *am*; Kh. *ị̄ᵉm* 'trousers' = K. *öm*; Kh. *kịᵉn-* 'to burn' = K. T. *köy-*, etc. But we will not include them here, since we are considering only the situation *before* the discovery of Khalaj. We have found the following new deviations (of monosyllabic roots) in 13.9:

Gagauz ǖn 'wool' = K. yuŋ̧, T. yüŋ̧, Y. suŋ̧
Qashqai, New Uighur īt 'dog' (C. yïtă) = K., Y. ˙it, T. it
WOD., Az. Nukha yāz- 'to write' = K., T. yaz-
New Uighur, Uzbek, Nogay, Kipchak-Uzbek bīt 'louse'
(C. pïytă) = K., T. bit, Y. bït.

Compare furthermore all examples of WOD., category C (with the exception of *gȫz* 'eye,' which we already had noted among the forms of QB, 13.7). These are 28 new exceptions. Thus our statistics show 160 deviations.

Finally we find the following variants in K. where I did not find correspondences in T. or Y.: *qï̄š-*, *qïš-* 'to bend'; *ȫz*, *öz* 'fat, grease'; *sǟr-*, *sär-* 'to get angry'; *sūd̄-*, *sud̄-* 'to spit'; *ẗīd̄-*, *ẗid̄-* 'to prevent, hinder'; *yām*, *yam* 'grain'; *yāt*, *yat* 'rain magic'; *yï̄š*, *yïš* 'valley.' See also K. *kǖp* 'vessel' = Osman *küp* (never *küb-* before vowels, thus < **küp*, Meyer). The final statistics before we consider Khalaj show 169 "exceptions." I think this figure can be called rather high, even when the graphic element in K. is taken into consideration.

13.11 *Vowel quantity in Khalaj and in Proto-Turkic.* Without knowing Khalaj one cannot give a definite solution to the many problems of PTu. vowel quantity.

13.11.1 *Khalaj, a solution to Proto-Turkic quantity.* As we have seen above, K. sometimes has a long vowel where T., Y. have a corresponding quantity (category A); on the other hand, K. sometimes has a long vowel where T., Y. have a short one (category B). We provisionally "solved" this problem by saying that in this last case T., Y. may have reduced the originally long vowel. This would be a simple scheme: category A = K. V̄ >T., Y. V̄; category B = K. V̄ >T., Y. V. But what is the reason for this double development? Why have T., Y. shortened the vowel in one case and not in the other? We see no cogent reason. Khalaj, however, can help us solve the problem easily. Let us first look at some lists:

Category A

K.	T.	Y.	KhM.	KhX.	KhT.
ōt 'fire'	ōt	uot	hụ̄°·t	hų̄°·t	hụ̄°·t
tōn 'clothes'	dōn	___	tụ̄°·n	tų̄°˒n	tụ̄°·n
qār 'snow'	g̬ār	xār	___	___	G̭ā̮ªr
tār 'narrow'	dār	tār	tā̮ªr	tā̮ªr	tā̮ªr

Category B

K.	T.	Y.	KhM.	KhX.	KhT.
qōl 'arm'	g̬ol	xol	qo̮l	qo̮˙l	qụ°·l
qōy 'sheep'	g̭oyun	___	qo̮n	qo̮˙n	G̭ụ°·n
āš 'food'	aš	as	___	___	ā̮š
bāš 'head'	baš	bas	ba̮˙š	ba̮˙š	bo̮˙š

[And we find bāš in QB, too.]

We complete this list with two examples of short vowels:

K.	T.	Y.	KhM.	KhX.	KhT.
at 'horse'	at	at	ha̮t	ha̮t	ha̮t
toq 'satisfied'	doq	___	___	___	tǫq, tǫx

13.11.2 The "medium quantity" in Khalaj. We see at first glance that we can formulate a rule as follows: where K. agrees with T., Y., we find in Khalaj moved long vowels or moved long diphthongs (symbol: /â/ ...); where K. disagrees with T., Y., we find in Khalaj level long (half-long) vowels or short diphthongs (symbol: /ā/ ...); /ā/ ... is, one might say, a "medium quantity" between /â/ ... and /a/ .... These vowels of category B may be shortened, particularly in KhM. (where qo̯l 'arm' presumably < *qo̯·l < *qu̯°l); but they remain sharply distinct from originally short vowels by having another quality (qo̯l 'arm' < qōl, but KhT. tǫq 'satisfied' < toq; also such examples as KhM. tǫqqų̈z 'nine' or hǫttųz 'thirty,' cf. 8.1, 2). And thus we can say: PROTO-TURKIC ORIGINALLY DID NOT HAVE TWO "QUANTITIES" BUT THREE. This threefold opposition of quantities solves the first question which we asked in 13.7: in such instances as K. qār 'snow' = T. gār, we must assume a quantity other than that in K. ās̆ 'food' = T. as̆. Whereas the first quantity became a long vowel in T., the second became a short one; it is, however, not identical to an originally short quantity which exists besides these two quantities (and has been short already in K.).

Contrary to my unwarranted scepticism in 1968.101-2, Khalaj has not only preserved long vowels: it gives the key to an explanation of PTu. "quantity" in general. And it seems to be the only Tu. language which has preserved exactly all three "quantities," whereas all other Tu. languages have preserved only two (or one). We provisionally may assume: /â/ ... where K., WOD., T., Y. have a long vowel; /ā/ ... where K., WOD. have a long vowel, whereas T., Y. have a short one; /a/ ... where K., WOD., T., Y. have a short vowel. Let us now make some comparisons which will illustrate our theory.

Some comparisons of Kh. with WOD.:

(1) WOD. yāt- 'to lie' (K. yat-, perhaps only graphic; cf. 13.6) = KhM. yā̯t- (but X. ya̯t-), but T. yat-, Y. śit- < *yāt- <* dë̄t-

(2) WOD. gȫz 'eye' (QB kȫz) = KhX. kö̯z (< *kö̯·z < *kȫz; short *ö > ǫ̈, cf. KhT. kǫ̈t 'anus'), but T. göz, Y. kös < *kȫz

(3) WOD. ūš 'three' (K. üč, perhaps only graphic; in the text ūč, cf. 13.6) = KhT., X. ụ̄š, M. ị̄č, but T. üč, Y. üs <*ūč

Some comparisons with K., besides those given above (1-3):

(4) K., QB bāš 'head' = KhT. bọ˙š, M., X. bạ˙š, but T. baš, Y. bas < *bāš

(5) K. ōr- 'to sickle' = KhT. họ̄ġraq 'sickle' < *ōrġaq, but T., Y. or- < *ōr-

(6) K., QB yēl 'wind' = KhT. yẹ˙l, but T. yäl, Y. säl < *yāl < *dāl

(7) K. būr-, bur- 'to smell' = KhT. bụrụn 'nose' [< *būran, short u is ụ in Ç̱ụš 'sparrow,' etc.], but T. burun, Y. murun < *būr-, *būran

(8) K. sīd-, sid- 'to urinate' = KhT. sị̄dȧk 'urine,' M., X. si˙däk, but T. siy- (?) < *sīd-

(9) K. sūw 'water' = KhT. sụ˙v, but T. suv (?), Y. ū (?) < *sūb (< *si̯ūb)

(10) K. t̄il, t̄il 'tongue' = KhM. tị˙l, but T. dil, Y. t̄il < *t̄īl

Two comparisons with other dialects:

(1) Qashqai, New Uighur īt 'dog,' C. yïtă (K. ˙it, perhaps only graphic, cf. 13.6) = KhT. ị̄t, but T. it, Y. ˙it < *īt < *i̯īt

(2) Gagauz ūn 'wool' (K. yuņ may be only graphic, cf. 13.6) = KhT. yụņ^k [< *yūņ; short u would become ụ, as in Ç̱ụš, cf. above], but T. yüņ, Y. suņ < *yūņ < *dūņ

Some examples where Kh. is the only language to have preserved /ā/ ...:

(1) KhM. hạ˙$^{\hat{i}}$- (but X. hạ̦$^{\hat{i}}$-) = T. ayt-, Y. ˙iy- (K. ay-, perhaps only graphic, cf. 13.6) < *āy- < *pēy-

(2) KhT. ha̯˙ġa̯ 'behind' = T. arqa (K. arqa, cf. 13.3). [Somewhat doubtful: the half-long vowel may be a substitutional lengthening for the dropped -r̲-]

(3) KhT., M. ȧ˙l (X. ȧl) 'hand' = T. äl (Y. älī, ilī, K. älig, Brahmi elig ~ älig) < *ǟl(äg)

(4) KhT., M. ȧ˙ri̦n 'lip' = T. ärin (K. erin) < *ǟrän? [K.'s e̲, rather than ä̲, may indicate an original *â̲r̲i̲n̲; â̲ sometimes is shortened in unstressed position in Kh., cf. 13.11.5; the same holds true for T. as in ī̲r̲ 'early,' but ä̲r̲t̲ä̲ id.; in K. the shortening may be only graphic]

(5) KhT. hi̦kmäk 'bread' [K. ä̲t̲m̲ä̲k̲ may be only graphic, cf. 13.6; Kh. i̲ cannot be derived from ä̲ since this vowel remains ä̲ or ȧ̲, but cf. KhT. h̲i̲˙̲r̲k̲ȧ̲k̲ 'male' = e̲r̲k̲ä̲k̲ elsewhere, cf. 13.11.5]

(6) KhT. čo̧la̧q 'weak' = T. čolaq [short o̲ would become o̧ in KhT., o̧ < o̧˙ < u̦°] < *čōlāq (or *čōlâq)

(7) KhT., M. qa̧˙ru̦n, X. qa̧˙rin 'bellow' = T. g̱arin, Y. xarin (Tuv. xirin, C. xirăm, K. qarin) < *qāran < *kē̄ram

(8) KhT. Ḉu̦lā̧q, M. qu̦la̧q (but X. qo̧lā̧qᶜ) = T. gulaq, Y. kulgāx, K. qul(q)aq < *qūlâq

(9) KhT. ti̦˙ʳsȧk 'elbow' = T. tirsäk (K. tirsgäk, cf. 13.3) [the half-long i̲ may be a substitutional lengthening for the reduced r̲; this possibility, however, is doubtful]

(10) KhT. tu̦°lo̯ 'hail' = T. doli (K. toli) < *tōlī

(11) KhM., X. yi̦˙l 'year' = T. yil, Y. sil (K. yil, cf. 13.6) < *yīl < *dīl

(12) KhT. yo̧rġā̧n 'blanket' = T. yorġan < *yōrġân < *dōrgân (?, cf. 14.7)

(13) KhT. yu̦mᵘšāq 'soft' = T. yumšaq [K. yumšaq; short u̲ would become KhT. u̦, cf. y̲u̲̦l̲d̲u̲̦Z̲ 'star'] < *yūmšāq <*dūmšā

(14) KhT. yo̧qqa̧r 'above' = T. yoqari (K. yoqaru) < * yōqqār < dōkgārū or dūkgārū

(15) KhM. kị^{e}n-, X. kö̤'n- 'to burn' = K., T. köy- (but Y. kȫɟör-) < *kȫń-.

At the end of 13.8 we said that Y. in some cases has ō, ȫ (which "should be" uo, üö); here we have the solution: ō, ȫ in this case is not < Ptu. *ô, *ö̂; (which become uo, üö) but < *ō, that is, Y. in some cases may have preserved PTu. /ā/ ..., namely in xōy(n) 'embrace,' kȫɟör- 'to cook,' ōl 'that.' Should such preserving of the PTu. long vowel be true of mīn- 'to mount,' ǖr- 'to drive on,' ūr- 'to beat,' sï̄s- 'to go astray,' sǖs 'face' (and, eventually, kīs- 'to get red,' sǖs 'a hundred'), too? At any rate, there is a chance that Y. has preserved /ā/ ... in sporadic cases (whereas T. always changes /ā/ ... to /a/ ..., and both languages in monosyllabic roots normally preserve /â/ ...).

Khalaj sometimes has preserved /â/ ..., too, where we do not find correspondences in other languages: KhT., M., X. ī^{e}m 'trousers' = K. öm (perhaps graphic, cf. 13.6); C. yĕm, Yellow Uighur yem, but not attested to in T., nor in Y.: must be < *i̯êmä. KhT. hā̤^{a}m 'cunt' = K. am (in the text erroneously em), surely in K. only graphic, not found in T. (which may be due to the well-known prudery of Soviet dictionaries). KhT. qā̤^{a}naq 'cream' = K. qanaq, qayaq, T. qaymaq, Y. xoymox, perhaps graphic in K. (cf. 13.6), in T. secondary shortening (cf. 13.8). KhM. qā̤^{a}nị 'who, which?' = K. qanū, qayū, T. xaysï, Y. xaya, xanna (a situation similar to qā̤^{a}naq).

However we also find some cases where /ā/ ... has been shortened in Kh., according to the parallel forms in K., WOD., Y.:

(1) KhT. harqā̤n 'thin' = Y. ï̄r-, ïr- 'to become thin' < *ārqân
(2) KhT. bȧg 'son-in-law = K. bā̈g < *bā̈g
(3) KhT. kṳ̈n ča̤lȧr 'east' = WOD. čāl- 'to beat' < *čāl
(4) KhT., M., X. da̤ġ 'not' = K. dāġ
(5) KhX. kȧlȧn yi̤l 'next year' = WOD. gā̈l- 'to come' < *kā̈l-

(6) KhT., X. kụn, M. kịn 'day, sun' = WOD. gün < *kün
(7) KhT. qa̤rrị 'old' = Az. Nukha ğārï < qārï (?, Wena̤reǰ qa̤
(8) KhT. tụrpa̤q 'soil,' tọpụq 'knee' = K. tōp, top 'ball' [?, cf Brahmi and Tu. in Tibetan script tupraq]
(9) KhT. tọx, tọq 'satisfied' = K. tōd- 'to be satisfied' < a root *tō-?
(10) KhX. ƀa̤r- 'to go' = WOD. vār-

The reasons for the shortening of these forms are different. For 2, 5 (and some other examples with *ā̱) cf. 13.11.5. In some other cases the shortening is due to the unstressed position, wher even /â/ ... sometimes is shortened, sometimes leaving a substitutional gemination (cf. *kûrïg 'dry,' T. gūrï >KhX. qụrrụġ; or *bâlā 'young animal,' T. bāla >KhT. balla). We find the same phenomenon in 7, 10, and without substitutional gemination in 1, 3; da̤ġ (5) may have been shortened because of being enclitic. In 8, 9 the connection with the roots *tōp, *tō- is not absolutely certain. Only kụn (6) is inexplicable, but cf. Kh. Wena̤reǰ kịn (or kị[5]

We may summarize as follows: we have to assume three categories of vowels in PTu., provisionally noted as /a/ ..., /ā/ ..., /â/ .... One may find further instances of /ā/ ... in 13.8 (beginning) and in 13.10 (category C, WOD.).

It is a most important fact that Kh. has preserved /ā/ ... even in unstressed position, i.e., in the first syllables of disyllabic words, such as a̤˙rịn 'lip,' tụ°lọ 'hail,' qa̤˙rụn 'bellow,' etc. Since Y. shortens all unstressed vowels (of roots) in such position and T. shortens all vowels /ā/ ... (though not /â/ ...) and K. normally shortens graphically, Kh. is in this case the only Tu. language which may distinctly testify for /ā/ ... in this position. Only some (very few) examples in other languages may be helpful in this respect, too: K. sōğon 'onion' (T. soğan), kölik 'shadow' (T. kölägä) may go back to PTu. *sōgōn, *kölāk (or a similar form); some other examples in K. are doubtful; cf. the words in K. Tercümesi quoted in 13.3; for Gagauz, Az. Nukha, Kirghiz ārï 'bee,' etc., cf. 13.9.

13.11.3 Oppositions /â/ ... : /ā/ ... : /a/ .... Do we find pairs of words with clear oppositions /a/ ... : /ā/ ... or /ā/ ... : /â/ ... or even /a/ ... : /ā/ ... : /â/ ... ? I think we can find such. Here are some examples, taken not only from Kh., but also from WOD. (13.10) and K. (13.8): āl- 'to take' (WOD.) : âl 'pink' (T. āl); ās- 'to hang up' (K.; T. as-) : âs 'ermine' (K., T. ās); bāš 'head' (K., Kh.; T. baš) : bâš 'wound' (T., K. bāš); qōl 'arm' (K., Kh.; T. g̱ol) : qôl 'plain' (K. qōl, T. g̱ōl) : qol- 'to ask' (K. 340, short also in QB 243 söküšmü qolur sän azu ögdimü 'whether thou mayest ask for cursing or for praising'); āš 'food' (K., Kh.; T. aš) : âš- 'to surpass' (K., T. āš-), etc.

When reading Gabain 1950. 292-357, one is astonished to see the enormous number of "synonyms." This number will be radically reduced when the following principles are applied:

(a) the well-known difference (opposition) of /a/ ... : /â/ ... (in the older transcription /a/ ... : /ā/ ...)

(b) the fact that PTu. did not have eight vowels but at least ten, perhaps even twelve (cf. 14.1, 14.3.3)

(c) the fact that in PTu. not only /â/ ..., /ā/ ... existed but also diphthongs /i̭â/ ..., /i̭ā/ ... (cf. 14.2, 14.4.1)

(d) the fact that not only two but three "quantities" existed: /a/ ..., /ā/ ..., /â/ ....

Instead of Gabain's 8 vowels (a, o, u, ï, ä, ö, ü, i), and instead of the commonly accepted 16 vowels (Gabain's vowels in short and long quantities), we must assume the existence of 50 (or even 60) vowels: Gabain's 8 vowels + ë, e, eventually o̤, ö̤ = 10 or 12; these x 3 because of the three quantities = 30 or 36; /i̭â/ ..., /i̭ā/ ... (but not /i̭a/...) gives 20 or 24 more vowels = 50 or 60 vowels.

13.11.4 The medium quantity in a Persian loanword. The following phenomenon is interesting: PTu. *bêl 'waist' (T., Y. bīl, K. bēl, Az. bel, C. pilĕk) is bị̄^{e}·l, bę̄^{e}l in Kh. But P. bēl 'shovel' (an older form prior to 1400 A. D.; later on we find bīl, but Tajik still preserves bēl) has become KhT. bị^{e}·l. We can see clearly that a simple length (ē) has become a short diphthong (ị^{e}); hence, bị̄^{e}·l must go back to something else. However, the normal development of Tu. *ǟ is ȧ·, ȧ in Khalaj.

13.11.5 The problem of Proto-Turkic ä/e. In Turcology an old problem exists: whether PTu. made a distinction between *ä and *e (the correspondences of *ä and *e in the modern languages existing, above all, in C., Az., T., and Y.). For literature see Räsänen 1949.88-90, also Thomsen 1957, etc. I cannot deal with this whole problem, which has raised so many controversies. Here is only a sketchy (incomplete) survey, to which I have attached some brief remarks.

(a) Poppe assumed (Islamica 1.410-4) that C. a = Az. ä < PTu. *ä, but C. i = Az. e < PTu. *e. This assumption is false since we find many examples like C. par- 'to give' = Az. ver- and C. kil- 'to come' = Az. gäl-: Poppe's correspondences are not the only existing ones.

(b) Németh assumed (Nyelvtudományi Közlemények 43.296-7) that Y. iä < PTu. *ǟ, Y. ī < *ē-. But Y. ī seems to occur (for Az. e, etc.) only in one monosyllabic word: bīl 'waist' (T. bīl, Az. bel, K. bēl, etc.). (Of course, Y. ī < PTu. *ī is frequent.)

(c) Räsänen 1949.89 distinguished PTu. *ǟ and *ē; *ǟ > Y. iä, T. ǟ, C. a; *ē > Y. ī, T. ī, C. i. He admitted, however, that there are many exceptions (e.g., T. īn- 'to descend' = C. an-). This "rule" is of no value since the "exceptions" have not been explained and are almost as numerous as the rule itself.

(d) Thomsen stated that Az. ä always goes back to a short *ä (= T., Y. ä) and that Az. e goes back either to a long vowel

(T. ī, ā̈, Y. iä, ī) or to a short ä in the neighborhood of y and before i in the following syllable. This theory practically meant that (except for some cases of assimilation) Az. ä/e did not reflect the qualities of PTu. vowels but their quantities. Thus Thomsen made the first real progress in this point. However, it must be added that we find some other cases of assimilation: before č, š, v (Az. keč- 'to pass' = T. gäč-, K. käč-; Az. deš- 'to bore' = T. däš-; Az. sev- 'to like' = K. säw-; we find the same development in loanwords, e.g., češmä 'source' < older čäšmä ← P. [čäšmä], etc.); furthermore Thomsen did not consider such cases as Az. gämi 'ship' = T. gā̈mi; Az. däli 'mad' = T. dā̈li; är 'man' = ā̈r, etc. See the justified criticism of Ligeti in Acta Orientalia Hungarica 7.115-7, 1957, a criticism which, however, is for the most part merely negative.

(e) Ščerbak 1963.25-6 affirmed that we find Az. e in closed syllables, ä in open syllables (beš 'five,' but bäzä- 'to adorn,' etc.). This theory is false, for we also find such examples as gäl- 'to come,' käs- 'to cut,' etc.; on the other hand, we find ešik 'threshold,' ešit- 'to hear,' de- 'to say,' etc.

(f) My own assumption is that the only language which has preserved a PTu. opposition *ä : *e is C. C. i = (e.g.) T. ä goes back to PTu. *e (C. kil- 'to come' = T., Az. gäl-, Y., K. käl-, WOD. gā̈l- <PTu.* kēl-; C. sik- 'to jump' = T., Az. säk-, Y. äkkiriä- < *sek-); C. a = (e.g.) T. ä goes back to PTu. *ä (C. kaś- 'to pass' = T. gäč-, K. käč-, Y. käs-, Az. keč- < käč-, WOD. gā̈š- < PTu. *kā̈č-; C. sas 'voice' = T., Az. säs < *säs; C. tan 'equal' = T. däŋ, Y. täŋ, Az. tän < *täŋ).

The situation is very simple for the short vowel /ä/ (by the way, also for /ā̈/, where we find the same situation). But it is more complicated for /ä̂/, cf. section (c) above. Thomsen said that to Az. e corresponds either Y. ī = T. ī, or Y. iä = T. ā̈, or Y. iä = T. ī, but he gave no rules under what circumstances we have to expect ī = ī, or iä = ā̈, or iä = ī.

In my opinion the regular development of PTu. *ā̂, *ē̂ in stressed position (in monosyllabic roots) is: *ā̂ >C. *a*, *ē̂ >C. *i*, e.g., *ā̂n- 'to descend' >C. *an-*; *ē̂r 'early' >C. *ir*. By the way, it can be proved that C. *i* in this case formerly was *e*: C. loanwords in Cheremiss and Votiak have preserved this *e*, e.g., Hill Cheremiss *eŕ* 'early' < older C. *er*, modern *ir*; Votiak *em* 'medicine,' modern *im*; and C. *a* < older *ȧ* < *ä*, preserved in Hill Cheremiss, e.g., *käp* 'form, pattern' (Votiak *kab*, Meadow Cheremiss *kap*, modern C. *kap*). We may compare also Hungarian *kép*, which *may be* old Bolgar, just as the other examples in Räsänen, *Finnisch-ugrische Forschungen* 24.246-55, 1937. So much for Chuvash. In CTu. *ā̂ and *ē̂ at first converged >*ǟ̂ (just as *ā and *ē converged >*ǟ). This *ǟ̂ normally developed as follows:

Y. $*e^{\ddot{a}}$ >iä

T. $*e^{\ddot{a}}$ >$*e^{e}$ >ē >ī

K., Brahmi $*e^{\ddot{a}}$ >$*e^{e}$ >ē

Az. $*e^{\ddot{a}}$ >$*e^{e}$ >*ē >e

Most Tu. languages $*e^{\ddot{a}}$ >$*e^{e}$ >ē >e>ä

(Some languages of the last group show a secondary development *ä* >*e* >*i*, or similar; this development is very recent, hence diachronically irrelevant: still in the sixteenth century Kazan Tatar, for example, had *ä* or at least *e* instead of *i*, cf. G. Doerfer, review in *Mitteilungen des Instituts für Orientforschung* 13.476, Berlin, 1967.)

We find for the most part such correspondences as Y. *kiäŋ* 'broad' = T. *gīŋ* (Kh. *kị̄*^{e}*ṇ*^{k}) = Az. *geniš* = Osman *geniş* (*gäniš*), etc

We have to consider, however, that in T. in unstressed position *ǟ̂ >*ǟ* (eventually shortened: >*ä*), and in Y. in unstressed position *ǟ̂ >*ī* (eventually shortened: >*i*).

All exceptions can be explained by assimilations (e.g., T. *īšik* 'threshold,' because of *š* and *i*^{2} at the same time), or by analogy (e.g., T. *gīǰä* 'night' in analogy to *gīč* 'late,' which, by the way, is the root of *gīǰä*; *ǟr* 'man' in analogy to **ǟrkäk* 'male' >*ärkäk*). Sometimes we have to consider that words must not be regarded in an isolated form (*status absolutus*) but within the context (*status constructus*): Y. *bīl* 'waist,' *iŋ* <*īŋ* 'upper cheekbone,' e.g., show *ī* since words signifying parts of the body normally occur with possessive suffixes (Y. *bīlim* 'my waist,' etc.), i.e., the **â* here normally is in an unstressed position; therefore we find Y. *bīl*, *īŋ* >*iŋ*, and T. *ǟŋ* (whereas T. *bīl* has preserved the *status absolutus* form).

I cannot note here how I explain all the exceptions (although "exceptions" generally are by far more important than "norms"). Here is but one instance. We find K. *bēš* 'five' < CTu. **bâš* = Y. *biäs* ("correct") = *bǟš* T. ("false," "incorrect," "exception"). The T. form seems to be contrary to my own rule given above, according to which the form should be **bīš*. But this exception can easily be explained when one considers that **bâš* often occurred in unstressed position (e.g., **bâš ǟ́b* 'five houses,' etc.). And in unstressed position **â* becomes *ǟ* in T., as I said. To be sure, this explanation looks like an *ad hoc* invention. But it can be proved if one but examines the details: C. has two kinds of numerals, those in unstressed position (*status constructus*), which occur immediately before a substantive (e.g., *ikĕ kil* 'two houses') and those in stressed position (*status absolutus*), which are used alone (e.g., as an answer to the question 'how many houses are there?' *ikkĕ* 'two'). The numerals in *status constructus* have a simple consonant (*ikĕ* 'two,' *pilĕk* 'five,' *śičĕ* 'seven,' etc.). The numerals in *status absolutus* have a geminated consonant (*ikkĕ*, *pillĕk*, *śiččĕ*). This system originally occurred in all Tu. languages. Some modern CTu. languages have preserved the *status constructus* form (e.g., Osman *iki* 'two,' *yedi* 'seven,' *sekiz* 'eight,' *dokuz* 'nine'); other CTu. languages have the *status absolutus* forms (e.g., Uzbek *ikki*, *yatti*, *sakkiz*, *toqqiz*). Which are the T. forms? They are *iki*, *yädi*, *sä́kiz*, *doquz*, i.e., the *status constructus* forms = the forms in *unstressed* position — and in unstressed position Proto-CTu. *ä̂ > T. ǟ, as I said. Accordingly, T. *bǟš* is well suited to *iki*, *yädi*, etc. We see, then, that this form is not an exception. It is interesting to see that Y. has *biäs*, i. e., the form in stressed position and, at the same time, has also other *status absolutus* forms: *äkki*, *ikki* 'two,' *sättä* 'seven' (but *ağis* 'eight,' *toğus* 'nine'); here *biäs* is well suited to the numerals surrounding it: *ikki*, *sättä*.

The following are some further proofs of my assumption:

(a) In T. we find *īr* 'early,' but *ärtä* id. The last word is derived from the same root (CTu. *ä̂r) as *īr*. But *ä̂ of this root has become ī in stressed position, *ä̂ > ä in unstressed position (for the secondary shortening of T. see above 13. 8).

(b) Nowadays we find *gīč* 'late,' but *bǟš* 'five' in the T. written language, forms where CTu. *ä̂ has developed in two very different ways (T. ǟ is pronounced ā!). But in Khorezmian T., which seems to have preserved an older stage, there is no distinction: Abdullaev 1967. 37 records *beš* 'five,' *geč* 'late' (also *bel* 'girdle,' *čel* 'frontier,' *sel* 'current,' *el* 'nation,' *yeddi* 'seven,' *yer* 'earth' = T. *bīl*, *čīl*, *sīl*, *īl*, *yäddi*, *yär*). See also 47-8: *gečä* 'late' (= T. *gīč*), *gēǰä* 'night' (T. *gīǰä*), *er* 'young man' (T. *ǟr*), *ēr* 'early' (T. *īr*), *eš-* 'to twist' (T. *īš-*), *ēš* 'companion' (T. ___, K. *ēš*), *bēz* 'cotton' (T. *bīz*, but *bäz* 'impudent' = T. *bäz*).

It is interesting to see that the Trukhmen forms in P. S. Pallas, *Linguarum totius orbis vocabularia comparativa*, Petropoli, 1787-9 also always have i for T. ǟ. This i may represent an ä (or ẹ), e. g., 237 'to cut' *kismjak´* (T. *käsmäk*), 99 'sea' *dingéz´* (T. *däŋiz*); but it seems strange to assume that it should be used for so open a sound as ǟ. We find not only 90 'evening' *kič´* (T. *gīč*), 116 'breadth' *kinlik* (T. *gīŋlik*), but also 89 'early in the morning' *irtja* (T. *ärtä* ~ *īr*, Az. *ertä*, *er*),

244 'give' bir´ (T. bär ~bā̈r). This system would mean that just the border dialects of T. have preserved an older ē (and, as it is well known, border dialects very often preserve archaic forms).

The older theory had many contradictions, e.g., that 'broad' should be reconstructed PTu. *kā̈ŋ according to Y. kiäŋ, but *kēŋ according to T. gīŋ. Our thesis has no inexplicable contradictions.

What concerns us at this point is that CTu. */ā̈/ has become short in T., Y., Az., as have all other vowels of the type /ā/ .... Therefore we find Kh. à˙l 'hand' (<*ā̈l, ā̈läg), but T., Az. äl, Y. älī, ilī (and C. ală, i.e., PTu. *ā̈l, ā̈läg), also WOD. gā̈l- 'to come,' but T., Az. gäl-, Y. käl-.

What about Khalaj? Normally corresponding to CTu. */â̈/ is ī̤˙^{e} (or ī̤^{e} or ē̤^{e}): kī̤˙^{e}čä 'night,' bī˙^{e}l 'waist,' kī̤˙^{e}ŋ^{k} 'broad,' etc. (T.=gīǰä, bīl, gīŋ, Y. kiäsä, bīl, kiäŋ, C. kaś, pilĕk). We find, however, hànlı̤^{G} 'broad,' hànsı̤z 'narrow' (cf. K. ēn, T. īn, Y. iän 'breadth'), yättı̤ 'seven' (T. yädi < yâ̈ti), presumably due to the unstressed position. In hı̤kmäk 'bread' (K. ätmäk) *â̈ seems to have become ı̤; for hı̤˙rkàk 'male', see below.

CTu. */ā̈/ is never represented by a long vowel (or a long diphthong) in Khalaj. We find either a half-long vowel (a) or even a short vowel (b):

(a) *ā̈l(äg) 'hand' = KhT., M. à˙l (X. àl) = K. älig, Brahmi älig, elig, T. äl, Y. älī, ilī, C. ală <PTu. *ā̈l(äg).
*ā̈rän 'lip' = KhT., M. à˙rı̤n = K. erin, T. ärin.
*yā̈l 'wind' = KhT. ye˙l = K. yēl, Brahmi yel, T. yäl, Y. säl. Presumably ye̤˙l < *yä˙l < *yā̈l [ä˙ assimilated after y, just as in Az. yär 'earth' >yer or Y. yär >*yer >sir].

(b) *ā̈kkī 'two' = KhT. àkkṳ̈, M., X. àkkı̤ = K., T., Brahmi iki, Y. äkki, ikki. Said to be long in QB (īki, cf. 13.7), â̈kkī?

*ǟb 'house' = KhT. hȧv = WOD. ǟv. Cf., however, Wena̯rej̆ hȧ˙v.
*bǟg 'prince' = KhT. bȧg = K. bǟg, T., Brahmi bäg.
*kǟč- 'to pass' = KhX. kȧšgụlị = WOD gǟš-.
*kǟl- 'to come' = KhX. kȧlȧn yịl 'next year' = WOD. gǟl-, K., Y., Brahmi käl-, T. gäl-.
*kǟlän 'bride' (< *kǟl-) = KhT. kȧlịn, M. kȧlịn, X. kȧlụ̈n = K. kälin, T. gälin.
*kǟd- 'to put on clothes' = KhT. kȧDmịšȧk 'we put on clothes' (unpublished material) = K. kǟd-, käd-, T. gäy-, Y. kät-, Brahmi käd-.
*kǟs- 'to cut' = KhT. kȧsȧr 'hatchet' = WOD. kǟs-.

I think the best explanation of this fact may be Persian influence: whereas P. ē has become Kh. $\underline{i}^{e}$ (cf. 13.11.4), T. ǟ has been shortened, since P. does not have ǟ or ā but only ȧ.

For some other instances of CTu. *ǟ found in K., we find no equivalent in Kh.: K. tǟg 'like' = T. däk, K. yēg 'best' = T. yäg, K. kǟnč = Az. gänǰ (not *genǰ).

A special problem arises with the word for 'man.' We must consider it together with the word for 'male.'

	man	male	
ATu.	är	erkäk	In Bang and von Gabain, *Analytischer Index* ... 22, Berlin, 1931, erroneously irkäk
Brahmi	ärän	irkäk(län-)	hǟrä is an error. Here we sometimes find i- instead of e-: iki 'two,' itig ~ etig 'decoration'
K.	är	erkäk	e according to erkek, derivation erkeklen- ~ irkeklen-
T.	ǟr	ärkäk	

Y.	är	irgäx
Az.	är	erkäk
KhT.	hȧr	hị˙ rkȧk

According to T. ǟr we should expect CTu. *är̂. But the odd fact is that all the other forms of Tu. languages clearly and conformably indicate är (*âr should be ATu. *er, Brahmi *erän, K. *ēr, Y. *iär, Az. *er, Kh. *hī˙ᵉr). It would seem to be evident that the word for 'male' is derived from 'man.' But must such derivation be true? The word for 'male' clearly goes back to *ârkäk, cf. the forms of ATu., Az., and Kh. (shortened < *hī˙ᵉrkȧk, in unstressed position). K., T. may represent a shortening which respectively is graphic (K.) or secondary (T. ärkäk < *ǟrkäk). I have the impression that the original CTu. word for 'man' was är, not âr (going back to *pärä, ä not e, being clearly from C. ar, p- from Kh. hȧr, -ä from Mo. ere). In T. it has been influenced by *ârkäk. It may be, however, that this word constitutes an example of what Ramstedt would call the pre-Altaic layer of Tu., i.e., a vowel gradation *pärä ~ *pârkäk; or är might even owe its origin to analogy with ärk 'might' (är in the RTu. inscriptions has the meaning 'knight, cavalier, champion'; 'man' seems to have been urï or orï) or to something else. The derivation remains unclear.

13.11.6 The diphthongal character of Turkic long vowels. Here I would like to make some comments on the nature of modern Tu. long vowels. I have always said that T. and Y. have preserved long vowels. Now I acknowledge that they have not. T. and Y. possess not long vowels but diphthongs. Jakobson 1962.261, quoting Julius Laziczius, Bevezetés a fonológiába, 1932, says that the so-called long vowels in these languages are "eigentlich Mischvokale, Bewegungsdiphthonge." According to A.P. Poceluevskij, Dialekty turkmenskogo jazyka 31, Ašxabad, 1936, all vowels of T. are diphthongs: ā rising, ı̄, ï̄, ū, ǖ falling (see also Räsänen 1949. 77, according to whom ǟ is pronounced ǟ^{a}; ï̄, ï̄^{i}; ı̄, ı̄^{i}; ū, ū^{u}; ǖ, ǖ^{i}. (I myself once heard in Bloomington, Indiana, āt 'name' pronounced ā^{a}t by a lady of T. origin). According to N. A. Baskakov, "Ob osobennostjax govora severo-kavkazskix turkmenov," Jazyki severnogo Kavkaza i Dagestana II. 143-4, Moskva, 1949, all long vowels in Trukhmen, the western T. dialect, are falling diphthongs. Finally, S. Kurenov, Osobennosti turkmenskogo govora Severnogo Kavkaza (Stavropolja) Avtoreferat kand. dissert. 7, Ašxabad, 1959, confirms this theory (cf. Ščerbak 1967. 15). In Y. the diphthongal character is evident in such cases as uo <*ô, üö <*ȫ, iä <*ä̂. The diphthongal nature of these dialects agrees precisely with the Kh. forms ụ̄^{o}, ọ̈̄^{ö}, ị̄^{e}, also ā^{a}, ụ̈̄^{ü}, etc.

13.11.7 The diphthongal character of long vowels in al-Kāšġarī. We find a possible confirmation of the diphthongal character of PTu. /â/ ... in K., too. Whereas 'horse' (at) is written اَتْ in K., 'name' (āt) is written اَات . Similarly we find words with ā-, such as اَاچ āč 'hungry,' etc. Now this form is not the regular transcription of ā-! ā- in Arabic words is written آ quite regularly, e.g., original p. 2 إِمَامٍ آخَرَ 'of another priest' (imāmin āxara), or آمَنُوهُ مِنْ فِرْقِهِمْ 'they believed that he belonged to their group' (āmanūhu min firqihim). However, we find a transcription اا in the middle of words, but here designating a new syllable, e.g., p. 3 طَآيِفَةٍ 'of the tribe' (ṭā'ifatin). These transcriptions indicate that اَات cannot be read āt but only as something like aat or āat, vowel sounds which would agree with T. ā^{a}, Kh. ā^{a}.

Here a question arises: were vowels really diphthongs in such words as قَارْ 'snow' < CTu. qâr? Do we have to read Karakhanid qā^{a}r? Here two possibilities exist:

(a) We must read $\underline{\bar{a}^{a}t}$, but can read $\underline{q\bar{a}r}$; in accord with Karakhanid shortening (cf. 13.7): $\underline{a^{a}t}$ or $\underline{a^{\cdot a}t}$, but $\underline{q\bar{a}r}$ (allegro $\underline{a^{\cdot}t}$, $\underline{qa^{\cdot}r}$). That an anlaut underlies special conditions and may give results other than an inlaut is well known. Tuv., for example, has preserved CTu. *ẽ as an i, but in anlaut it always has a- (cf. 14.1); CTu., having all PTu. i̭-diphthongs in anlaut, in inlaut has only i̭-diphthongs with back vowels (cf. 14.4.1), etc.

(b) The other possibility is that also in inlaut we would have to read $\underline{a^{\cdot a}}$ or $\underline{a^{a}}$ (allegro $\underline{a^{\cdot}}$), e.g., $\underline{qa^{\cdot a}r}$ or $\underline{qa^{a}r}$ 'snow,' not $\underline{q\bar{a}r}$. This reading would agree with K. (cf. 13.6), who prefers to write open syllables as plene, closed syllables as defective. The writing قَارْ in this case would mean that we must read $\underline{qa^{a}r}$; i.e., the first a is not immediately followed by a consonant. It is obvious that no truly open syllable exists, but only something similar to one.

I cannot decide which of these two possibilities is correct. Against (b) is the fact that PTu. /ā/ ... also is written as plene in K., e.g., bā̈g بَاكْ. Here presumably there is no diphthong, but we find nevertheless a plene transcription. Provisionally, I prefer thesis (a).

13.11.8 Turkman -t-, etc., unchanged after Proto-Turkic */ā/ .... As we have seen, PTu. */â/ ... changes T. -p-, -t-, -k-/-q-, -č- >-b-, -d-, -g-/-ġ-, -ǰ-; e.g., *ât 'name,' *âtïŋ 'of the name' >T. āt, ādïŋ. This change holds true even when */â/ ... is secondarily shortened: T. äd-il- 'to be done' (< *ä̂d-il-, from *ä̂t- >ät- 'to do'); gid-iš 'march' (< *gä̂t-iš, from *gä̂t- >git-, *ä̂ assimilated to i under the influence of the frequent form gitti 'he went, he is gone,' just as äki 'two' >iki); ġuǰaq 'embrace' (< *qûčaq, from qûč- >quč- 'to embrace'); buġa 'bull' (< *bûqa, K. buqā).

But PTu. */ā/ ... never causes this change. This fact is clear proof that */ā/ ... must be distinctly separated from */â/ .... Here are some instances. In T. we find that it 'dog' (Kh. ï̄t, CTu. *ï̄t, cf. 13.9) never occurs with a -d- (e.g., āv iti 'hunting-hound'); at- 'to throw' (WOD. āt-, CTu. *āt-) has the passive form at-ïl- (not *ad-ïl-); gač- 'to flee' (WOD. ǧāš-, CTu. *qāč-) has the cooperative form gač-ïš-; üč 'three' (WOD., Kh. ǖš, CTu. *ǖč) has the ordinal number üčünǰi; *ǟkki 'two' has become iki, not igi; yat- 'to lie' (WOD. yāt-, Kh. yāt-, CTu. *yāt-) has the cooperative form yat-ïš-; oq 'arrow' (K. ōq, oq, CTu. *ōq) is oq + ï with the possessive suffix; sap 'handle' (K. sāp, CTu. sāp) is sap + ï with the possessive suffix, etc. We may include here also K. kǖp 'vessel' = Osman küp, which is küp-ü with the possessive suffix, not *küb-ü.

The law which says that long vowels cause voiceless stops and affricates to become voiced holds true only for PTu. */â/ ..., not for */ā/ .... Hence these two vowels must represent two different categories.

13.11.9 Vowel quantity in non-initial syllables. One previously has assumed, according to the thesis of two vowel quantities in Tu., that PTu. had either short or long vowels in non-initial syllables. The strange fact is that T. and K. disagree enormously on this point. Whereas in T. (and in Y.) the vast majority of vowels of non-initial syllables is short, in K. (and QB) almost all vowels in open syllables and many vowels in closed syllables are long in this position. The difference between K. and T. is even greater on this point than in the first syllables; e.g., 'he did not open' would be in Karakhanid ačmādï̄ (if one literally renders the plene transcription as long vowels) = T. ačmadï, etc. Tekin 1967.165-170 has given a list of vowel lengths in suffixes. This list is correct; its only shortcoming is that Tekin gives no general summary, no general rule. The simple rule is that all vowels of open non-initial syllables (and many of closed ones) are "long" in QB, with the exception of those which have a fourfold set of allophones ï/i/u/ü; that is, a/ä, u/ü, ï/i always are long (ağïrlā- 'to honor,' čïqarmā 'do not bring out,' birāgü 'one of them,' ölürüm 'my dying,' tapuġčï 'servant,' qalïrï 'his remaining'); but the passive suffix -ïl-/-il-/-ul-/-ül-, for example, never is long, nor is the accusative suffix .ïġ/.ig/.uġ/.üg, etc. (for the correct pronunciation cf. 14.4.4).

Let us state another fact: long vowels in T. and/or Y. sometimes do correspond to Karakhanid "long vowels" (cf. T. according to Dmitriev in Issledovanija po sravnitel'noj grammatike tjurkskix jazykov I. 190, Moskva, 1955 and Biišev 1963. 63-5); e.g., the comparative suffix (QB) +rāq/+rāk (Tekin No. 26) is also long in T. (the same form). But, as I said, in other cases short vowels in T. correspond to Karakhanid "long vowels," e.g., the plural suffix QB +lār/+lār (Tekin No. 27) is short in T.: +lar/+lär. This difference seems to prove that we must distinguish two categories of "length" in this case. Even Y., by the way, makes a clear distinction between such cases as ī in kälī 'mortar' and -i in kisi 'person'; in Karakhanid the vowels would be long in both cases (short vowels in open last syllables do not occur in Karakhanid, except for some affective exclamations). Taking into account the short vowels also (as in QB at+ïm 'my horse' = T. at+ïm), we get the following three categories:

(a) T. long vowel = QB long vowel (e.g., +rāq)
(b) T. short vowel = QB long vowel (e.g., +lar/+lār
(c) T. short vowel = QB short vowel (e.g., +ïm).

The situation in K. is similar to that of QB, i.e., the transcription in K. gives results similar to those of the meter in QB. For example, we find (Tercümesi II. 220-11) qïz + lār 'girls,' or

(II. 138-2) kävil:sūn 'he may chew' (= Tekin No. 19). To be sure, in the samples we find even short vowels written as plene, e.g. (I. 69), kōṇlūm 'my heart' or (45) kōrklūg tonūg 'the beautiful coat' (accusative); but normal transcriptions such as qïzïg 'the girl' (accusative), qïzïm 'my girl' prevail here, i.e., normally the possessive suffix +ïm/+im/+um/+üm 'my' and other suffixes with fourfold allophones are short. (In QB, too, they are always short, e.g., Verse 186, "... sözüm oġluma sözlädim," ᴗ - - / ᴗ - - / ᴗ - , 'I told you my word, O son.') The situation is clear in the headwords of K. where, for example, we find (I. 188-9 alïšūr 'he takes together with others.' Here the cooperative suffix -ïš-/-iš-/-uš-/-üš- is written as defective, the aorist suffix -ur/-ür as plene (the aorist suffix sometimes is written as plene, sometimes as defective, the cooperative suffix always as defective). The same holds true for the meter in QB: Tekin's list does not contain one case of a suffix with the fourfold set treated as long. (However, besides išlā- 'to work,' the vowel is written as defective in closed syllables: išläl- passive, iälän- reflexive, išläš- cooperative, išlät- causative; this situation may be partly graphic.) And now let me begin our explanation of these facts:

(a) T. long vowel = QB, K. long vowel < PTu. */â/ ...
(b) T. short vowel = QB, K. long vowel < PTu. */ā/ ...
(c) T. short vowel = QB, K. short vowel < PTu. */a/ ...

*/â/ ... may occur in inlaut (e.g., comparative suffix -rÂK) and in auslaut (Y. kälī 'mortar' < *kälî, etc.); */ā/ ... may occur in inlaut (imperative suffix third person :sŪn) and in auslaut (dative suffix .KĀ); */a/ ... may occur in inlaut (passive suffix -ïl-/-il-/-ul-/-ül- < -ăl-/-ĕl- < unstressed -al-/-äl-, possessive suffix -ïm/-im/-um/-üm < -ăm/-ĕm < unstressed -am/-äm), but it never occurs in auslaut (we do not find the fourfold allophone -ï/-i/-u/-ü in Uighur Tu., only -ï-/-i-/-u-/-ü-).

Now we have to consider that Mo. often has a final -*a*/-*e* (or -*an*/-*en*) where Tu. has a final consonant. I think that here Mo. has preserved archaic Tu. *-*a*/-*e* in auslaut (or rather *-*ă*/-*ĕ*, since sometimes other vowels occur in forms which seem to be assimilated, a proof for a reduced -*ă*/-*ĕ*. Compare Mo. *qadum* 'in-law' = Middle Tu. *qādïn*, the Mo. form presumably < Old Bolgar **qâd́ŏm* or a similar form < **qâd́ăm*, *ă* being assimilated to *m*; Mo. *qonin* 'sheep' = Middle Tu. *qōn*, *qōy*, ATu. *qōń*, the Mo. form presumably < Old Bolgar **qṓńĭn* or a similar form < *qṓńăn*, *ă* being assimilated to *ń*; Mo. *küčin*, later *küčün*, 'force' = Middle Tu. *kû̈č*, the Mo. form presumably < Old Bolgar **kû̈́č̌ĭn* or a similar form <**kû̈́čĕn*, *ĕ* being assimilated to *č*).

I maintain that we have to assume Uighur *ï*/*i*/*u*/*ü* < older Tu. (RTu.) *ă*/*ĕ* and PTu. -*a*/-*ä* > -*ă*/-*ĕ* zero, and this for four reasons:

(1) The existence of an original -*ă*/-*ĕ* is assumed because we find /â/ ... and /ā/ ... both in inlaut and auslaut, whereas we find /a/ ... only in inlaut. Were this situation original, it would be extremely surprising. That in Mo. -*a*/-*e* has not been added secondarily has been proved in Doerfer JSFOu. Here is but one hint. To Tu. *küzän* 'polecat' Mo. *kürene* corresponds; and there exist many other words where we find in Tu. -*n*, in Mo. -*na*/-*ne*. But it seems quite unlikely that Mo. has *attached* (added) -*a*/-*e* in this case: -*n* is a frequent auslaut in Mo.; a word like **küren* would have an absolutely "Mongolian" shape (cf. *mören* 'river,' *morin* 'horse,' *ǰirin* 'two,' *oron* 'place,' a Tu. loanword, etc.) Contrary to the opinion of Sir Gerard Clauson and A. M. Ščerbak, I assume that Mo. has preserved the older situation. At any rate, the mere argument of system would be cogent enough (and the dropping of short or even reduced vowels in auslaut is a well-known development, cf. Old English *nama* 'name' >Middle English *nāmə*>New English *ne·ⁱm*).

The fact that ï/i/u/ü goes back to a reduced vowel is clear because this form never occurs in auslaut. In the Uighur auslaut we find -ā/-ǟ, -ū/-ǖ, -ï̄/-ī (and -ō/-ȫ), but never -ï/-i/-u/-ü. Why? This phenomenon is inexplicable when one assumes that Uighur represents the oldest stage of Tu.; but it is quite easy to explain according to my thesis: Uighur -ï-/-i-/-u-/-ü- goes back to older -ă-/-ĕ-. So we may assume an older -ă/-ĕ, which may have disappeared, in contrast to -ă-/-ĕ-.

(2) That ï/i/u/ü goes back to an older reduced vowel is clear because of its fourfold set of allophones, the only fourfold set existing in Uighur. Here we always find twofold sets of allophones: ā/ǟ (e.g., the dative suffix qōl.qā 'to the arm,' kȫl.kǟ 'to the lake'); ï̄/ī (e.g., the denominal noun suffix +qï̄/+kī); ū/ǖ (e.g., the deverbal verb suffix -ġū/-gǖ: bar-ġū 'he must go,' kǟl-gǖ 'he must come'; we also find ō/ȫ, by the way). But compare the fourfold set of allophones in at-lïġ 'having a horse,' ät-lig 'having flesh,' qōl-luġ 'having an arm,' kȫl-lüg 'having a lake' (ï after a, ï; i after ä, e, i; u after o, u; ü after ö, ü, but cf. 14.4.4.) Why do we have a fourfold set in this case alone? This phenomenon is inexplicable according to the terms of the older thesis. According to our thesis, however, it is easily explained: a reduced vowel can easily adopt the timbre of its phonetic surroundings. By the way, I should not exclude the possibility that -ă-/-ĕ- already had some labial allophones (without phonemic value), e.g., -ŏ-/-ŏ̈- or -ă-/-ă̈, after labial vowels, cf. 14.4.4.

(3) A further reason is inherent in the transcription of K. and the meter of QB. Whereas "full" vowels (u/ü, o/ö, ï/i, a/ä) normally are written as plene in K. (almost always in open, very often in closed syllables) and are long according to the meter in QB, ï/i/u/ü is written mostly as defective in K. and is always treated as short in QB (cf. above). Thus we see clearly that

'i/i/u/ü has another, a shorter quantity than, for example, u/ü in the imperative suffix :sūn/:sǖn, a/ä in the plural suffix +lār/+lǟr, or 'i/i in the aorist suffix :ïr/:īr.

Now I would like briefly to deal with another point (though it is not so relevant to my purpose). I think that the transcription of the RTu. inscriptions also proves that 'i/i/u/ü must be distinguished from the full vowels (and must be read ă/ĕ), contrary to Meyer 1965. 183-203, who affirmed that RTu. has the same system as Uighur, namely not ă/ĕ, but 'i/i/u/ü. Meyer has not considered the fact that the vowels of the Uighur fourfold set are almost never written in RTu. but occur regularly in the later Runic manuscripts (biliṇlär 'ye may know' instead of bilṇlr, etc.). The few examples where vowels of the fourfold set are written can be readily explained, as in the word qūnčuyūġ (I transcribe RTu. written vowels as "long" vowels) 'the princess' accusative (cf. Talât Tekin, A Grammar of Orkhon Turkic 37, Bloomington, 1968), easily identified as qunčuyŏġ; furthermore, since these written vowels occur only in the neighborhood of q, k, ġ, g they may be merely graphic. By the way, some forms said by Tekin to contain "connective vowels" have or may have full vowels indeed: bōdūn 'nation,' ōlūr- 'to sit,' cf. Y. olor-. But, in contrast to Meyer's rule (rounded vowels in suffixes written only after unrounded vowels of the root, unrounded vowels of suffixes written only after rounded vowels of the root) we often find rounded "full" vowels in all positions, cf. Tekin 37: the causative suffix, for example, and other suffixes are written as plene even after rounded vowels: bōlčūn 'he may be,' bōšġūrmïš 'he taught,' qōntūr- 'to settle (somebody else),' etc. (and this not only after q, k, ġ, g). And we also find (Tekin 35) adăñčïġ 'extraordinary' (traditionally transcribed adïnčïġ), qōnayïn 'I shall settle down' (Tekin 59), whereas the suffix of the converb is written as defective, cf. René Giraud, L'inscription de Baïn Tsokto,

Paris, 1961.34, e.g., būlmayăn 'without finding' traditionally transcribed bulmayïn. We see that a clear distinction is made between ï and ă, that is, ï/ï written after unrounded vowels. But we never find written, for example, the vowel of the perfect first person singular (:tm); nor do we find it after rounded or unrounded vowels. I think even here the situation is clear enough; I agree with Tekin's denomination of "ï/i/u/ü" as "connective vowels" (63), but I think that we must conclude that they are the RTu. reduced vowels ă/ĕ, disregarding whether or not they had labial allophones.

(4) The last reason is the well-known elision of the middle syllable in Turkic. In late sources elision may affect almost all vowels (at least, all closed vowels), above all, of suffixes; e.g., K. yandru 'again' <yanduru (with a full vowel u). But in words of older texts it concerns only some cases, such as uġur 'opportunity,' oġul 'son,' aġïz 'mouth,' (cf. Gabain 1950.44), also burun 'nose,' köŋül 'heart,' qarïn 'bellow,' boyun 'body.' We find the same instances even in modern dialects (cf. PhTF, "chute des voyelles," p. 758), e.g., Osman burun 'nose,' but burn + u 'his nose.' We find forms with elision also in K.: III. 55-18 uġrï 'his opportunity' (from uġur), I. 220-17 oġlï 'his son' (from oġul), I. 193-8 aġzï 'his mouth' (from aġïz), I. 375-7 burnï 'his nose' (from burun), II. 188-19 köŋlï 'his heart' (from köŋül), II. 288-7 qarnï 'his bellow' (from qarïn), II. 233-4 boynï 'his body' (from boyun). And we find the same cases in Brahmi texts, cf. Gabain, Türkische Turfan-Texte VIII, Berlin, 1954: oġlï, aġzï, köŋlï, qarnï, boynï. In these examples we find u after o, u; ü after ö; ï after a, that is, the same distribution as in the fourfold set of vowel harmony! Thus, these must be the same vowels as in, for example, the suffix +lïġ/+lig/-luġ/-lüg. And this identity is confirmed by the fact that in Manichaean texts (where we find a/ä [= ă/ĕ?] instead of ï/i/u/ü, especially

after a/ä, e.g., bartam 'I went,' kältäm 'I came') we find aġaz instead of aġïz. How can we explain that u, ü, i were dropped just in these words (e.g., aġïz 'mouth,' aġzī 'his mouth'), but never, for example, u in such words as aġūz 'first milk' or sïġūn 'deer' (why never *aġzī 'her first milk')? This phenomenon is inexplicable on the basis of the older thesis. In our view the explanation is quite simple: we have to assume older forms uġăr, oġăl, aġăz, burăn, köŋĕl, qarăn, boyăn. And, quite naturally, the reduced vowels were dropped in unstressed syllables: òġălī́ 'his son' > oġlī, etc.

These are four proofs of an older RTu. ă/ĕ, which has been dropped in auslaut and in the middle of trisyllabic words (Uighur forms such as oġulī 'his son' are an analogous restitution following the pattern aġūz 'first milk' : aġūzī = oġul 'son' : X, X becoming oġulī).

It seems strange, by the way, that we find no old CTu. or old Bolgar non-long vowels except -ă/-ĕ reflected in Mo. loanwords, e.g., Mo. miŋgan 'a thousand' ← Tu. *bïŋăn > bïŋ > bïŋ (PTu. form presumably *bḯŋan). It is very possible that in the oldest stage of Tu. (proto-proto-Turkic, so to speak) we had other short vowels in auslaut. It may be, for instance, that *pä́rĕ 'man' < *pä́rä goes back to older *pä́rü, or *bḯŋăn < *bḯŋan goes back to *bḯŋun. In this case we ought to write something like ȣ, that is, "some vowel of indefinite timbre." But this thesis, though not refutable, would be merely a glottogonic speculation. We have no proof whatever for *pä́rü, bḯŋun: Mo. hints only of *pärĕ, *bïŋăn.

Now let us summarize PTu. vowels of non-initial syllables:

/â/ ... Karakhanid long vowel, T. long vowel, RTu. often written;

/ā/ ... Karakhanid long (or rather half-long) vowel, T. short vowel, RTu. often written;

/a/ ... Karakhanid and T. short vowel, RTu. almost never written, -/a/ ... in all attested Tu. languages dropped, preserved in Mongolian.

However, I should not exclude the possibility that in older Tu., in a period of transition, only /â/ ... was pronounced as a long vowel, /ā/ ... already being short (but a full vowel), /a/ ... reduced (or dropped, in auslaut), in other words, that every vowel of a non-initial syllable was reduced one degree. The reason may have been that non-initial syllables were unstressed, in contrast to modern Tu.

What about the vowels of non-initial syllables in Khalaj? PTu. -/a/ ... has been dropped, too (hȧr 'man,' Mo. ere, not *hȧrȧ). The short vowels in closed non-initial syllables (/a/...) often have been rounded, cf. 11, e.g., kȧlṳ̈n 'bride,' ča̮qụr 'pale,' qa̮˙rụn 'bellow'; they never occur as long vowels. But also PTu. /ā/ ... is shortened in Khalaj, just as in T. and Y.: ȧkkṳ̈, ȧkkị 'two,' etc. We find long vowels only in the following examples: *bağïrsôq 'bowels' (bọġa̮rsa̮˙q, bọġa̮rsụq); *pïrâq 'far' (?ịra̮q, hịrā̮q, yịrā̮q); *ôtčâq 'hearth' (hū̥°ča̮q, hū̥°ča̮˙q); *qūlâq 'ear' (Ḉụlā̮q, Ḉụla̮qᶜ, qụla̮q, qọlā̮q); *sïčġân 'mouse' (sịčġā̮n, sịčġā̮n, sị⁴čġā̮n); *tâlâq 'milt' (tā̮lā̮q); tâpân 'sole' (tā̮ᵃpā̮n); *tabïšġân 'hare' (ta̮vụšġa̮˙n, tọvụšġa̮n, tọu̯ụšġā̮n); *tôrâq 'dried milk' (tū̥°ra̮q, tụ°ra̮˙q); *tōprâq or *tuprâq 'soil' (tụrpā̮q); *uzâq 'long' (ụzā̮q); *yāġâq 'nut' (yaġā̮q, yọġa̮˙q, yaġa̮˙q); *yïlân 'snake' (yịlā̮n); *yōrġân 'blanket' (yọrġā̮n).

Thus we find mainly endings -ân, -âq, which often agree with T., K.: yïrâq 'far,' yïlân 'snake.' But we also find deviations: T. gulaq 'ear' (Y. kulgāx, K. qulaq, QB qulāq). Here are the correspondences in T., Y., K.:

*bağïrsôq	___	___	bagirsaq
*pïrâq	yïrāq	ïrāx	yïrāq

*ôtčâq	ōǰaq	ohox	očaq
*qūlâq	g͉ulaq	kulgāx	qulaq (QB qulāq!)
*sïčġân	sïčan	___	sïčġān
*tâlâq	dālaq	(tāl)	talāq
*tâpân	dāban	___	tapan (in the text "taban")
*tabïšġân	tovšan	___	tawïšġān
*tôrâq	___	___	___
*tuprâq	topraq	___	toprāq (or rather tuprāq)
*uzâq	uzaq	___	uzaq
yāġâq	___	___	yaġāq
*yïlân	yïlān	___	yïlān
*yōrġân	yorg͉an	___	yoġurqān

Instead of *yōrġân we may prefer another original form, e.g., *yoġurqân. It seems probable that we find -âq in suffixes of parts of the body, since we find in QB adāq 'foot,' qulāq 'ear,' and in K. talāq 'milt.' Thus K. qulaq may be a graphic shortening (cf. 13.6); in K. uzaq the vowels must be long (or at least full) since the word is derived from uzā- 'to be long,' etc. On the whole, the Karakhanid situation agrees with Khalaj quite well; only *tâpân, *ôtčâq deviate, but even here a graphic shortening may exist in K. With T. Khalaj normally disagrees; we find only T. yïrāq, yïlān; but this situation can be secondary: in Y. we find kulgāx (= QB, Kh.) against T. g͉ulaq. However, the situation is sophisticated. On the whole, I am not so sure whether T. shows a secondary shortening in such forms as sïčan, dālaq or whether we have to assume /â/ ... only in such cases where even T. has a long vowel (yïrāq, yïlān), whereas in such cases as T. sïčan, dālaq = K. sïčġān, talāq we have to assume an original /ā/ ..., quite normally preserved in K., shortened in T. (just as in the first syllables). However, Kh. has /ā/ ...

in these cases, whereas it generally changes /ā/$_2$ ... > /a/ ..., a situation which seems to be a contradiction.

PTu. /ā/$_2$ has been preserved in some cases in WOD., too: *yalvār-* 'to beg,' and many aorist forms as *gidä̅riz* 'we go' (contrary to Korkmaz 203, note 11).

13.12 *Attempted reconstruction of Proto-Turkic quantity.* We shall try to reconstruct the older (or oldest) situation of vowel quantities in Turkic.

13.12.1 *Former attempts.* It is clear that all the older attempted reconstructions, based on only two quantities, must be false. Ščerbak 1967, for example, offers a good refutation of Biišev's thesis */â/ ... < */a^{i}/ .... But his own thesis is not much better. He gives on p. 46 the following pattern for the development of *āt* 'name' : *at* 'horse.' **át*/*at´* (in the first case a stressed vowel, in the second case a stressed consonant) > **āt*/*att* or **a:t*/*at:* (which is the same) > modern languages *ād*/*at*. This theory is untenable even without the evidence provided by Khalaj: Ščerbak considered only monosyllabic words. But we find the same opposition of long and short vowels also in disyllabic words, such as T. *bö̅ri* 'wolf,' *āla* 'colored' : *g̦ara* 'black,' *kiši* 'person.' Applying Ščerbak's thesis to these words, we must assume that in *bö̅ri* the vowel was stressed, in *qara* the consonant *r*, that is, **bö´ri*, **qar´a*. But it is rather unlikely that a consonant between two vowels would be stressed. Concerning Ščerbak's connection between short vowels and gemination, we find in Kh. several instances where just *long* vowels have produced a secondary (substitutional) gemination, cf. *balla* 'small' = T. *bāla* < **bâlā* 'young animal'; *qạrrị* 'old' = Az. dialect of Nukha *g̦ārï* < **qārï̄* (T. *g̦arrï*); *qu̦rru̦ġ* 'dry' = T. *g̦ūrï* < **qûrï̄*

But my own remarks in *Journal de la Société Finno-Ougrienne* 65.16 have also been erroneous: mere tonality without quantity is not a sufficient explanation.

13.12.2 The possibilities of explanation. How may we explain the quantities in Kh., for example, in tọq 'satisfied,' qụ°l 'arm,' tū̥°n 'clothes'? (We provisionally reconstructed *toq, *qōl, *tôn.) There are many possibilities:

(1) Something like ancient Greek o : ώ : ῶ, i.e., short vowel : simple (acute) length : moved (circumflex) length. We may write o : ō : ô or even o : ō : ō°;

(2) o : o˙ : o:, i.e., short : half-long : long;

(3) o : uo : uō, i.e., short : short diphthong : long diphthong (a : aa : aā, etc.);

(4) o : oó : óo, i.e., short : rising diphthong : falling diphthong.

This last possibility would be compatible with the following fact: in Osman (and other Oghuz languages) we find not only ā`tï´ņ 'of the name' > adın, i.e., -t- > -d- after long vowels, but also qa`natī´ņ 'of the wing' > kanadın, i.e., -t- > -d- in the third syllable of trisyllabic words. We may explain this phenomenon as follows: *a`atï´ņ 'of the name' > adın, *qànatï´ņ 'of the wing' > kanadın, but *a`tï´ņ 'of the horse' > atın, and also *yaa`tur 'he is lying' > yatır. In the first case an unstressed syllable (or part of a diphthong, two morae) was before -t-; in the second case a stressed syllable (or part of a diphthong, one mora) was before -t-. But the same fact may be explained by possibility (1), as well.

We may consider still other possibilities. On the whole, I think it is rather useless to reflect here too much: we do have taped recordings of Khalaj but we have none of PTu. And, by the way, these explanations are all rather similar (cf. Jakobson 1962.119 ff.). I, for my part, am inclined to accept solution (1), which seems to be the least artificial (it resembles, by the way, the system reconstructed for Indo-European languages, cf., for example, Hans Krahe, *Indogermanische Sprachwissenschaft*, Berlin, 1943.35). We may assume three "quantities": (1) one-mora (short) vowels, (2) two-morae (long) vowels with a level (or acute) intonation, (3) two-morae (long) vowels with a moved (or circumflex) intonation. This explanation agrees quite well with Kh. and even with T., Y., K. (cf. 13.11.6, 7).

13.12.3 Monosyllabic roots ending in vowels. In 13.4 I said that monosyllabic roots ending in a vowel are always long in Tu. And indeed we find: K. bā- 'to bind' = T. bā-ġ-la-, Y. bāy-; K. bū 'this' = T., WOD. bū (Y. bu may be a secondary shortening, since PTu. *bô often is proclitic, i.e., unstressed); K. bū 'steam' = T. būġ; K. sā- 'to count' = T. sāy-; K. sï̄- 'to break' = T. sï̄ndïr-; K. tē- = T. diy-, Y. diä, WOD. dē-; K. yā 'bow' = T. yāy, Y. sā; K. yē- 'to eat' = T. iy-, Y. siä-; K. yū- 'to wash' = T. yuv- (= yū^{u}-), Y. sūy-. Even a correspondence such as K. nǟ 'what' = T. nä is no genuine exception, because we find such derivations as T. nǟlär (plural), nǟmä 'whatever' : nä must be a secondarily shortened form, used perhaps in affective expressions (cf. Essen 1953.119, lines 23-6). For more examples of this type see Ščerbak 1967.43-4.

We surely never find short vowels in the position mentioned. Do we find an opposition /â/ ... : /ā/ ... ? I think we do. Compare the following examples: K. qōd- 'to put,' qōn- 'to settle' seem to go back to a root *qō-. The origin must be *qō-, not *qô-, since we have T. goy-, Y. xot-. A similar case may exist in WOD. gȫr- 'to look,' gȫz 'eye' (= QB kȫz); the root seems to be *kȫ- (T. gör-, göz, Y. kör-, kös). It is hard to say whether or not K. tōd- ~tod- 'to become satisfied' = T. doy-, Y. tot- is among these examples (cf. K. toq 'satisfied' = T. doq). We may cite furthermore K. sīz 'ye' (and, presumably, *bīz 'we'). Since +z is a plural suffix in this case and since we find ATu. si.ni 'thee,' bi.ni ~mi.ni 'me' (and other such case forms, too), we may reconstruct a root *sī (and, analogically, *bī). Even K. yaq- 'to burn (something else)' and yan- 'to burn,' yal- 'to flame' may go back to *yā-, also yük 'burden,' yǖd- 'to burden.' The vowels normally are short in K., but the shortness may be graphic. (This explanation is not certain, however.) The root *ā+ 'that' seems to belong here, too: it is short in T. (anča 'so much'), but it is long in Yükneki (cf. 13.7); in verse 446 we find ānï 'him.' We may find some other examples of this type, too; however, it is not my task to deal with all of them here. At any rate, I think we have to assume PTu. roots of the type consonant + /â/ ... and of the type consonant + /ā/ ..., but none of the type consonant + /a/ ....

13.12.4 Summary. Here is a survey about the development of PTu. vowel quantities in K., WOD., T., Y., and Kh.

(A) Monosyllabic roots

PTu.	K. lento	K. allegro	WOD.	T.	Y.	Kh.
/â/ ...	/ā/ ...	/a˙/ ...	/ā/ ...	/â/ ...	/â/ ...	/â/ ...
/ā/ ...	/ā/ ...	/a˙/ ...	/ā/ ...	/a/ ...	/a/ ...	/ā/ ...∼/a˙/ ...
/a/ ...	/a/ ...	/a/ ...	/a/ ...	/a/ ...	/a/ ...	/a/ ...

Notes: (1) K. â- (in anlaut) has become a^{a} or $a^{\cdot a}$ (lento) ∼ a˙ (allegro), cf. 13.11.7.

(2) In WOD. I do not know whether or not a distinction is made between /ā/ ... and /â/ ....

(3) For T., Y. /â/ ... cf. 13.11.6.

(B) First syllables of polysyllabic roots

PTu.	K. lento	K. allegro	T.	Y.	Kh.
/â/ ...	/a˙/ ...	/a/ ...	/â/ ...	/a/ ...	/â/ ...
/ā/ ...	/a˙/ ...	/a/ ...	/a/ ...	/a/ ...	/ā/ ...∼/a˙/ ...
/a/ ...	/a/ ...		/a/ ...	/a/ ...	/a/ ...

Notes: (1) K. in this case does not seem to have had a^{a} in anlaut; at least there is no hint of such.

(2) Very few examples of polysyllabic words are given for WOD. but in Az. Nukha such an example is found, cf. 13.9. For WOD. cf. Korkmaz āltĭ 'six,' āltĭn 'gold,' kā̆ndi 'self' (all of them doubtful for various reasons, and we find no correspondence to T. forms with long vowels).

(C) Non-initial syllables of polysyllabic roots

PTu.	K. lento	K. allegro	T.	Y.	Kh.
/â/ ...	/ā/ ...	/a˙/ ...	/â/ ...	/â/ ...	/ā/ ...
/ā/ ...	/ā/ ...	/a˙/ ...	/a/ ...	/a/ ...	/ā/ ...
/-A-/	/V̈/		/V̈/	/V̈/	*/V̈/
/-A/	zero		zero	zero	zero

Notes: (1) PTu. /-A/ has been preserved in no living Tu. language; but its existence is attested to in old Tu. loanwords in Mongolian.

(2) /ā/ ... may be /a˙/ ... or even /a/ ... in Karakhanid.

(3) /V̈/ means the fourfold set ï/i/u/ü (found in Uighur, too, but cf. 14.4.4), this form <older (RTu.) ă/ĕ, eventually ă/ĕ/ă/ä̆ or even ă/ĕ/ŏ/ö̆ (cf. 13.11.9).

(4) No material has been found for WOD.

(5) In T. /ā/ ... sometimes may not be /a/ ... but /ā/ ... when used in inlaut before some suffixes, cf. Biišev 1963.54: ōbada 'in the village' (= Karakhanid o˙pādā) becomes ōbadāqï 'he who is in the village' with the suffix +KI. Other cases are assimilations or analogous constructions (e.g., analogous

to ōyla- 'to think' is ōylāp 'thinking'; also aq- 'to flow,' aqīp 'flowing').

(6) In Kh. /V̈/ often becomes u̯/ü̯, cf. 13.11.9.

13.12.5 Reflexes of Proto-Turkic quantity in Chuvash. At last let us investigate the correspondences of PTu. /â/ ..., /ā/ ... and /a/ ... in Chuvash. We find long vowels preserved in Bolgar loanwords in Hungarian (from about the eighth century), cf. Räsänen, "Über die langen Vokale der türkischen Lehnwörter im Ungarischen," Finnisch-ugrische Forschungen 24.246-55. However, this material is not reliable enough: (1) it often is unclear whether a word is of Tu. origin at all (szél 'wind,' nyár 'summer,' for example, are not, in my opinion); (2) even when it is clear that a word is Tu., it is not always clear whether it is just Bolgar or whether it belongs to another Tu. language (e.g., Pecheneg). Why, for example, must szál 'float' be a loanword from Bolgar? Nothing about it is typically Bolgar. Furthermore Hungarian has many secondary long vowels, cf. Gyula Décsy, "Der gegenwärtige Stand der finnougrischen Lautforschung," Mitteilungen der Socictas Uralo-Altaica 2.42-3, Hamburg, 1968. I did not find any reliable examples of /ā/ ... in the Bolgar words in Hungarian. /â/ ... has several Bolgar examples with long vowels, e.g., sár [šār] 'yellow' = C. šură <PTu. *si̯â´rag. On the whole, we cannot do much with this material.

Volga Bolgar (thirteenth/fourteenth century) has preserved the old distinction of quantities, cf. Doerfer 1967.58: ǰāl 'year of life' = T. yāš; ǰūz, later ǰūr (or čūz, čūr) 'a hundred' = Y. sūs; wo̢n 'ten' = T. ōn; xīr 'daughter' = T. g̱īz; töätĭm 'fourth' = T. dōrt 'four'; ǰiäti 'seven' (or čiäti) = T. yädi < *yâtē, etc. (but säkkăr 'eight' = T. säkiz, etc.). We find two examples of PTu. /ā/ ..., apart from the examples quoted above (which reflect PTu. /â/ ...): وچ vüč 'three' = WOD. ūš, Kh. ūs, īč (perhaps only graphic, avoiding ووج , i.e., two wāw, one after the other). Furthermore we find كوان ، كُوان ، كُوان 'day' in the older inscriptions 3, 14, 16, 24, 27, 30, 31, 33 (1291 to about 1357 A.D.); in two late inscriptions we find كن (47, from 1340), كون (48, from 1355/6). We may read *küọ̈n (later *kün) = WOD. gǖn.

The C. loanwords in Finnic languages (dating from about the fifteenth/sixteenth century) give no satisfying result since Cheremiss and Votiak have undergone too many changes, etc.

In modern C. we find reflexes of old quantities in the following cases (I speak only of monosyllabic roots):

(1) ȫ̂ has been preserved as ăva: K. kȫk 'blue' = C. kăvak, K. tȫrt 'four' = C. tăvată, etc. (the correspondent ü only in Tatar loanwords, such as K. kȫl 'lake' = C. kül ← Tatar kül or older köl). Short ö after or before k normally is ă: C. kăk 'root' = T. kök, C. tăk- 'to pour' = T. dök-. But PTu. /ȫ/ seems to be u in this case: kur- 'to look' = WOD. gȫr- (T. gör-), kuś 'eye' (originally 'his eye') = WOD. gȫz (T. göz). If this analysis is correct, what about kuś- 'to rove' = T. göč-, kut 'backside' = T. köt? The first word may contain a long vowel, since we find gȫč- in Khorezmian Tu. (Abdullaev 48), which material, however, is not entirely reliable, as we have seen. The second example cannot be explained. Does it go back to old *kȫt? Is C. in such cases the only Tu. language to have preserved a reflex of PTu. *ȫ?

(2) To PTu. kǖ̂- in C. kĕ- corresponds, to kü-,ku-, e.g., C. kĕr 'autumn' = T. güyz (Tuv. küs); kĕt- 'to guard' = T. güyt-; on the other hand, kul- 'to laugh' = T. gül-. For kǖ- we find ku-, cf. kun 'day' (Volga Bolgar kü̯ön) = WOD. gǖn, T. gün (Tuv. xüʾn). But is this correspondence correct? What about kĕl 'ash' = T. kül, K. kül? Is it a Tatar loanword? (The many Tatar loanwords, about two-thirds of the C. vocabulary, cause many difficulties.

(3) To PTu. *î* in C. *ĕ* corresponds (cf. Räsänen 1949.91), to *i*, *i*: C. *pĕr* 'one' = Y. *bīr*; *kĕr*- 'to enter' = T. *gīr*- (and *tĕn* 'belief' ← P. *dīn*!); C. *pin* 'a thousand' = T. *müņ* <*miņ*, K. *miņ*; C. *śip* 'thread' = T. *yüp*, older *yip*; C. *čik*- 'to stick' = K. *tik*-, T. *dik*- (but *ĕś*- 'to drink' = T., K. *ič*- in anlaut). What about PTu. /ī/? It has converged with /i/: *sirĕn* 'your' = K. *sīz* 'ye,' T. *siz* (and, *mutatis mutandis*, *pirĕn* 'our'). But if this derivation be correct, what about *pĕl*- 'to know' = K., T. *bil*-? Is it older **bīl*-, too?

Obviously we cannot do much with this material. However, it is not impossible that C. has preserved the PTu. oppositions /â/ ..., /ā/ ..., /a/ ... in several cases. Research should be continued in this area.

14
ETYMOLOGICAL DICTIONARY OF TURKIC WORDS IN KHALAJ

14.1 *Importance of several Turkic languages.* For the reconstruction of ATu. (particularly, quantity of vowels) I used, above all, K., T. (according to N. A. Baskakov *et alii*, *Turkmensko-russkij slovar´*, Moskva, 1968), and Y. (according to Ė. K. Pekarskij, *Slovar´ jakutskogo jazyka*, Leningrad, 1917-30), sometimes also Az. and other Tu. languages (mostly according to Radloff, and Az. according to Azizbekov 1965); furthermore, I used for the reconstruction of quantity the indications of WOD.

For the reconstruction of PTu. (and CTu.) I used Y. for some questions, above all *-*ē*/-*ë̄*, respectively *-*ī*/-*ï̄* of non-initial syllables: -*ē*/-*ë̄* has become *ä*/*a* in Y., whereas -*ī*/-*ï̄* has become *i*/*ï*, e.g., Y. *alta* 'six' (most Tu. languages *altï*) < **altë̄*, Y. *sürbä* 'twenty' < **yi`gärmē´*, but Y. *äkki*, *ikki* 'two' < **äkkī*.

Still more important for the reconstruction of PTu. is C. (according to M. Ja. Sirotkin, *Čuvašsko-russkij slovar´*, Moskva, 1961). Chuvash gives us the possibility of reconstructing *i̯*-diphthongs. Here is one instance: whereas C. *xur* 'goose' = CTu. *qâz* gives a reconstruction of PTu. **kâz*, the word (that is, the group of words of such a type as) C. *yun* 'blood' = CTu. *qân* gives a reconstruction of PTu. **ki̯ân*. I also used the older (Bolgar) stages of C. (Volga Bolgar according to G. V. Jusupov, *Vvedenie v bulgaro-tatarskuju ėpigrafiku*, Moskva and Leningrad, 1960, and Hungarian Bolgar according to Zoltán Gombocz, *Die bulgarisch-türkischen Lehnwörter in der ungarischen Sprache*, Helsinki, 1912). Sometimes C. helps us to determine whether to reconstruct PTu. *-*n(A)* or *-*m* or **mA*, cf. Doerfer 1967: PTu. *-*n* and *-*nA* are

-n both in C. and CTu. (C xuran 'kettle' = CTu. qâzġān); *-m is -m in C., but -n in CTu. (C. xïrăm 'bellow' = CTu. qā'ran ~qē'ran); *-mA is -m both in C. and CTu. (C. yĕm 'trousers' = CTu. ấm, C. yat+ăm 'my name' = CTu. â't-am). C. is (just as are Y. and Tuv.) relevant for reconstructing PTu. *ē/e: CTu. *a, PTu* ē >i in C. (whereas PTu. *ï has become ĕ in this language) and/or Y. and/or Tuv. (e.g., PTu. sēp 'handle,' CTu. sāp = C. s̈ipă, Y. up < *ïp, Tuv. s̈ip; PTu. dēt- 'to sleep,' CTu. yāt- = Y. s̈it-, Tuv. č̈it-; but sometimes only one of these languages has i; Tuv. especially never has i- in anlaut, e.g., C. il- 'to take,' Y. il- = Tuv. al-, similar to CTu. āl-, whereas PTu. has had *ēl-. For the reconstruction of PTu. *e C. is the only relevant Tu. language, cf. 13.11.5.

14.2 Proto-Bolgar loanwords in Mongolian. The oldest attestable Tu. stage is represented by the Bolgar loanwords in Mongolian, which, however, represent an archaic dialect, not PTu. itself. For Mo. I used the well-known dictionaries, above all the reconstructions in TM., cf. here the bibliography (e.g., Ko, RKW). Mo. represents to a great extent the same dates as C., e.g., i̯-diphthongs are represented by i in Mo. (CTu. sâ'raġ 'yellow' = C. šură = Mo. šira < *sira ← Bolgar *s̈iară^{g} or similar <PTu. *si̯â'rag). The (unstressed) auslaut vowels (and auslaut vowels + n) have been preserved exclusively in Mo., e.g., CTu. kȫk 'blue' = C. kăvak would not tell us whether we have to reconstruct PTu. *kȫk or *kȫ'kä, but Mo. köke shows that the last form is correct (in regard to the preservation of Tu. auslauts in Mo., the auslaut vowel is always -a/-e, cf. 13.11.9). Even Tu. *ē sometimes has been "preserved" (in the form of i), e.g., CTu. yāz- 'to write' = C. śir- = Mo. ǰiru- (← Old Bolgar *dēr̯z-) gives a reconstructed PTu. *dēz-. The distinction between *e and *ä, however, does not occur in Mo. The only

language to have preserved PTu. unstressed -An is Mo., e.g., CTu. bïŋ 'a thousand' = Mo. miŋgan proves PTu. *bḯŋan. The difference between ō/ȫ and ū/ǖ in non-initial syllables is well preserved in Mo. (e.g., CTu. yaqū 'fur' = Mo. daqu ← PTu. *dagku, but CTu. bälgö 'sign' = Mo. belge ← PTu. *bälgȫ, cf. TM I. 9-12). Sometimes ō/ȫ have been preserved in ATu. and Middle Tu., above all after o/ö; e.g., ATu. and Middle Tu. still have ortō 'center,' orō 'ditch,' botō 'young of a camel,' sōġōn 'onion,' törȫ 'law,' etc. Most more recent Tu. languages tend to change ō/ȫ > a/ä, i.e., orta, ora, bota, soġan, törä. Sometimes we find alternances, as in boġoz 'throat' = Osman boğaz, but Taranči boġuz. In Mo. we find botogan, soġongina (with a diminutive suffix), torqa(n), törö, boġorla- 'to strangle.' But ō/ȫ may be reconstructed even after other vowels, e.g., K. töpȫ 'hill' = T. däpä = M. dege.re 'above' (dege-dü 'superior,' etc.) ← PTu. *täpȫ; modern Tu. *baltu ~ *balta = Mo. balta ← PTu. *baltō; ATu. tusu = Mo. tusa ← PTu. *tusō, etc., cf. TM headwords 587, 592, 777, 134, 792, 884, 872, 78.

Another good means of recognizing the opposition PTu. ō/ȫ : ū/ǖ is Brahmi texts. Here the opposition is clear and strict; the perfect passive participle, e.g., has -oq/-ök (art-oq 'more,' ār-oq 'tired,' süz-ök 'filtered,' yār-oq ~ yar-uq 'bright, splendid), whereas the causative suffix, for example, has -ur-/-ür- (ič-ür- 'to let drink,' kǟl-ür- 'to bring,' tur-gur- 'to cause,' ün-tür- 'to bring out.' However, there are two difficulties: (1)There is already a perceptible tendency of o/ö becoming u/ü, cf. above yaruq, also cases such as kertü ~ kertö 'true,' qayu ~ qayo 'who.' In rare cases one may find a word only with -u/-ü although its PTu. form may have ended in -ō/-ȫ. (2) After o/ö of the first syllable even -ū/-ǖ often become o/ö, the distinction between ō/ȫ and ū/ǖ in this case being abolished (cf. öl-ör- 'to kill' instead of öl-ür-, pol:or 'he becomes' instead of bol:ur).

We find the same situation in ATu. in Tibetan script, cf. Sir Gerard Clauson, *Turkish and Mongolian Studies*, London, 1962. 97-100, e.g., o_2 preserved in alqo 'all' (= Brahmi alqo, ālqo, ālqu. This is not a converb of alq-!, contrary to Gabain 1950.135: the converb would be alqu, not alqo); törö.g 'law' (accusative) (= Brahmi törö); tözön 'noble' (= Brahmi tözöṃ); ötönü 'demanding' (= Uighur ötünü), etc. Thus o/ö is not unambiguous in Brahmi Tu.; it stands for PTu. ō/ȫ, for PTu. ū/ǖ (only after o/ö), and for ŏ/ö̆ < ă/ĕ <PTu. unstressed a/ä (only after o/ö).

Compare also some developments in the modern Tu. languages. Normally ō/ȫ$_2$ becomes u/ü in Tuv. (often even in Khakass, sometimes in New Uighur or in other Tu. languages), a/ä in most Tu. languages, cf. PTu. *baltō 'axe' (→ Mo. balta), TM I.199: Tuv., Khakass, New Uighur, Čulym *baltu, all other dialects (including Altay Tu.) balta (Y. balta < baltō; however, even PTu. *-ū/ǖ becomes -a/-ä in Y., e.g., saǧa 'fur' < yaqū, cf. Mo. daqu ← PTu. *dagku); the form balto has been preserved in Ket, cf. V. N. Toporov, "Materialy k sravnitel'no-istoričeskoj fonetike enisejskix jazykov, 1, Arinsko-enisejskie sootvetstvija (čast' pervaja)," *Ketskij Sbornik*, Moskva, 1968. 277-330, p. 287 baltó 'topor' (but altún 'zoloto,' which in spite of Mo. altan must have been PTu. *ëltūn, since we find altun in all Tu. languages, but iltăn in C.; in Mo. it is presumably a loanword from an old Tu. dialect where ëltūn may have become altōn?, or is PTu. *ëltōn correct and modern Tu. altun, also Brahmi altun, an inter-Tu. loanword?). Here are some other instances: ortō 'middle' = Tuv. ortu, Khakass ortï < *ortu, all other dialects (including New Uighur) orta (TM II. 141); orō 'cave' >Tuv. oru, most other dialects *ora (II. 144); torqō 'silk' >Tuv. Khakass *torqu, most other dialects *torqa (II. 478). That ō/ȫ$_2$ >a/ä is the normal development is clear also from such examples as qâp = tôn 'a kind of clothing' >qaptan (III. 186-7); säkäz ôn 'eighty' >*säksän (K. still säksön); toqaz ôn 'ninety' >*toqsan (K. still toqson), etc. To this belongs PTu. *olpōq 'a kind of garment' = Tuv. olbuq, Y. olbox, Taranči olpaq, Kirghiz olpoq = Mo. olbog (TM II. 111).

PTu.	RTu.	ATu.	"Khorezmian Tu." Period
o-a	o-ǎ	o-ŏ	o-u
o-ō	o-ō	o-ō	o-o ~o-u [in suffixes u]
o-ū	o-ū	o-ū ~ o-ō (ọ̄?)	o-u

In suffixes we find variants, e.g., Brahmi bolzun ~bolzon (perhaps *bôl:zọ̄n < *bôl:zūn?) 'he may be,' which in the modern languages have become u. Furthermore suffixes developed differently from second syllables of roots, cf. ortō 'center' >Khorezmian Tu. ortu or orto (modern languages mostly *orta, but Tuv. ɔrtu); but the participle -oq/-ök, for example, became -uq/-ük in all languages; in analogy to a-ō >a-u we find o-ō >o-u, too (Kh. sịdäk 'urine,' however, < *sîd-ök). For o-ō some modern languages go back to an older o-u (Tuv., for instance), others to o-o >later o-a (and this sometimes secondarily o-o again).

A similar explanation is found in Sir Gerard Clauson, "Three Notes on Early Turkish," Türk Dili Araştırmaları Yıllığı, Belleten, Ankara, 1967.1-37. However, Sir Gerard is mistaken on this point: he overestimates Kirghiz, which, because it has such forms as orto 'center' "seems in this respect to be the most archaic living Turkish language" (p. 14); i.e., Sir Gerard thinks that Kirghiz has *preserved* *o* in *orto* and similar words where the other Tu. languages have changed it >*a* (*mutatis mutandis* for Kirghiz *ö*). But it is clear that Kirghiz also originally had **a*/*ä* which, by way of assimilation, it only secondarily changed >*o*/*ö* (after *o*/*ö*). Here I offer two proofs:

(1) We find *o* in loanwords after *o*, where it *must* go back to older *a*, e.g., *dorbo* 'bag' ← P. *tōbra* (← Indian *tōbra*); *dosondo* 'friend' ← P. *dōst* 'friend' + Mo. *anda* 'friend' (hendiadyoin); *počto* 'post' ← Russian *počta* (older loanword, even *počta* is attested to in Kirghiz as a younger loanword); *moldo* 'who is able to write and read' ← P. *molla̤* 'priest' (= Osman, T. *molla*, Kazakh *molda*).

(2) We find *o* in Kirghiz suffixes after *o*, where it *must* go back to older *a*, e.g., *qol.do* 'at the arm' (*qoldo bar* 'imuščij'), *qol.ġo* 'to the arm,' etc., respectively < ATu. locative .*dĀ*, dative .*KĀ*. And so with many other instances.

Kirghiz does not lead us back to any older stage of Tu. Let us come back to Mo.

Mo. furthermore is important for the reconstruction of PTu. **p*- (e.g., Tu. *öküz* 'ox' = Mo. *hüker* gives a reconstruction of PTu. **pö´käz* >Old Bolgar **pö̆´kärz* → Mo. **pükär* >**fükär* > *hüker*). However, such cases are rare, cf. TM I. 93, 97 (an important case is Tu. *oyma* 'felt boot' = Mo. *hoyimasun* = Manchu *fomon* < **poimo(n)*; hence we may reconstruct PTu. **poyma*). Mo. is likewise important for reconstruction of Tu. *y*- as an original **d*- (PTu. **d*- >**d´*- >**ǰ*- >*y*-, e.g., ATu. *yaġï* 'enemy' = Mo. *dayisun* gives PTu. **daġï*; later loanwords are such as Mo. *ǰol* 'luck' ← **ǰôl* < **dôl*, etc., cf. TM I. 97-8, ATu. *yôl* 'way, luck'). Perhaps Mo. has preserved PTu. *o̤* and *ö̤*, cf. 14.3.3.

14.3 *Three unsolvable problems*. However, in our reconstruction some points will remain unclear. We will distinguish (a) three unsolvable problems and (b) four points which have been theoretically solved but which often are practicably unrealizable. Here are the three unsolved problems:

14.3.1 Lambdacism and rhotacism. Since we do not possess taped recordings of PTu., we cannot say whether PTu. had z or ŕ or ř or whatever, nor whether it had š or ž or ĺ or whatever. It is obvious that for CTu. qâr 'snow' = C. yur and for CTu. qâz 'goose' = C. xur we have to reconstruct two different PTu. consonants, but we cannot say which. At any rate, CTu. has preserved two different ancient phonemes (converged in C., Mo., Tungus). The special phonetic character of this phoneme is rather irrelevant for a reconstruction: what we can reconstruct is never a sound; it is always only a phoneme. We likewise cannot say, for example, whether ATu. or PTu. /a/ was a or a^6 or a̲ or a^3 or $ȧ^4$ or even ȧ. In principle, the problem is not different from that of the z-ŕ-ř problem.

It is impossible to deal here with this vast problem. I wish to say only that I am not convinced that this problem will ever be solved. It cannot be solved (as some have tried to solve it) on the basis of mere reflection; we would have to wait for old texts (e.g., of 1000 B.C.); and since these do not exist (and the chance that they will be discovered is extremely slight), this problem remains unsolvable. For the sake of simplicity I shall write (not reconstruct) z, š. (There is a slight — but very slight — chance that these forms are preferable, cf. TM I.523. Even such Hungarian forms as borjú 'calf,' bölcső 'cradle,' older belcsé seem to represent not Bolgar *buraǧu, *bišiǵ [contrary to Gombocz' opinion, the form should be *biliǵ, since CTu. -š- is normally C. -l-] = CTu. buzāǧū, bêšik, but something like Bolgar *buřzāǧū, *belžig.)

14.3.2 d- ~ t- in Old Bolgar. The second problem is whether or not we have to reconstruct d- or t- in Old Bolgar, cf. TM I. 97. Normally Mo. t- corresponds to a Tu. t-. But we find the following exceptions: ATu. talōy 'ocean' = Mo. dalay, ATu. töpȫ (T. däpä) = Mo. deġe- 'above,' ATu. tȫrt 'four' = Mo. dörben, and (78) ATu. tôz 'birch bark' = Mo. durusun. These four examples are sufficient to show that a problem exists, but they are not sufficient to prove that PTu. had d- apart from t-. We cannot exclude the possibility that Mo. got these words from a Bolgar dialect which early changed t- > D- or that, for example, Tu. had unaspirated t-, while Mo. had d- and (aspirated) t'- and, having no t- itself, sometimes rendered Tu. t- as t'-, sometimes as D-, etc. Therefore I simply reconstruct t-, even in this case, i.e., PTu. *talōy, *täpȫ, *tȫrt, *tôz (without totally excluding *dalōy, *däpȫ, *dȫrt, *dộz, and without excluding the fact that at least Old Bolgar had something like *Dalōy, *Däpȫ, *Dȫrt, *Dộrz). It sometimes is said that the Oghuz dialects in particular have preserved an old (PTu.) distinction between t- and d-; but the development t- > D- > d- surely is secondary in Oghuz (I shall prove this point in Wiener Zeitschrift für die Kunde des Morgenlandes 62). Here I will say only this much: the above progression can be shown, among other things, by the development of old loanwords in Oghuz; e.g., Indian tōbra 'bag' (R. L. Turner, A Comparative Dictionary of the Indo-Aryan Languages, London, 1966, No. 5972) became P. tōbra, the modern Osman dorbacik (TM headword 947). Here d- is apparently secondary. The same holds true for P. tağār 'vessel' > Osman dağarcık (TM headword No. 905).

14.3.3 Existence of closed o, ö in Old Bolgar. The third unsolvable problem is that of the existence (or non-existence) of o, ö (or ọ, ộ) in PTu. Normally to Tu. o corresponds Mo. o, e.g.,

Tu. bōz 'grey' = bora; to Tu. u corresponds u, e.g., Tu. qudruq 'tail' = qudurga. The same holds true for ö = ö, ü = ü. But sometimes to CTu. o corresponds Mo. u, to Tu. ö corresponds Mo. ü, as shown in the following examples: (TM I. 99) qoč 'ram' = quča; bodō- 'to color' = budu- ($\bar{o}_2$ after u >u in contrast to Tu. *tusō 'profit' = Mo. tusa!); qopūz 'lute' = quhur, quġur, (100) ökäz 'ox' = hüker; (78) qobï̄ 'luck' = qubi; tôz 'birch bark' = durusun; (182) opā 'make-up, powder' = uha; (435) qozï̄ 'lamb' = qurigan; (II. 289) bö̂rk 'cap' = bürgü; (III. 9) čōq 'mass' = čug; (239) sôr- 'to ask' = sura-; (547) qôzġāl- 'to be irritated' = quruġulǰa-; also ? (K.) ǖd 'time' (T. öylä 'midday') = Mo. üde 'midday'; tôrōq 'meager, hungry' (K. erroneously turuk, but cf. Radloff Altay Tu. toro 'hungry,' torïn- 'to hunger, to become emaciated') = turugan ($\bar{o}_2$ after u >u, as above; false in TM I. 104); K. töz- 'to endure' (T. döz-) = türe-. These sixteen examples again are sufficient to show that a problem exists, but not sufficient to prove that PTu. must have had the special intermediate vowels ọ, ö̤ between o/ö and u/ü. (I think, however, that the chance of such vowels having existed is a bit greater than that of d-'s having existed, point 2 above.) Even here the possibility cannot be excluded that Mo. borrowed these words from a special Bolgar dialect with ọ/ö̤ or ọ/ö̤ (whereas, for example, Mo. bora 'grey' = Tu. bōz is from another Bolgar dialect) or that a uniform Bolgar ọ/ö̤ sometimes (perhaps at different periods or through different mediators, etc.) gave o/ö, sometimes u/ü. For my part, I regard the existence of ọ/ö̤ as rather likely, but it cannot be proved with absolute certainty. So I simply write o/ö.

May we find ọ/ö̤ in certain cases where Tu. dialects have variants o ~u, ö ~ü, e.g., Brahmi "üt" = üd 'time' = T. öy.lä, or Brahmi ürt- 'to cover' (Kazan Tatar ŏrt- < ürt-) = most Tu. dialects ört-?

Fortunately these three problems present no practical difficulty in our process of reconstruction: we simply write respectively z, š; t-; o/ö, leaving aside other possibilities (ŕ, ĺ, D-; o̤/ö̤).

14.4 Four problems not generally solvable. But there are four other points far more relevant to reconstruction. Our reconstructions cannot always be definitive, because C. and Mo., the most important languages for reconstruction, have preserved but a little part of the original Tu. vocabulary. Most of the Tu. words in C. are (or, at least, can be) old Tatar loanwords (e.g., ančax 'only,' instead of *unśax, etc.). And the Old Bolgar or Old CTu. loanwords in Mo. are few, even fewer than are words inherited from PTu. in C. Practicably the four following problems often remain unsolvable, due above all to the lack of C. and M. correspondences.

14.4.1 Diphthongs /i̯â/ .... Long vowels may or may not contain a diphthongal part. The only Tu. language to have preserved traces of such diphthongs is C. i̯-diphthongs occur in C. only after q-, t-, s- and in vocalic anlaut (occurrence after k- seems rather doubtful). Here is an enumeration of all PTu. diphthongs attested to by C. (I shall give one example); */i̯â/ (/i̯ā/) in C. čul 'stone' < PTu. *ti̯âš >CTu. tâš; */i̯ë̂/ (/i̯ë̄/) in śunat 'wing' < PTu. *ki̯ë̂ńat >CTu. qânat; */i̯ï̂/ (/i̯ï̄/) in yĕnĕ 'sheath' < PTu. *ki̯ï̄n >CTu. qï̄n; */i̯ô/ (/i̯ō/) in šïra- 'to ask' < PTu. si̯ôra- >CTu. sôra-; */i̯û/ (/i̯ū/) in šïv 'water' > PTu. *si̯ūb >CTu. sūb (the development is similar to that of PTu. *sï/si and of PTu. *tï/ti, which respectively have become šĕ and čĕ in C.). Note that we find only back vowels, never front vowels. It may be (though it is not certain) that this situation reflects PTu. In anlaut we find * /i̯â/ (/i̯ā/) in yus 'ermine' < PTu. *i̯âs >CTu. âs, yat 'name' < early *yät < PTu. *i̯ât >CTu. ât; */i̯ï̂/ (/i̯ï̄/) in yïtă 'dog' <

PTu. *i̯ī̈t >CTu. ī̈t, also C. yĕr 'trace,' yar- 'to send' (?); */i̯ä̂/ (/i̯ä̅/) in yal 'village' < PTu. *i̯ä̂l >CTu. ä̂l; */i̯ê/ (/i̯ē/) in yĕm 'trousers' < PTu. *i̯êmä >CTu. ä̂m; /i̯ë̂/ (/i̯ë̄/) in yïvăś 'tree' < i̯ë̄gač >yïġač and similar forms. I found no example for */i̯ô/, */i̯î/. I suppose that in anlaut after i̯ all vowels were possible in PTu.

C. very often is able to solve this problem, e.g., CTu. qâz 'goose' < PTu. *kâz (because of C. xur), but CTu. qân 'blood' < *ki̯ân (because of C. yun). But what if a C. correspondence is lacking? For instance, Tu. qâš 'eyebrow' has no C. correspondent; hence it may go back to PTu. *kâš and to *ki̯âš, as well. In this case of doubt I reconstruct the form without i̯ (in our given example: kâš), writing after the reconstructed form ~ 1.

Mo. sometimes helps us solve this problem; cf. above where Mo. šira 'yellow' = C. šură gives PTu. *si̯ârag. Sometimes it has preserved diphthongs with i̯ where C. has lost them or where no C. correspondence can be found, e.g., Mo. biraġu 'calf' (written language) ~bura'u (Secret History) ← Old Bolgar *bi̯ūrzāġū < PTu. *bi̯ūzāġū = C. păru, Hungarian borjú, CTu. buzāġū, T. buzav; Mo. šinqor 'falcon' ← Old Bolgar (= PTu.) *si̯ōŋqōr > CTu. sōŋqōr (C. not attested to); Mo. nidurġa 'fist' (written language) ~nudurġa (Secret History) ← Old Bolgar (= PTu.) *di̯ūdūrqa = CTu. yudrūq (C. not attested to), cf. TM I. 361-2.

14.4.2 Proto-Turkic *ä and *e. C. often solves the problem of PTu. *ä, *e: e.g., *säs 'voice,' but *kēl- 'to come,' cf. 13.11.5. But for ATu. ä̅b 'house,' e.g., we find no C. correspondence (avlan- 'to marry' seems to be a loanword from CTu.; the normal C. word for 'house' is kil). We may reconstruct PTu. *pä̅b(ä) and *pēb(ä), as well. In this case I reconstruct the form with ä (in our given example: *pä̅b(ä)), writing after the reconstructed forms ~ 2.

14.4.3 Unstressed auslaut in Proto-Turkic. The problem whether a PTu. word had or had not an auslaut vowel is often unsolvable, e.g., our example *pǟb 'house' ~2, given above. Here we have the following means of solving this problem:

(a) When both CTu. and C. have -m, we must reconstruct PTu. -mA, cf. above (CTu. *ä̂m 'trousers' = C. yĕm gives PTu. *i̯êmä).

(b) When CTu. has -n and C. has -m, we must reconstruct PTu. -m, cf. above (CTu. qāran 'bellow' = C. xïrăm gives PTu. *kë̆ram).

(c) Since unstressed -An became zero in modern Tu. (e.g., PTu. bïŋan 'a thousand' >bïŋ, biŋ), Uighur Tu. -ïn/-in/-un/-ün (<-ăn/-ĕn) in suffixes must go back to PTu. *-AnA. The deverbal suffix -ïn/-in/-un/-ün has labial harmony, i.e., the vowel goes back to an unstressed ă/ĕ < unstressed *a/ä (cf. kǟlin 'bride,' tütün 'smoke,' from kǟl- 'to come,' tüt- 'to smoke'). Hence we have to reconstruct kǟlin 'bride' (C. kilĕn) < PTu. *kēlänä.

(d) Mo. often is especially helpful. For example, using Mo. ere 'man' we can reconstruct Old CTu. *ä´rä (not *är) (and Kh. hȧr proves that the PTu. form is *pä´rä). For discussion of the fact that the Mo. vowel is correct and not secondarily added, see 13.11.9. On the other hand, Mo qadum 'in-law' shows that we have to reconstruct PTu. *qâ´dam, not *qâ´dama. Sometimes we may even reconstruct not only -A, but -An (e.g., CTu. âm 'cunt' = Mo. aman 'mouth' gives PTu. *â´man).

(e) Sometimes we may draw a conclusion by analogy. Since to CTu. tôrōq 'meager' (from tôr- 'to become emaciated') Mo. turugan corresponds and to CTu. köšīk 'curtain' (from köšī- 'to cover') Mo. köšige corresponds, it seems justifiable to reconstruct the ATu. perfect participle suffix -ŌK (after vowels -K) as PTu. *-ŌkA(n). (However, did this form have or not have an -n? And what about Mo. bölög 'part' = ȦTu. bölök: is this a later loan?)

Another example. Since C. -Ăm corresponds to some designations of parts of the body ending in modern Tu. in -ïn/-in/-un/-ün, we may reconstruct unstressed *-Am in all such cases, i.e., from CTu. qāran 'bellow' = C. xïrăm (giving PTu. *kēram) we may reconstruct *būram 'nose,' etc., as well. (However, the following is not perfectly clear: to Tu. tâpân 'sole' C. tupan corresponds; this word may be a loanword from Tatar, but it may be an old inherited form, as well. In this case a reconstruction of PTu. *tâpâm would be doubtful.) According to Mo. ulağan 'post horse' = Tu. ulā-ġ we may assume a deverbal suffix -GAn, etc. However, conclusions by analogy are always doubtful.

It must be said that C. -Ă is not relevant to the reconstruction of the PTu. forms. C. -Ă seems to be a diminutive suffix, often secondarily added to substantives (less frequently to adjectives, never to verbs); e.g., CTu. ït 'dog' = C. yïtă (= little dog), etc.; cf. V. Kotvič, Issledovanija po altajskim jazykam, Moskva, 1962.44, and Ščerbak 1967.40 (-Ă in such numerals as vună 'ten' = Volga Bolgar wǭn or wān seems to be an analogy to such forms as ikĕ, ultă, śičĕ 'two, six, seven'). That this -Ă is secondary and not relevant to the reconstruction of the PTu. form can be proved by a Chinese loanword (cf. TM headword 1230): Chinese tsʿit 'lac' >tsʿir → Tu. sïr, C. sără; this -ă must be secondary.

Due to the lack of Mo. (and C.) correspondences, we often cannot decide whether a PTu. word had or had not an auslaut vowel, e.g., CTu. ǟb, Kh. hȧv 'house' < PTu. *pǟb (pēb) or *pǟbä (pēbä)? ; CTu. ät 'flesh,' Kh. ȧt < PTu. *ät or *ätä? In this case we reconstruct the forms without auslaut vowels (in our given case: *pǟb, *ät), writing after the reconstructed form ~3 (hence ät ~3, but pǟb ~2, 3, since here even the problem ä/e exists, cf. above).

14.4.4 Vowels in non-initial closed syllables. The fourth problem is that of vowels in non-initial closed syllables. Sometimes the vowels are clear: Ā is always clear (e.g., PTu. *ki̯ẽńāt ~3 'wing'). Ū, Ō are always clear after an unrounded vowel (e.g., PTu. *ẽltōn 'gold,' according to Mo. altan, ATu. altūn, also in the well-known suffix PTu. -ŌkA, etc.). Ī is always clear after a rounded vowel (ATu. bulı̄t 'cloud' gives PTu. *bulı̄t ~3). But Ū, Ō after a rounded vowel, and Ī after an unrounded vowel often are unclear. I mean that one cannot know whether they go back to PTu. Ū, Ō, Ī or to A. For example, does Uighur Tu. būrun 'nose' go back to older *būrūn or to *būran? (both must become būrun >burun in modern Tu.); does Uighur âlı̈n 'front' go back to older ATu. *âlı̄n < PTu. *âlı̄n or *âlı̄na, or does it go back to PTu. *âlana? This latter solution seems doubtful at first glance, but the problem can be solved in the following cases:

(a) If a/ä in Manichaean Tu. corresponds to Uighur ı̈/i/u/ü, we have to assume unstressed a/ä (cf. TM I. 23-5, Gabain 1950.5, 49; also cf. beneath). For example, Uighur Tu. aġı̈z 'mouth' must go back to *a´gaz because we find Manichaean Tu. aġaz.

(b) The RTu. script often preserves full vowels (seldom reduced ă/ĕ < unstressed a/ä), cf. TM I. 23-5; the same conclusion may be arrived at from a thorough investigation of the material given by Talât Tekin, A Grammar of Orkhon Turkic, Uralic and Altaic Series 69, Bloomington, 1968.34-8. However, even full vowels are frequently not written, cf. 13.11.9.

(c) If the vowel ı̈/i/u/ü is dropped in unstressed position, we may reconstruct *A; e.g., Uighur Tu. oġul 'son,' oġlı̄ 'his son' gives PTu. *o´gal.

(d) Sometimes we may draw conclusions by analogy. For example, in K. all terms of parts of the body with -n have unrounded ı̈/i after unrounded vowels and rounded u/ü after rounded vowels, cf. Doerfer 1967.59: būrun 'nose,' bı̈qı̈n 'hip,' qārı̈n 'bellow,' ārin 'lip,' ušun 'shoulder-blade,' âl'in 'front,' yar'in 'shoulder-blade,' yilin 'udder,' boyun 'neck' (K. ~boy'in seems to be an assimilation to -y-), bükün 'blind gut,' tulun 'place between ear and mouth,' boġun 'finger-joint,' ägin 'shoulder.' Such consistency can hardly be coincidental.. Hence we have to reconstruct -A- in the second syllable (and -m according to C., also to Mo. egem 'shoulder): PTu. *bū'ram 'nose,' *bï'kam 'hip,' etc.

(e) Y. seems to have preserved a distinction between A and Ō, Ū, Ī in some cases, e.g., kömör 'coal' (Osman kömür), but kömüs 'silver' (Osman kümüş). Since to Uighur ï/i/u/ü in suffixes, ï/i/u/ü in Y. corresponds (e.g., +ïm/+im/+um/+üm 'my' = the same in Y.), we may assume that kömör must represent PTu. *kömōr (or *kömūr?; at any rate, not *kömär), whereas kömüs represents PTu. *kö'mäš. However this case is not absolutely clear since Y. sometimes even changes genuine Ū >a, e.g. PTu. *dagkū 'fur' (with -ū according to Mo. daqu) >Y. saġa (not *sagï). This means that Y. kömör may go back both to kömōr and to kömūr, but not to *kömär. And kömüs must go back to *kömäš. For a similar case see TM I. 100: Tu. öküz 'ox' = Mo. hüker may be reconstructed as PTu. *pököz and *pökäz (not as *pöküz, because of Mo. hüker, with e_2); Y. oġus shows that *pökäz is the correct PTu. form (*pököz should have become Y. *oġos).

(f) Mongolian furnishes a good proof. However, its proof can be used only in combination with Tu. facts. We have the following correspondences (cf. TM I. 99-100):

Old CTu., Old Bolgar	Mo.
-Ā-	-A-
-Ū-	-U-
-Ō-	-A- (after I, O: O)
-Ī-	-i-
-A-	-A-

We see that Mo. -A- is ambiguous: it may go back to -Ā-, -Ō-, and -A-. However, Mo. often excludes false possibilities, as above: one may think that Tu. öküz goes back to *pökǖz, but Mo. hüker excludes this possibility (which is also excluded by Y. oġus). Let me cite another instance: the suffix -dürük in CTu. kömüldürük 'strap around the horse's chest' can, theoretically, go back to ATu. +dȫrȫk/ +dȫrǖk/ +dȫräk// +dǖrȫk/ +dǖrǖk/ +dǖräk// +därȫk/ +därǖk/ +däräk. Mo. kömüldürge shows clearly that only Uighur +dǖrük < ATu. +dǖräk (< PTu. *+dǖrkä) is correct

However, we often cannot reconstruct the genuine form. For example, what about ï in Uighur tabïšġân 'hare'? All our instances given above fail: (a) the word is not attested to in Manichaean Tu.; (b) the transcription without vowels in the Runic script does not prove much: many full vowels are not written there; (c) -ï- is dropped in no Tu. language, but it cannot be, for phonological reasons; (d) an analogous form does not seem to exist; (e) Y. has not preserved tabïšġân; (f) Mo. taulai 'hare' proves nothing; perhaps it is not connected with tabïšġân at all. In this case we reconstruct the forms with unstressed a/ä (in our given example: PTu. *ta`bašgâ´n), writing ~4 after the reconstructed form. (Roots with short, later reduced a/ä seem to occur more frequently in Tu. than do those with long vowels in the non-initial syllables.)

I am not sure, by the way, that in Uighur we have to read ï/i/u/ü. The only two scripts which are sufficiently clear in marking vowel qualities are Brahmi and Tibetan. They do not follow the pattern ï/i/u/ü (which seems to be a "crypto-Osmanism," i.e., which has been reconstructed this way because this form occurs in modern Osman). Actually we find the following situation. In Uighur script we find [illegible], [illegible], which are read ï/i, u/ü. In Manichaean instead of these sounds (cf. beneath) we very often find a/ä, especially after a/ä of the first syllables (e.g., tart:ap 'pulling' ~tart:ïp; käl:äp 'coming' ~käl:ip). I think we have to read ĕ/ĕ in this case (just as e, an intermediate sound between ä and i, in RTu. sometimes is spelled i, sometimes ä, I suppose that ĕ sometimes is written a, sometimes ï, and e sometimes is written ä, sometimes i). As to a instead of ï, we find the phenomenon in Brahmi, too, cf. ahir ~agar 'heavy' (a only in text I); tūrmāqag 'the standing' (accusative), etc. Here we also find o after o, ö after ö (e.g., yollog 'knowing the way,' köŋöllög 'having a heart,' in all texts). I see no cogent reason why the situation in the contemporary documents in Uighur script must have been different; that is, I should suppose the following development of PTu. /A/ of non-initial syllables:

PTu.	RTu.	ATu.	Khorezmian Tu. period
-a	___	___	___
-ä	___	___	___
-a-	ă	ĕ ~ ï̆, ŭ ~ ŏ	ï, u
-ä-	ĕ	ĕ ~ ĭ, ü̆ ~ ö̆	i, ü

Notes: (1) RTu. may have had ~ŏ, ~ö̆ after rounded vowels.

(2) ATu. may have had the following:

ĕ after a, ï̆ after ï, ŭ after u, ŏ after o;

ĕ after ä, ĭ after i, ü̆ after ü, ö̆ after ö,

that is, an almost complete assimilation. ĕ, however, may soon have become ĭ, as in Brahmi script we find mostly i.

(3) Between ATu. and Khorezmian Tu. a period may have existed in which the stress changed from the first to the last syllable (perhaps attested to by Karakhanid). Then also the reduced vowels were stressed, and so were lengthened and became full vowels (just as in the Russian Church

Slavonian unstressed reduced vowels were dropped, whereas stressed reduced vowels became full vowels: sŭnŭ [sŭ´nŭ] 'sleep' > son, etc.).

Here is a complete list of vowel changes (non-initial syllables) in older Turkic:

PTu.	RTu.	ATu.	Khorezmian Tu. Period
-a	———	———	———
-ä	———	———	———
-a-	ă	ë̆ ~ ï̆, ŭ ~ ŏ	ï, u
-ä-	ĕ	ĕ ~ ĭ, ü̆ ~ ö̆	i, ü
-ā(-)	ā	ā	a
-ō(-)	ō	ō	u ~ a
-ū(-)	ū	ū	u
-ï̄(-)	ï̄	ï̄	ï
-ë̄(-)	ë̄(?)	ë̄(?)	ï
-ǟ(-)	ǟ	ǟ	ä
-ȫ(-)	ȫ	ȫ	ü ~ ä
-ǖ(-)	ǖ	ǖ	ü
-ī(-)	ī	ī	i
-ē(-)	ē	ē	i

Notes:

(1) I omit the development of -â(-), etc., which must have been quite similar to that of -ā(-), etc.

(2) ATu. means Runic manuscripts (not the inscriptions, which = RTu.); manuscripts in Uighur, Brahmi, Tibetan, Manichaean, perhaps even Arabic; scripts (Karakhanid).

(3) For the preservation of -ē, compare Brahmi yte 'seven'; -ë̄(-) is unclear. Since there is no special sign for it, it can be reconstructed

only on the basis of Y. and Kh. (e.g., altē̈ 'six').

(4) For -ō, -ȫ respectively -ū, -ǖ cf. 14.2.

(5) In Karakhanid the vowels may have been half long: a˙ instead of ā, etc.

(6) In early Manichaean texts the vowels are all as in RTu.; later on they converge with Uighur.

(7) In RTu. ŏ, ö̆ presumably did not yet exist.

Let me add still another word about the Manichaean a/ä instead of the Uighur "ï/i/u/ü." Meyer 1965.199 explains: "Das a/ä des n-Dialekts ersetzt nur ï/i, nicht die gerundeten Vokale, und zwar nur nach einem a/ä der vorausgehenden Silbe. Die Notationen a/ä des n-Dialekts sind offenbar als ein Assimilationsphänomen zu beurteilen." This theory that a/ä occurs only after a/ä of the first syllable and is a simple assimilation is false. To be sure, we often find a after a, ä after ä, but this phenomenon is no miracle, since a_1 and $ä_1$ are frequent vowels in Tu. (more frequent than o_1, $ö_1$, etc.; the percentage in K. is a_1, 29%; $ä/e_1$, 16%; u_1, 13%; o_1, 10%; i, ï, ö, ü, each 8%). But we often find a after other back vowels, and ä after other front vowels. Here are some other instances, communicated to me mostly by Dr. Peter Zieme, Berlin: (the abbreviations are obvious for every Turcologist, I think, e.g., M = Albert von Le Coq, Türkische Manichaica aus Chotscho, etc., cf. the bibliography in Gabain 1950.225 ff.)

(A) a/ä after ï/i

kiši.näŋ M I 8/14-15; özi.näŋ M III No. 32 v 8; anïġ.aġ Xᵛāstvānīft 28; isig.äg W 46; tämir.äg M I 8/12; t(ä)ŋri.äg M III No. 6 II v 15; aġrïġ.aġ U 297 v 3; tumlïġ.aġ U 297 v 9; tämir.än M I 8/11; yigit.än M III No. 6 III r 17; yïd.an M III No. 32 v 5 [cf. also TT VI 292 yïd.an yïpar.an]; ilʾig + (ä)mäz M I 10/4; iš + äŋäz.(ä)n M I

10/13; ïd:aŋ TT II A 51; ät'iz:äŋ Man. Erz. I 34; ig+säz Man. Erz. I 10 (= M II 1209/9); ad(ï)rt+laġ M I 26/16; tir(i)l:äp M I 15/9; qat(ï)l:ap M I 16/6; kir:äp Man. Erz. I 24 (= M II 1210/6); äšid:äpü (or :äpp?) U 268 r 10; Also M III No. 6 I v 1 (buši) biräŋ (= bêrăŋ). We may count here even M I 36/21 bal(a)q.aġ 'the fish' (accusative) = "normally" (Uighur) balïq.ïġ, but we find in the same texts balaq 'fish' instead of balïq (but balïq 'town').

(B) a/ä after u/ü:

qatun.naŋ M III No. 13 III title; kọŋül.näŋ M III No. 13 III v title, - v 6; yaruq.un yašuq.an M III No. 8 VII v 14; yụz'üŋüz.än M I 10/9; küč.äg M III No. 8 II 14.

Zieme adds: "Vgl. auch -maš (?) bei Bang, Türkische Bruchst. einer Georgspassion, S. 70" and "Auch in buddhistischen Texten kommen A (= a/ä)-Formen statt u/ü/ï/i vor, z.B. Maitrisimit, U III, U IV u.a." Compare the relics of ATu. ă/ă, etc., in New Uighur, PhTF. 539.

14.5 Graphic signs. These many unclear points seem to be little satisfying. But we can reconstruct only according to a given material. Where the material fails, we can give only provisional, no definitive, reconstructions. (We shall mark definitive reconstructions by //, hereby disregarding, however, the three unsolvable problems.) After all, we have made some progress. Before knowing Khalaj and the Chuvash -n/-m law (cf. 14.1 above), we could reconstruct CTu. (or modern Tu.) üzüm 'raisin' as *üzämä, *üzǖmä, *üzäm, *üzǖm, *püzäma, *püzǖmä, *püzäm, *püzǖm. Now we see that only *püzäma or *püzǖmä can be correct (we reconstruct püzämä ~4). This restriction of eight possibilities to two is better than nothing, after all. (And the etymological assumption of üzüm from üz- 'to cut off' would leave *püzämä as the only possibility.)

Here again is a short list of graphic signs which we have used in our reconstruction of PTu.:

//	The reconstruction is definitive.
~1	It is unclear whether a simple long vowel or a long vowel with a preceding i̯ has to be reconstructed.
~2	It is unclear whether we have to reconstruct ä or e (in first syllables).
~3	It is unclear whether or not we have to add a/ä to the auslaut consonant.
~4	It is unclear whether we have to reconstruct PTu. a/ä (becoming ă/ĕ in RTu., ï/i/u/ü in most of the modern Tu. languages) or full vowels ū/ǖ, ō/ȫ, ï̄/ī.

14.6 Preface to the dictionary. The following list is not a complete dictionary of Khalaj, a work which will be published only after all the material has been assembled. In the meantime, I think this index will be sufficient for scientific comparative purposes. It contains all inherited Tu. words in Khalaj; hence it excludes not only P. (or other) loanwords, regional words, baby words, but also Az. loanwords. The basic form we give at first is that of Old CTu., which is quite similar to RTu., only that we have â, not ê as in RTu. and that we have a/ä in non-initial syllables, not ă/ĕ as in RTu. (or ï/i/u/ü as in later Tu. languages). The principal means of reconstructing Old CTu. is K., T., Y.; with the help of Kh., C. (and sometimes Y., Tuv.) we reconstruct PTu. (with asterisks). Then we give the Kh. forms.

14.7 The dictionary.

âč 'hungry' (K., T. āč, Y. ās) < *ë̂č ~3 (C. v̈iś- 'to be hungry,' v̈iśă 'hungry') = ā̯^{a}č T. 268

âčïġ 'bitter,' from âčï̄- 'to be bitter' (K. ačïġ, T. āǰï, Y. asï̄) < *pi̯âčï̄gan // (C. yüśĕ) = hā̯^{a}ču̧x 'salty' T. 273, 'bitter' T. 276, hā̯^{a}ču̧^{q}x 'bitter M. 20, hā̯^{a}či̧^{q}x id. X. 20

adāq 'foot' (K. ad̄aq, T. ayaq, Y. atax) < *padāk (or rather *padâk, cf. 13.11.9) ~3 (C. ura) = ha̯da̯q T. 59, ha̯da̯qï̄ a̯^{6}sDo̯ 'shank' T. 62, ha̯da̯qị̈̄ i̯üzü 'instep' T. 64, ha̯da̯qị̈̄ a̯sDo̯ 'sole' T. 65, ha̯da̯q qā̯^{a}bo̯ 'shoe' T. 221, ha̯da̯G̯ M. 22

aġāč 'tree' ~ (y)ïġāč (K. yïġāč, yïġač, T. aġač) < *pi̯ëgāč ~3 (C. yïvăś) = ha̯ġa̯č T. 113, 'wood' 114, 'tree' M. 21, 58 (X. 21)

almï̄lā 'apple' (K. almïlā, T. alma) < *almï̄lā // (C. ulma, Mo. alima, Hungarian alma must not be Bolgar, perhaps Pecheneg) = a̯^{6}lu̯mla̯ T. 115, M. 4, a̯^{6}lo̯mla̯ X. 4

altē̈ 'six' (K. altï̄, T. altï) < *altē̈ // (C. ultă, Y. alta, Volga Bolgar الطا altï or altë) = a̯lta̯ T. 304, M. 96, a̯^{6}lta̯ M. 96

altmaš 'sixty' (K., T. altmïš) < *altmaš ~3, 4 (C. utmăl) = altmu̧š T. 314, a̯^{1}tmi̧š M. 106, a̯ltmi̧š X. 106

âm 'cunt' (K. am, in the text erroneously em) < *pâman ~1 (Mo. aman 'mouth') = hā̯^{a}m T. 50

amrût (?) 'pear' (T. armït) < *almarūt ~3 [cf. G. Doerfer, <u>Türkische Lehnwörter im Tadschikischen</u>, Wiesbaden, 1967. 26-7] = amrū̧^{u}t T. 116 (← Persian?)

aqār 'rivulet,' from aq- 'to flow' < *i̯āk- ~3 (C. yux-) = aG̯G̯a̯ʼ r, aqGa̯ʼ r T. 13. [The quantity of the vowel is unclear. We find K., T. <u>aq</u>-; Biišev 34 has T. <u>āq</u>-, Az. <u>aġ</u>-, but these forms are false: they must be T. <u>aq</u>-, Az. <u>ax</u>-. But the

C. form attests to a long vowel, since in this language i̬ stands only before long vowels. Therefore the most probable PTu. form is *i̬āk-.]

arq 'excrement' (K. arq) < *park ∼3 = hạrq T. 70

ārqā 'behind' (K. arqā, T. arqa) < *pārkā ∼1 = hạ˙ġạ T. 288

arqālaq 'long clothes of men,' from arqā = (a^{r}xạlụq, arqạlụq) T. 216 (← Az., probably)

ārqân 'thin' (T. arqān, arřiq, K. ařiq) < *pērkân ∼1,3 (Y. ïr-, ïr- 'to get thin,' C. ïrxan) = harqān T. 251

ast 'beneath' (K., T. ast) < *ast ∼3 = hạdạqị̄ a^{6}sDọ 'shank' T. 62, hạdạqị̄ ạsDọ 'sole' T. 65

āš 'soup' (K. āš, T. aš, Y. as) < *āš ∼1,3 [C. yaška proves nothing: C. l should correspond to CTu. š] = āš T. 208

at 'horse' (K., T., Y. at) < *pat ∼3 (C. ut, the relation to Mo. agta is doubtful) = hạt T. 71, M. 7, X. 7, 25

ây 'moon' (K., T. āy) < *pêy ∼3 (C. uyăx, Y. ïy, Volga Bolgar ayïx) = $hā^{ai}$ T. 159, išqi̦^{4} 'moonshine' T. 160

āy- 'to say' (K. ay-, T. ayt-) < *pēy- ∼3 (Y. ïy-, C. ïyt- 'to ask') = hạ˙^{i}d^{u}lạ^{6}r 'they said' M. 27, hạ^{i}maq X. 27

ǟb 'house' (RTu. äb, K. äw, T. öy, WOD. ǟv) < *pǟb ∼2,3 = hȧv T. 177, M. 30, hö̦^{ü} X. 30, Wenạreǰ hȧ˙v (unpublished material)

äčkō 'goat' (K. äčkü, T. gäči) < *äčkō ∼2 (for -ō cf. Mo. ešige) = ȧ^{k}či̦ T. 80, ȧčči̦ M. 2, ȧkk'ü̦ X. 2

ägrī (or rather ägrē) 'crooked,' from äg- 'to bend' (K., T. äg-) < *ägä- // (C. av-, Mo. ége-) = äyri̦ T. 241

äkkī or ä̂kkī (cf. 13. 7) 'two' (K. ikī, T. iki, Y. äkki, ikki) < *ekkī or *êkkī // (C. ikkĕ, Volgar Bolgar اكي eki) = àkkụ T. 300, àkkị M. 92, X. 92; (àkk^{i}-ọttụz 'sixty') X. 106, (àkk^{i}-ọttụz-ọ˙n 'seventy') X. 107

ǟl(äg) 'hand' (K. älig, Brahmi älig ~elig, T. äl, Y. älī, ilī) < *ǟl(äg) ~3,4 (C. ală) = à˙l T. 52, M. 3, àl X. 3

älgǟk 'sieve,' from älgǟ- 'to sieve' (K. älgǟ-, T. älä-) < *pälgǟ- // (C. ala-) = hà^{i}làk T. 190, hàlyäk´ M. 31, hä^{i}làk X. 31

älläg 'fifty' (K. ällig, T. älli) < *älläg ~3,4 (C. allă, Volga Bolgar ال, آلُو älü) = àllị^{y} T. 313, à´llị M. 105, àllị^{g} X. 105

ä̂m 'trousers' (K. öm, in the text erroneously üm, Yellow Uighur yem, Old Osman em, öm, in the text erroneously im, üm, etc.) < *i̯êmä // (C. yĕm) = ī^{e}m T. 218, M. 43, X. 43

ä̂n- 'to go down' (T. īn-) < *ä̂n- ~3 (C. an-, Az. en-) = ī^{e}nà^{k} 'on foot' (literally 'let us go down') M. 87

ä̂nǟ 'going down,' from ä̂n- = ī^{e}nä T. 298

ä̂nläg 'broad,' from ä̂n 'breadth' (K. ēn, T. īn, Y. iän) < *pä̂n ~3 (C. an) = hànlị^{G} T. 263, (hànlị^{g}x) M. 29

ä̂nsäz 'narrow, thin,' from ä̂n 'breadth' = (hànsịz said to be Az.) T. 262, (hànsịz) X. 28, cf. dāġ

äŋ̦är 'yesterday, evening' (Karaim äŋ̦ir 'evening,' K. iŋ̦ir, rather eŋ̦ir, 'twilight') < *äŋ̦är ~2,3,4 = à´ŋ̦gịr 'yesterday' T. 166, à´ŋ̦gị^{r} M. 5, à´ŋ̦^{g}ụr X. 5; à´ŋ̦gịr kī^{e}čä 'last night' T. 167, à´ŋ̦gị^{r} kī^{e}čä M. 5, à´ŋ̦^{g}ụr kī^{e}čä X. 5

är- cf. ärǖr

är or ä̂r 'man' (T. ǟr, K., Y., Az., Brahmi, Uighur är) < *pärä or pä̂rä // (C. ar, Mo. ere) = hàr T. 12, M. 56, hàrị

(< hȧrịṇ?) X. 57, hȧrịm X. 57. [For the quantity of the vowel cf. 14.4.2. Is Hungarian *érdem* 'virtue' a proof that it has been long?]

ǟrän 'lip' (K. erin, T. ärin) < *ǟräm ~1,2 = ȧ˙rịn T. 29, M. 6

â̈rkǟk 'male' (K., T. ärkäk, Az., Uighur erkäk, cf. 14.4.2), perhaps from â̈r = hị˙rkȧk T. 246

ärǖk 'plum, apricot' (K. ärük, T. ärik) < *ärǖk ~2,3 = ȧrịk 'apricot' T. 118

ärǖr 'is,' from är- 'to be' (K. är-) < *är- ~2,3 = hā^{a}čị^{q}x daġ šịrịn är 'it is not bitter, it is sweet' X. 20 (är < ärǖr)

â̈šäk 'door, threshold' (T. ī̈šik) < *â̈šäk ~3,4 (C. alăk) = ī^{e}šịk 'door' T. 180, M. 41, ī^{e}šịk X. 41

äšgǟk 'donkey' (K. äšgäk, T. äšäk) < *äšgǟk ~2,3 [the relation to Mo. *elǰigen* is doubtful] = ȧšGä T. 72, M. 8, X. 8, ȧškä X. 8

ät 'flesh, meat' (K., T., Y. ät) < *ät ~3 (C. aš < *at+šě 'his flesh,' cf. baġarsôq, bāš, kȫz) = ȧt T. 67

â̈t- 'to do' (K. ēt-, T. ät-, äd-, Y. īt-, Az. et-, Brahmi ät-) < *â̈t- ~1,2,3 (C. not found) = ī^{e}tt^{i}lä^{l}r 'they did,' ī^{e}t^{i}räk 'we shall do' M. 32, bȧdiẹtmä 'angry' (literally 'ill-doing') M. 59

ätǟk 'seam' (K., T. ätäk) < *pätäk ~2,3 = hȧtȧk T. 224

â̈tmǟk 'bread' < *pâ̈tmǟk ~1,2,3 = hịkmȧk T. 206, hịk'mäk' M. 33, hịkmȧk X. 33. [The original form seems to have contained a -*t*-, not a -*k*-, cf. K. *ätmäk*. But we often find forms with *ö*: K. *ötmäk*, Chaghatay *id.*, ATu. (Manichaica III 12, 5) *id.*, Altay Tu. *ötpök*, from such a form as Mo. *ödmeg*. However, according to Kh. the form with *ä* seems to be older. Osman *ekmek* is quite recent, where we may find an assimilation to -*k* and/or an analogy to *äk*- 'to sow.']

bâčānāq 'brother-in-law' (T. bāǰa) < *bâčānāk ~1, 3 (C. puśana) = ba̤˙ǰanax T. 18, ba̤˙ǰa̤nax X. 57

baġarsôq 'bowels' (K. baġïrsuq, Az. baġïrsaq) < * bëgarsôk ~ 3, 4 (C. pïrša̋ < *bëgar-sï, derived from bëgar, the basic form of bëgarsôk) = bo̤ġa̤rsa̤˙q T. 45, bo̤ġa̤rsu̯q M. 13

bâlā 'young animal' (K. balā, T. bāla) < *bâlā ~1 = balla 'small' T. 252

bār- 'to go' (K., T., Y. bar-, WOD. vār-) < *bë̄r- ~3 (C. pir-) ṳqa̤ ƀa̤rmi̯š 'went to sleep' X. 86

barmāq 'finger' (T. barmaq) < *barmāk ~3 (C. pürnä presumably in analogy to t̄ïrn̯āq 'nail,' see below) = ba̤rma̤q T. 56, šāba̤rma̤q 'thumb' T. 57

bāš 'head' (K. bāš, T. baš, Y. bas) < *bāš ~1, 3 (C. puś < *pul-še < *bāš-sï 'his head') = bo̤˙š T. 23, ba̤˙š M. 15, X. 15. The Kh. form bo̤˙š may be explained as follows: bāš > bā⁵š > bā̤š > ba̤ᵃš > bo̤ᵃš > bo̤ᵒš (or bo̤ᵃš) > bo̤ᵒš > bo̤ᵒš > bo̤ᵒš (or bo̤ᵒš) > bo̤ᵒš > bo̤˙š.

bat- 'to sink' (K., T., Y. bat-) < *bat- ~3 (C. put-) = kṳn ba̤tȧr 'evening' (literally 'the sun is sinking') T. 172, 'west' T. 174

bädük 'big' (K. bädük, T. bäyik), from bädü- 'to be big' < *bädük ~2, 3 = bi̤di̤k T. 253, bi̤di̤k ha̤ġa̤č 'big tree' M. 58

bäg 'prince' (K. bäg, T. bäg, Y. bī) < *bäg ~2, 3 = bȧg, bȧG 'son-in-law' T. 17

bâl 'waist' (K. bēl, T., Y. bīl) < *bêl ~3 (C. pilĕk) = bi̤ᵉ˙l T. 48, M. 12, (X. 12)

bärk 'strong' (K. bäk, bärk, T. bärk, Y. bärt) < *bärkä // (C. parka, Mo. berke) = bȧk T. 283. [However, since in Mo. a word cannot end in two consonants, a vowel must be added; therefore PTu. *bärk would also be possible.]

bâš 'five' (K. bēš, T. bǟš, Y. biäs)] *bêš ~3 (C. pilčk, Volga Bolgar بيال presumably beäl) = bị̄ᵉš T. 303, M. 95, X. 95

bîr 'one' (K. bīr, bir, T. bir, but on-bīr 'eleven,' Y. bīr) < *bîr ~3 (C. pĕr, Volga Bolgar بر bir) = bị̄ T. 299, M. 91, X. 91

bïldar 'last year' (K. bïldïr, T. bildir) < *bïldar ~3 (C. pĕltĕr) = bị́ldịr T. 169, bụ̈ldụ̈r M. 89

bïŋ 'a thousand' (K. miŋ, T. müŋ, Kazakh mïŋ, Osman bin) < *bïŋan // (C. pin, Mo. miŋgan) = mịn T. 319, mịŋᵏ M. 111

bô-kǖn 'today,' literally 'this day,' from bô 'this' (Brahmi bo, K. bō or bū, T. bū, Y. bu); for the second part of the word cf. kǖn = bẹ́ịịn T. 162, 165, M. 16, bụ̈́ịᵘn X. 16

bô-yïl 'this year,' cf. bô-kǖn and yïl = bụ́ịịl X. 89

boğōz 'throat' (K. boğoz, T. boğaz, New Uighur boğuz) < *bogōz // (C. pïr, Mo. boğor+la- 'to strangle') = bọğụz T. 40, M. 14, X. 14

bōyan 'neck' (K. boyun, boyïn, T. boyun) < *bōyam (C. măy?) = bọyụn T. 39 (Bạġ-e yäk bụyụn)

bōyandūraq 'yoke,' from boyan = bụndᵘruq, bọⁱndïrụq T. 139

bôrē 'wolf' (K. börī, T. bōri) < *bôrē ~1 (Y. börö) = bị̄ᵉrị T. 85, bị̄ᵉrị¹ M. 11, bị̄ᵉrị¹ X. 11

bôrk 'hat' (K. börk, T. bōrük) < *bôrk or *bộrk ~3 (Mo. bürgü) = bọ̈ᵒk T. 220, bịriậk M. 18, bịriậk X. 18 (in Čạhäk börk, unpublished material)

bulït 'cloud' (K. bulït, T. bulut) < *bulït ~3 (C. pĕlĕt 'heaven') = bụlụt T. 152

būran 'nose' (K., T. burun, Y. murun), from būr- 'to smell' (K. būr-, bur-) < *būram ~1 = bụrụn T. 28

busuq, cf. pišik

bût 'thigh' (K., T., Y. būt) < *bût ~1,3 (C. pĕśĕ < *bût-si) = bụ̄ᵘ·t T. 60

bûtā 'shrub' (K. butiq, butaq, T. pūdaq < pūtaq < būtāq) = bûtā ~1 = pụ·ta T. 216

bûz 'ice' (K., T. būz, Y. būs) < *bûz ~1,3 (C. păr) = bụ̄ᵘ·z 'cold' T. 279, 'cool' T. 281

čāl- 'to beat' (K., T. čal-, WOD. čāl-) < *čāl- ~1,3 (C. śul- 'to cut') = kụn čạlȧr 'east' (literally 'the sun beats') T. 173

čaqar 'pale, faint' (K., T. čaqïr) < *čaqar ~3 = čạqụr M. 73

čây 'river' (T. čāy) < *čāy ~ 1,3 = čạ̄ᵃⁱ T. 147

čōlāq 'cripple' (K., T. čolaq) < *čōlāq ~ 1,3 = čọlạq 'weak' T. 284

dāġ 'not' (K. dāġ) = hạvụl dạ⁶ġ 'is not good' T. 239, hạ⁶vụl dạġ M. 19, hạvụl dạġ X. 19, hạ̄ᵃčịᑫx dạġ 'is not bitter' X. 20, hȧnsịz ụzạ̄q dạġ '<u>hȧnsịz</u> means <u>not far</u>.' [For the etymology cf. Doerfer 1968.106-7.]

ilgä̅r(ü̅) (or yilgä̅rü̅?) 'before' (T. iläri, from the root *il; cf. K., T. ilk 'first,' with directive suffix .gä̅rü̅) < *il.gä̅rü̅ // (C. ĕlĕk 'formerly') = yịlgȧr T. 287, ịlyä¹r M. 40, ị¹lgär X. 40

ïrâq (or yïrâq?) 'far' (K. yïrāq, T. ïrāq, Y. ïrāx) < *pïrâk ~3 = ?ịrạ̄q 'far' T. 265, hịrạ̄q M. 90, yịrạ̄q X. 90

ïs(s)ï̄ġ 'warm' (K. isig, T. ïssï), from ïs(s)ï̄- 'to become hot' < *pïs(s)ï̄gan // = hịssịʸ T. 280, hịssị M. 34, hịssịᵍ́ X. 34

ïšï̄q 'shine, light, bright' (T. ïšïq), from ïšï̄- 'to shine' < *ïšï̄qa(n), ïšï̄- // = hạ̄ᵃⁱ ịšqị⁴ 'moonshine' T. 160, ị⁴šị⁴q 'bright' T. 242

ï̄t 'dog' (K., T. ïit, T. it, but Qashqai, New Uighur īt) < *i̯īt ~ 3 (C. yït, yïtă) = ịt T. 73

käč- 'to pass,' cf. käčäglī

käčä 'felt' (K. käčǟ, Oghuz, T. käčä, Az. keča <käčä) < *keč(č)ǟ (C. kĕśśä) = käčä T. 203 (← older Az.?)

k̂äčǟ 'night' (K. kēč, kēčǟ, T. gīč, gīǰä, Y. kiäsä), from k̂äč 'late' < *k̂äč(ǟ) // (C. kaś, Hungarian késő 'late') = kị̆ᵉčä T. 163, å'ŋgịr kị̆ᵉčä 'last night' T. 167, kịᵉčä M. 47, X. 47

kǟčäglī 'passed, past' (from kǟč- 'to pass,' K. käč-, T. gäč-, Y. käs-, WOD. gǟš-) < *kǟč- ~3 (C. kaś-) = kåšgụ̈lị i̯ịl 'last year' KhX. 89 < *kǟčgüli < *kǟčügli < *kǟčĕglī <*kǟčäglī

kǟl- 'to come' (K., Y. käl-, T. gäl-, WOD. gǟl-) < *kēl- ~3 (C. kil-) = kålån yịl 'next year' (literally 'the coming year') X. 89

kǟlän 'bride' (K. kälin, T. gälin) < *kēlänä // (C. kin, older kilĕn) = kålịn T. 15, kålịn M. 46, kålụ̈n X. 46

k̂äŋ 'broad' (K. keŋ, T. gīŋ, Y. kiäŋ) < *k̂äŋ ~2,3 = kịᵉŋᵏ M. 29

käs-, cf. käsǟr, käsäk

kǟsǟr 'hatchet,' from kǟs- 'to cut' (K., T. käs-, WOD. kǟs-) < *kǟs- ~3 (C. kas-) = kåsår T. 229

kǟsäk 'clothing,' from kǟs- = kåsịk T. 215, 'long clothes of men T. 216

kindäk 'navel' (Brahmi kindik) < *kindäk ~3,4 (Hungarian köldök?) = kụ̈ndụ̈k (< *kindük < kindik) T. 44, X. 48, kịndịkᶜ M. 48

kirpäk 'eyelash' (K., T. kirpik) < *kirpäk ~3,4 (C. xăpră̆k) = kịprịk T. 25

kis(s)ē 'wife' (K. kis, kisī, kissī) < *kis(s)ē // < qā^a dun kịssị 'sister-in-law' T. 19

kišī 'person' (K. kišī, T. kiši, Old Osman giši, Y. kisi) < *kišī // = kịšị^5 'woman' T. 13, kịšị M. 56, X. 56, kịšị̄ babasụ 'woman's father-in-law' T. 21

kôk 'blue, heaven' (K. kȫk, T. gȫk, Y. küöx) < *kôkä // (C. kăvak, Mo. köke, Hungarian kék ← Bolgar *köäk or similar form) = kọ̄^ö·k T. 157, 'above' T. 297, kụ̄^ö·k T. 294, kī^e·k M. 51, kọ̄^ö·k X. 51

kôkȫrčgän 'dove' (K. kökörčgün, in the text erroneously kökürçkün, T. gȫgärčin) < *kôkȫrčgänä // (C. kăvakarčăn, Oirot Mo. kögöljirgene) = kọ^ö·kȧrčịk T. 100, gȧ^5 ụȧ^r čịn M. 55

kôl 'lake' (K., T. kȫl, Y. küöl) < *kôl ~3 (C. kül, but the C. word probably ← Tatar, and the Tu. word in general may be a loanword ← Middle P. kōl, Cf. TM III. 645-6) = gọ̄^ö l, gọ̄^ö·l (← Az. ?)

kȫń- 'to burn' (K. köy-, kön-, T. köy-, Y. kȫǰör-, köynör-, kȫynör-, kȫnyör-, köynyör- 'to cook') < *kȫń- ~3 = kị^e·ndị 'it burnt' M. 50, kọ̈·nmäk X. 50

köt 'anus' (K. köt) < *köt ~3 (C. kut) = kọt T. 51

kȫz 'eye' (T. göz, Y. köz, WOD. gȫz) < *kȫz ~3 (C. kuś < *kur-šė < *kȫz-si 'his eye') = kọ^2 z T. 24, kị^1 z M. 49, kọz X. 49

küdāgū 'bridegroom' (K. küdāgū), from *küdā- // 'to wed' = kịdȧịị M. 46

küdān 'wedding' (K. küdän), from *küdā- 'to wed' = kụdȧn T. 16, X. 54, kịdȧn M. 54

kül 'ash' (K., T., Y. kül) < *kül ~3 (C. kĕl) = kụl T. 198

kǖn 'day, sun' (K., Y. kün, T. gün, WOD. gǖn) < *kǖn ~3 (C. kun, Volga Bolgar كُوَان küọn) = kụn 'sun' T. 158,

X. 52, 'day' T. 162, kịn M. 52; kụ̈n ba̱tȧr 'evening' T. 173, 'west' T. 174, kụ̈n č̱alȧr 'east' T. 173, Wena̱reǰ kī̤⁵n (unpublished material)

kǖndû̈z 'day' (K. kündüz, T. gündīz), from kǖn 'day' < *kǖndû̈z ~3 'midday' (C. kăntăr; V. G. Egorov, Ėtimologičeskij slovar' čuvašskogo jazyka, Čeboksary, 1964. 99-100 explains this as kǖn- tû̈z '[when the] sun [is] straight [over one's head],' but cf. K. tǖz, tüz, T. düz, Y. tüs: 'straight' is PTu. *tǖz, not *tû̈z, i. e., we ought to find a T. form *gündiz, not gündīz) = kụ̈ndụ̈z T. 62

kürgǟk 'oar' (K. kürgäk, T. küräk) < *kürgǟk ~3 (C. kĕräśä < kürgäčäk, with a diminutive suffix) = kụ̈rǵȧk, kụ̈ryȧk T. 237, kịryäk M. 53

ôčôq ~ôtčôq 'hearth' (from ôt 'fire,' cf. Suvarnaprabhāsa otčoq) (K. očaq, T. ōǰaq, Y. osox) < *pôtčôk ~1, 3 = hū̜ᵒčaq T. 195, hū̜ᵒča̱˙q M. 37

oġal 'son' (K., T. oġul, Y. uol) < *ogal (C. ïvăl, Volga Bolgar اول ëvăl?) = o̜ġụl T. 5

ôn 'ten' (K., T. ōn, Y. uon) < *ôn ~3 (C. vună, Volga Bolgar وان wo̜n) = ᵘo̜˙n T. 308, ṳo̜n M. 100, o̜˙n, ᵒō̜n X. 100

ôn-bîr 'eleven' cf. ôn and bîr = o̜n bī̤ T. 309, o̜²˙ n bī̤ M. 101, o̜n bī̤ X. 101

ōrġāq 'sickle,' from ōr- 'to sickle' (K. ōr-, T., Y. or-) < *pōr- ~1, 3 = hō̜ġraqᶜ, hō̜ġraqx, hō̜ġrax T. 135

ôt 'fire' (K., T. ōt, Y. uot) < *pôt ~3 (C. vut, the relation to Mo. hočin 'spark' is doubtful) = hū̜ᵒt T. 154, M. 35, hū̜ᵒt X. 35

ôtan 'wood, timber,' from ôt 'fire' = hū̜ᵒtụn X. 21

ottaz 'thirty' (T. otuz) < *pottaz ~3 (Y. otut, C. vătăr, Volga Bolgar وطر votor) = ho̜tDụz T. 311, ho̜ttụz M. 103, X. 103

ôl 'wet' (K., T. ōl, Y. üöl) < *pôl ~3 (Az., New Uighur höl, Uzbek hol, T. dialect according to Ligeti hōl) = họ̄^{ö}·l T. 256, hị̄^{e}·l M. 36, X. 36

pišik 'cat' (or rather *bušuq?) (T. pišik, Uzbek mušuk, etc., cf. Doerfer 1968.87) = pụ̦šụ̦q T. 74

qâdan 'relative by marriage' (K. qadïn, T. g̰āyïn) < *kâdam ~1 (Mo. qadum ← Old Bolgar *qâdŏm or similar form, C. huń ← Tatar) = qā̰^{a}dụ̦n kịssị̦ 'sister-in-law' T. 19, qā̰^{a}dụn 'brother-in-law' M. 57, qā̰^{a}dị̦n àbä 'mother-in-law' M. 57 = qā̰^{a}dïn àbà ~qā̰^{a}dụn àbà X. 57, qā̰^{a}dïn ba̰ba̰ 'mother-in-law' X. 57, qā̰^{a}dïn hàrịm 'sister-in-law' X. 57)

qâńāq 'cream' (K. qanaq, qayaq, T. g̰aymaq, Y. xoymox) [cf. Räsänen 1949.208; the Tu. forms end in -maq, -mïq, -muq, -moq in analogy to such words as, for example, bulamaq, cf. TM II.321] < *kâńāk ~1,3 = qā̰^{a}naq T. 210, M. 61, X. 61

qânāt 'wing' (K. qanat, T. g̰ānat) < *kị̂êńāt ~3 (Y. kiǰat, kïyiat, kïnat, C. śunat) = qànàt T. 106 (← Az.?)

qâńō 'which' (K. qanū, qayū, Brahmi qayo, T. xaysï, Y. xaya 'what kind?' xanna 'where?') < *kâńō ~1 = qā̰^{a}nị M. 60, qā̰^{a}nị̦ X. 60

qâp 'vessel, bag' (K. qāp, T. g̰āp) < *kâp ~1,3 = ha̰da̰q qā̰^{a}bo̰ 'shoe,' literally 'foot vessel' T. 221

qâr 'snow' (K. qār, T. g̰ār, Y. xār) < *kị̂âr ~3 (C. yur) = Gā̰^{a}r T. 148

qarā 'black' (K. qarā, T. g̰ara, Y. xara) < *karā // (C. xura, Mo. qara) = G̰a̰ra T. 290, M. 1

qāran 'bellow' (K. qarïn, T. g̰arïn, Y. xarïn, xarïṇ) < *kēram // (C. xïrăm, Tuv. xïrïn) = qa̰·rụ̦n T. 43, M. 62, qa̰·rïn X. 6

qarāṇġūlaq 'dark(ness),' from qarā = qạrā̊lụx T. 243

qarġū 'reed' (Old Osman qarġu, T. ġarġï) < *karġū // = qạrġọ T. 188

qārī 'old' (K. qarī, T. ġarrï) < *kērī ~1 (Y. kïrïy- 'to grow old,' Tuv. qïrï-, Az. dialect ġārï 'old woman') = qạrrị M. 63, qạ˙rrị Wenạrej̆

qâš 'eyebrow' (K. qāš, T. ġāš, Y. xās) < *kâš ~1,3 = Ġạ̄ᵃš T. 26

qatīq, qatōq 'turn,' from qat- 'to add (to the meal)' (K. qat-, T. ġat-) < *kët- ~3 (Y. kïtar-) = qạtụq T. 213

qatmā 'cord,' from qat- 'to add' = qạtma T. 227

qatōq, cf. qatīq

qïl 'hair' (K. qïl, T. ġïl, Y. kïl) < *kïl ~3 = qịl T. 36 'down'

qïrq 'forty' (K., T. qïrq) < *kïrk ~3 (C. xĕrĕx, Volga Bolgar خرخ xïrx) = qị⁴rq T. 312, qị⁴rq M. 104, qïrq X. 104

qî̈sġā 'short,' from qî̈s- 'to shorten' (K. qïs-, Y. kïsay-, T. ġīsġa) < *kî̈s- ~1,3 = qïsqȧ T. 261

qî̈z 'daughter, girl' (K. qïz, T. ġīz, Y. kīs) < *kî̈z ~3 (C. xĕr, Volga Bolgar هير xīr) = qịⁱ˙z T. 6, qị̄⁴ᶻ M. 65

qōl 'arm, sleeve' (K. qōl, T. ġol, Y. xol) < *kōl ~3 (C. xul) = qụᵒ˙l T. 223, qọl M. 68, qọ˙l X. 68

qolay 'easy, comfortable' (T. ġolay 'near, close; relative,' Osman kolay 'easy') < *kolay ~3 = qulạ 'short' M. 66 ('at easy reach' > 'near' > 'short'), qọlạⁱ 'near' M. 90

qōń 'sheep' (K. qōn, qōy, T. ġoyun) < *kōńan // (Mo. qonin ← Old Bolgar *qōńĭn or similar form) = Ġụᵒ˙n T. 78, qọn M. 70, qọ˙n X. 70

qudġū 'fly' (K. qudġū) < *kudgū // = qụdᵘġụ T. 109, qụdġị⁴ M. 74

qudrūq 'tail' (K. qudruq, T. g̬uyruq, Y. kuturuk) < *kudūrka // (C. xürä, M. qudurg̬a) = qụdᵘ̓rụq T. 92, qụrdụq M. 67, X. 6

qūlāq 'ear' (K. qulaq, qulxaq, qulqaq, T. g̬ulaq, Y. kulgāx) < *kūl(k)āk ~3 (C. xălxa, perhaps <qūl, with a diminutive suffix +qāq; Mo. qulki 'inner ear' < *qūl+qï 'being in the ear'?) = G̬ụlāq, G̬ụlāqᶜ T. 27, qụlāq M. 69, qọlāqᶜ X. 69

qûrïġ 'dry,' from qūrï- 'to dry' (K. qurï-, qurū-, quruġ, T. g̬ūrï) < *kûrï-, kûrïgan // (C. xăr-) = qụrrụĠ T. 257, qụrrụᵍ̇ M 71, qụrrụġ X. 71

qûrt 'worm' (K. qurt, T. g̬ūrt) < *kûrt ~1, 3 = G̬ụᵘ̓t T. 111

quš 'bird' (K. quš, T. g̬uš, Y. kus) < *kuš ~3 = G̬ụš 'sparrow' T. 103, M. 72, X. 72

sač 'hair' (K., T. sač, Y. as) < *sač ~3 (C. śüś <čuč <čoč < čạč <sạč <sač or similar form) = šạč T. 37

saq(q)āl 'beard' (K. saqal, T. saqg̬al) < *sak(k)āl ~3 (C. suxal, Hungarian szakál(l) must not be a Bolgar loanword, perhaps Pecheneg) = sȧqqȧl T. 34 (← Az.?)

sâraġ 'yellow' (K. sarïġ, T. sārï) < * si̯ârag // (C. šură, Mo. šira, Hungarian sár <Bolgar *sïârä or similar form) = sāᵃrụx T. 291, sāᵃrọᵍ̇, sārọᵍ̇ X. 73

säkkäz 'eight' (K. säkiz, säkkiz, T. säkiz) < *säkkäz ~3 (Y. ag̃is, C. sakkăr, Volga Bolgar سکر säkkăr) = säkkịz T. 306, M. 98, X. 98

säkkäz ôn 'eighty,' from säkkäz and ôn = sẹⁱ(x́)sȧn T. 316, saⁱsan M. 108 (<säksän <säksön K.)

sīdȫk 'urine,' from sīd- (K. sīd-, sıd-, T. siy-) < *sīd- ~3 (C. šĕr-) = sịdȧk T. 69, sị̇dȧk M. 75, X. 75

sipärgä̅, cf. süpärgä̅

sïčġân 'mouse' (K. sïčġān, T. sïčan, from sïč- 'to shit') < *sïčgân ~3 (C. šăši with another suffix) = sịčgḁn T. 75, sịčġḁn M. 76, sị^{4}čġḁn X. 76

sïġar 'cow' (K., T. sïġïr) < *sïgar ~3,4 = sị^{4}ġị^{4}r T. 76, M. 77, sïġïr X. 77

sïgarčïn 'starling,' from sïġar (?) = sïġïrčïn, sïġïrčịġọ, sïġïr-čịụọ T. 104

soġïq 'cold,' from soġï- 'to get cold' (K. soġï-, soġuq, Brahmi soġïq, T. sovuq, Y. uox 'strength, hardness') < *soġï-, soġïqa(n) // = sọụụq 'hard' T. 282

sūb 'water' (K. sūw, T. suv, Y. ū) < *sịūb ~3 (C. šïv) = sụ·^{v} T. 146, M. 78, sụ̄ X. 78

sūbsaz 'thirsty,' from sūb = sụ^{v}sụzȧm 'I am thirsty' T. 146, sụ·^{v}sụz 'thirsty' T. 269

süpärgä < sipärgä 'besom,' from sipär- 'to sweep' (K. süpür-, süpürgö, T. süpür-, süpürgi, Osman sipir-, sipirge) < *sipär-, *sipärgö (C. šăpăr-, šăpăr, Hungarian seper) = sụpụrġä T. 205. [Perhaps Tu. sipär- is connected with Mo. sirbe- 'to sweep,' which might be a metathesis < *siprä-. Another explanation would be that Tu. *sirpä- regularly became Mo. sirbe-, and after the elision of unstressed -ä, sirpä- itself became *sirĕp-, and this, with a metathesis, sipĕr- (sipir-). I am inclined to prefer the explanation with Tu. *siprä-, because *sirpä- would have become, according to the Tu. phonetic laws, simply *sirp-. Furthermore in Mo. *sibre- was impossible for phonologic reasons (a cluster -br- does not exist in Mo, cf. ab- 'to take,' but ab,u:ra 'in order to take,' not *ab:ra, etc.); hence (if not the insertion of a vowel) a metathesis was inevitable in Mo. But compare also Mo. šigür 'besom,' West Middle Mongolian ši′ür- 'to sweep,' ši′ürgü ~ ši′ür 'besom.' Perhaps this is a more recent loanword.]

sǖr- 'to send, to drive ahead' (K., T. sür-, Y. ǖr-) = sịrd^{i}lä^{l}r 'they sent' M. 42, (sụ̈rmåk) X. 42, Wenạrej̆ (unpublished material) sī^{5}rmịš, etc.

sût 'milk' (K. süt, T. süyt, Y. ǖt) < *sût // (C. sĕt, Mo. sün, a reconstructed singular, T. sût being regarded as a plural form; for the method cf. TM III. 58) = sụ̄^{ü}·t T. 209, sī^{i}·t M. 6

tabašġân 'hare' (K. tawìšġān, T. tovšan) < *tabašgân ∼3, 4 = tạvụšġạ·n T. 83, tọvụšġạ̄n M. 81, tọụụšġạ̄n X. 81

tâġ 'mountain' (K. tāġ, T. dāġ, Y. tïa) < *tâg ∼3 (C. tu) = tạ̄^{a}ġ T. 144, X. 79

tâlâq 'milt' (K. talāq, T. dālaq, Y. tāl) < *tâlâk ∼1, 3 = tạ̄lạ̄q T. 4

tâm 'roof' (K., T. tām) < *tâma // = dạ̄^{a}m ịstụ̈ T. 184 (← Az.?)

tâpân 'sole' (T. dāban, Osman taban < tāban < tāpan) < *tâpân ∼3 (C. tupan, perhaps a Tatar loanword) = tạ̄^{a}pạ̄n 'ankle' T. 6

târ 'narrow, tight' (K., Y. tār, T. dār) < *târ ∼1, 3 = tạ̄^{a}r T. 26 M. 80, X. 80

tâš 'stone' (K. tāš, T. dāš, Y. tās) < *tịâša // (C. čul, Mo. čila+ġun) = tạ̄^{a}š T. 143

tämär 'iron' (K. tämür < ATu. tämir, tämär, T. dämir) < *temär ∼3 (Y. tämir, timir, C. timĕr; Mo. temür is a Middle Tu. loanword) = tȧmịr T. 155

täpȫ 'hill' (K. töpȫ, in the text erroneously tüpü, T. däpä, Y. täbä töbö) < *täpȫ ∼2 (C. tüpä presumably ← Tatar) = tȧBȧ 'mountain' M. 79

tärî 'skin' (K. tärī, T. däri, Y. tärī, tirī) < terî // (C. tir) = tȧrị T. 66

tilkǖ 'fox' (K. tilkǖ, T. tilki) > *tilkǖ // (C. tilĕ) = tụ̈lkụ̈ T. 87

tīrs(g)ǟk 'elbow' (K. tirsgäk, T. tirsäk, Osman dirsek) < *tīrsgǟk ~3 = tị·ʳsäk T. 54

tišī, cf. t́išī

t́īl 'tongue' (K. t́īl, t́il, T. dil, Y. t́il) < *t́īl ~3 (C. čĕl-xä) = tịl T. 31, tị·l M. 82, tịl X. 82

t́irŋāq 'nail' (K. t́irŋaq, T. dirnaq) < *t́irŋāk ~3 (C. čĕrnä) = tị²rnaq T. 58

t́îš 'tooth' (K. t́īš, T. dīš, Y. tīs) < *t́îš ~ 3 (C. šăl < śiš < ŝîš < čîš < t́îš) = tị·š T. 32

t́išī 'female' (mostly tiši, but Y. t́iśi, K. t́išī ~tišī) < *t́išī // = tịšị T. 247

t́îz 'knee' (K. tīz, T. dīz) < *t́îz ~3 (C. čĕr) = tịz T. 61

toġrï or toġrē 'straight' (Chaghatay toġri, T. doġrï, Old Osman doġrï) < *togrē (Y. tuora 'opposite') = toġru T. 240 [why not *toġra?, loanword ← Az., i. e., contamination with Az. doġru?]

tōlï 'hail' (K. tolï, T. dolï) < *tōlï ~1 = tu°lo T. 150

tôlū or tôlō 'full,' from tôl- 'to become full' (T. dōl-, Y. tuol-) < *tôl- ~3 (C. tul-), tôlu or tolō = tu°la T. 286. [The vowel in 'full' is unclear. Some Tu. languages attest to *tôlō > tola, namely Kh.; furthermore (Radloff III.1191) Chaghatay, New Uighur, Taranči tola 'plenty'; New Uighur, Sagay (Khakass) 'full,' also Uzbek Borovkov tola, Kirghiz Judaxin tolo, Altay Tu. Baskakov tolo (presumably also Brahmi tolo). K. is unclear: tolū or tolō? Other languages attest to tolū with certainty or, at least, with a great probability: Khwarezmian Tu. Borovkov tolï, tolu, Codex Comanicus tolu, Houtsma tolu, Tuḥfat az-Zakīya tolï; modern languages: Az. dolu, Bashkir tulï, Y. tolu, tolū, Karakalpak toli, Karaim tolu, Karachay tolu, Kazakh toli, Kazan Tatar tuli, Kumyk tolu, Nogay toli, Osman dolu, C. tulli, T. dōli, Tuv. dolu, Salar tol, tʿolj, Yellow Uighur tolu, tolo, Khorezmian T. dōlь. This may be a case of -$ō_2$ > a ~ u, cf. 14.2. But another explanation is possible, too: *tolō may be the original form, preserved in Kh., etc., whereas *tolū (at least in many cases) either may have been contaminated by toluġ <tôl-aġ or may directly go back to toluġ, cf. Ananjasz Zajączkowski, Najstarsza wersja turecka Ḫusräv u Šīrīn Quṭba III, Warszawa 1961.182 toluġ. A. K. Borovkov, Leksika sredneaziatskogo tefsira XII-XIII vv., Moskva 1963.308 has (besides tolu, toli) toluġ, too. These texts are not much more recent than K., Y. tolū; furthermore the Kipchak and Oghuz Tu. forms can go back immediately to toluġ, too. And Tuv. dolu may be a regular development of *tôlō, cf. 14.2.]

tôn 'shirt' (K. tōn, T. dōn) < *tôm // (C. tum) = tụ̄ᵒn T. 217, M. 84, tụ̄ᵒn X. 84

toņaz 'pig' (K. toņuz, T. doņuz) < *toņaz ~3,4 = tọņguz T. 84

tōpïq 'ankle' (presumably from tōp ~3, K. tōp ~top, T. top; K. topïq, T. topuq, Y. tobuk) < *tōp ~3, tōpïq (Mo. toyig ← *tōpïq, later Mo. tobug ← Middle Tu. topuq) = tọpụq T. 63

tōprâq 'ground, soil' (or rather tuprâq, so Brahmi, Tibetan, Kh.), perhaps from tōp (cf. tōpïq), cf. TM II.600-1 (C. tupă) = tụrpāq T. 142

toq (tōq?) 'satisfied' (K. toq, but cf. tōd- 'to become satisfied,' T. doq) < *tok ~3?, *tōk ~3? (cf. 13.12.3) = tọx, tọq T. 267

toqqaz 'nine' (K. toquz, T. doquz) < *tokkaz ~3 (Y. toġus, C. tăxă, Volga Bolgar طخور toxur) = tọqqụz T. 307, M. 99, X. 99

toqqaz ôn 'ninety,' from toqqaz and ôn = Dọxsan T. 317, tọqxsa M. 109 (toqsan toqson K.)

tôrâq 'dried milk' (Old Osman doraq, Chaghatay toraq) < tôrâk ~1,3 (perhaps a loanword from P., cf. TM III. 210-1) = tṳ̄^{o}·ra̱q T. 214, tṳ^{o}ra̱·q M. 83, X. 83

tȫrt 'four' (K. tȫrt, tört, T. dȫrt, Y. tüört) < *tȫrt ~3 (C. tăvată, Volga Bolgar توات töät, Mo. dör+ben) = tọ̄^{ö}·rt T. 302, X. 94, tị̄^{e}·rt M. 94

tȫš 'chest' (K. tȫš, T. dȫš, Y. tüös) < *tȫš ~3 = tọ̄^{ö}·š, Dọ̄^{ö}·š T. 41, tọ̄^{ü}·š X. 85

tuprâq, cf. tōprâq

tûz 'salt' (K. tūz, T. dūz, Y. tūs) < *tûz ~3 (C. tăvar; Mo. dabusun has nothing to do with this word, cf. TM II 510-1) = tṳ̄^{u}·z T. 207

türk 'mighty, flourishing' (K., T. türk 'Turk') < *türk ~3 (cf. TM II headword 888) = tṳ̈rkä^{r}? (literally 'is far') X. 90 ('mighty' > 'far reaching (what concerns might)' > 'far'?)

tǖ, diminutive tuk 'down (of birds, etc.)' (K. tǖ, T. tüy, Y. tǖ, many languages *tǖk) < *tǖ(k) ~3 (C. tĕk) = tṳ̄^{ü}k T. 36

ū or û 'sleep' (K. ū, T. ūqï, Y. ū) < *ū or *û // (C. ïyxă) = ṳ̄ča̱ 'in (during' sleep,' ṳ̄qa̱ ƀa̱rmị̧š 'he went to sleep' X. 86

uzâq 'long' (K. uzaq, T. uzaq, from uzā- or uzâ- 'to become long,' cf. Y. usā-) < *uzâ-, *uzâka(n) // (C. vărax) = ṳ̧zā̱q T. 260, X. 28 (cf. dāġ)

ǖč 'three' (K., T. üč, Y. üs, WOD. ǖš) < *ǖč ~3 (C. viśśĕ, Volga Bolgar وج vüč) = ṳ̄š T. 301, X. 93, ị̄č M. 93

ǖn- 'to ascend, to rise, to grow' (Brahmi ün-, K. ǖn-, Y. ǖn-; T. ȫn- presumably influenced by ȫr- 'to grow') < *ǖn- ~1,3 = hị̄nȧk 'to mount a horse' (literally 'let us mount'), cf. Minorsky 419 Kondurud hat̄imï hündüm 'I mounted my horse,' 421 Xoräka̱ba̱d hat̄i hindim 'I mounted the horse' ürän̦ 'bright' (K., Y. ürün̦) < *pürän̦ ~3,4 = hụrụ̈n 'white' T. 289, hịrịn M. 39, hụrụ̈n X. 39

üst 'above' (T. üst) < *üst+ ~3 = dā̰^{a}m ịstụ̈ 'roof' (literally 'roof-above') T. 184 (← Az. ?)

üzäm 'grape' (K., T. üzüm) < *püzämä ~4 = hụ̈d̄ụ̈m T. 121

yâġ 'the fat' (K., T. yāġ, Y. sïa) < *dâg ~1,3 (C. śu) = ya̰˙ġ T. 6

yaġâq 'nut' (K. yaġāq), perhaps rather yāġâq < *dāgâk ~1,3 = yaġā̰q T. 122, yo̰ġa̰˙q M. 88, yaġa̰˙q X. 88. [M. 88 may show that the original form is *_dāgâk_ ~1,3. We perhaps should prefer to reconstruct PTu. *_dḗgâk_ because of the Hungarian form _dió_.]

yaġaš 'rain' (from yaġ- 'to rain,' K., T. yaġ-) < *dag- ~3 (C. śu-) = ya̰^{6}ġụš T. 149

yâġlaġ 'fat, thick' (from yâġ, cf. above) = yā̰^{a}ġlụx T. 275

yaġūq 'near' (from yaġū- 'to approach,' K. yaġū-, yaġuq, T. yovuq) < *dëgū-, *dëgūka(n) // (C. śivăx) = yọġụq T. 266, yọ^{u}˙q X. 90

yan̦ë̄ 'new' (K. yan̦ï̄, T. yan̦i) < *dan̦ë̄ // (Y. san̦a, C. śĕnĕ) = yẹn̦gị 'next year' T. 169 (but presumably ← Az., modern yeni, older yän̦i)

yaq(q)ā 'collar' (K. yaqā, T. yaqa, Y. saġa) < *dak(k)ā // (C. śuxa, Mo. ǰaqa) = yaqqa T. 222

yastūq (K. yastuq, T. yassïq) = ya̰˙sDụq T. 202

yâšal < *yâššal [cf. C. Brockelmann, _Osttürkische Grammatik der islamischen Litteratursprachen Mittelasiens_, Leiden, 1954. 137, from _yâš_ 'wet,' K. _yāš_, _yaš_, T. _yāš_, Y. _sās_] < *dâš ~1,3 = yā̰^{a}šụl T. 292

yāt- 'to lie' (K., T. yat-, WOD. yāt-) < *dē̄t- ~1,3 (Y. śit-, Tuv. čit-) = yḁtma 'to (go to) sleep' M. 86, yḁtmïš 'slept' X. 86

yä̅l 'wind' (K. yēl, T. yäl, Y. säl) < *dēl ~3 (C. śil, Hungarian szél is a genuine Hungarian word, not ← Old Bolgar) = yẹ'l T. 153

yälä̅k 'feather' (T. yäläk) < *dälä̅k ~2,3 =(yȧlȧk) T. 107

yäņäl 'light' (Altay Tu., T. yäņil, Chaghatay yeņil, Baraba yiņil) ~yüņäl > yüņül (analogy to yüņ 'down' = 'light as down,' Chaghatay, Az. yüņül) < *däņäl ~3,4 (C. śămăl < yüņül) = yụņgụl T. 254. [The Kh. form may be derived from yüņul, but also a development yäņäl > yäņil > yeņil > (assimilated) yiņil > yịņụl (i_2 > ü is quite frequent) > yụņụl (assimilated) cannot be excluded, cf. kindik]

yâtmäš 'seventy' (T. yätmiš) < *dêtmäš ~3,4 (C. śitmĕl) = yätmịš T. 315, yätmịš M. 107

yâttē 'seven' (K. yetī, yättī, T. yädi) < *dêttē // (C. śiččĕ, Volga Bolgar جياتِ čiäti, Y. sättä) = yättị T. 305, X. 97, yättị M. 97

yigärmē 'twenty' (K. yigirmā̆ ~yigirmī = yigirmē, T. yigrimi) < *digärmē ~4 (Y. sūrbä, C. śirĕm, Volga Bolgar جرم، جيارم ǰirmi, ǰiärmi) = yịịirmị T. 310, yịⁱrmị M. 102, yịgịrmị, X. 102

yïl 'year' (K., T. yïl, Y. sïl) < *dïl ~3 (Mo. ǰil may be < *dil, but may be even a younger loanword) = yịl, ịịl T. 164, yị'l M. 89, X. 89; bu'ịịl 'this year' X. 89, kȧlȧn yịl 'next year' X. 89, kȧšgụli ịịl 'last year' X. 89

yïlân 'snake' (K., T. yïlān) < *dïlân ~3 (C. śĕlăn, "Danubian Bolgar" dilom is devious, just as are all the other reconstructions of this document) = yịlān T. 112

yïlqï 'cattle' (K. yïlqï, T. yïlqï, Y. sïlgï) < *dïlkï // = yịlqï 'wether' T. 77

yïrâq, cf. ïrâq

yôllā- 'to send,' from yôl 'way' (K., T. yōl, Y. suol) < *dôl ~ 1,3 (C. śul, Mo. ǰol 'luck' is a rather recent loanword) = yọ˙lla̠⁶maq X. 42

yōq(q)ār(ū), cf. yūq(q)ār(ū)

yōrġân 'blanket' (T. yorġan) < *dōrgân ~1,3 = yọrġa̠n T. 201. [But cf. K. yoġurqān. This may show that an original form *dogarkân or something similar is by far more probable. In this case the Kh. form may be a loanword < older Az. with preserved long vowels, as in *gôl instead of kôl 'lake.' Or are these old Oghuz loanwords?]

yuldaz 'star' (K. yulduz, T. yïldïz, Y. sulus) < *duldaz ~3,4 (C. śăltăr) = yu̹ldu̹Z T. 161

yūmšāq 'soft' (K., T. yumšaq, from yumšā- 'to be soft,' K.) < *dūmšā-, *dūmšāka(n) ~1 = yụmᵘšaq T. 285

yūn̹ 'wool' (K. yun̹, T. yün̹, Y. sun̹, Gagauz ūn) < *dūn̹ ~1,3 (C. śăm; Mo. nun̹gasun does not belong here, cf. TM 89-90) = yụn̹ᵏ T. 91

yūq(q)ār(ū) or yōq(q)ār(ū) 'above, upwards' (K. yuqar, yuqarū according to Uzbek yuqa̠ri, New Uighur žuqur, žuquri, in the text erroneously yokar, yokaru, but cf. Brahmi yoqaru, T. yoqarï; original form probably yūq.ġārū >yūqqārū > yuqaru >yoqaru, the KhT. form < *yōq.ġār) < *dūk.gārū or < *dōk.gārū ~1,3 = yọqqa̠r T. 297

yün̹äl, cf. yän̹äl

yü̂z (or yǖz?) 'face' (K. yǖz, T. yüz, Y. sǖs 'front') < *dü̂z or *düz [whether Mo. <u>dürsün</u> 'appearance' belongs here is unclear for semantic reasons] = ha̯da̯qī̤ iṳzṳ 'instep' literally 'face of the foot') T. 64

yü̂z or yǖz 'a hundred' (K. yǖz, but only in a sample, T. yüz, Y. sǖs) < *dü̂z or *dǖz ~3 (C. śĕr, Volga Bolgar جوز , later جور čür͜z > čür) = yṳ̄z T. 318, X. 110, yị˙z M. 110

15
PHOTOGRAPHS

1. A valley near Khalajistan's capital, Dästgerd

2. Our car in a narrow "street" of Dästgerd

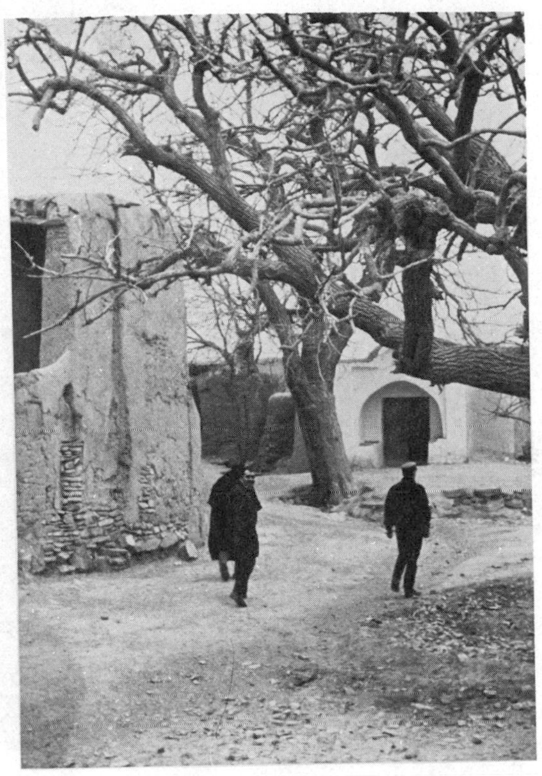

3. A walk in the village of Mouǰa̰n

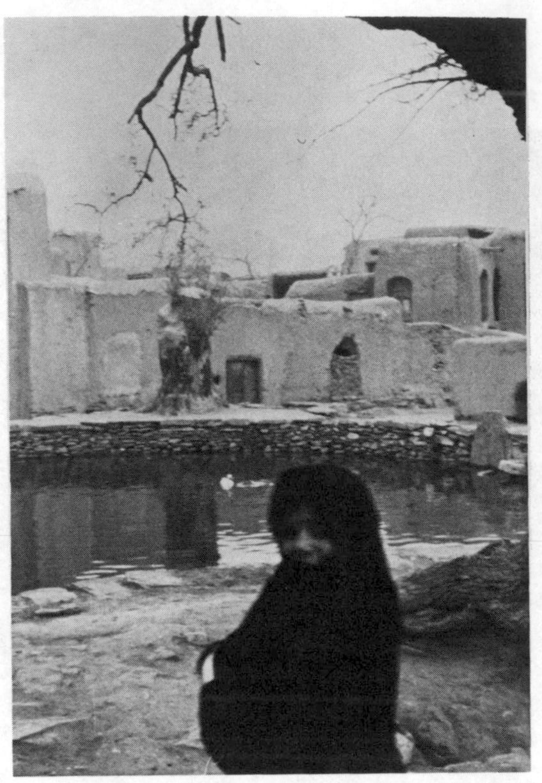

4. A young Khalaj beauty at the laundry pool of Mouǰa̱n

5. Khalaj women washing dishes in Mouǰa̧n

6. Sight-seeing in Moujan

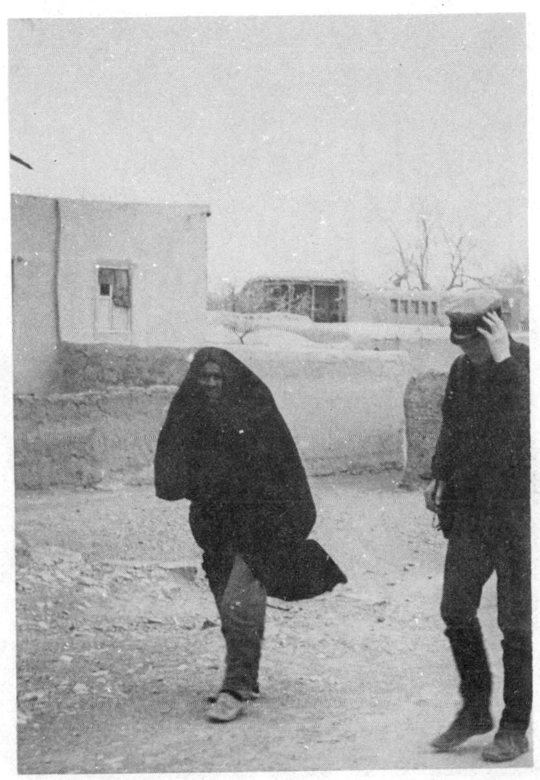

7. The chief of Mouǰa̮n leading our expedition (only Wolfram Hesche is shown) to the school. The wind at that time, early March, was extremely cold and strong.

8. The entrance portal of the school of Mouǰan

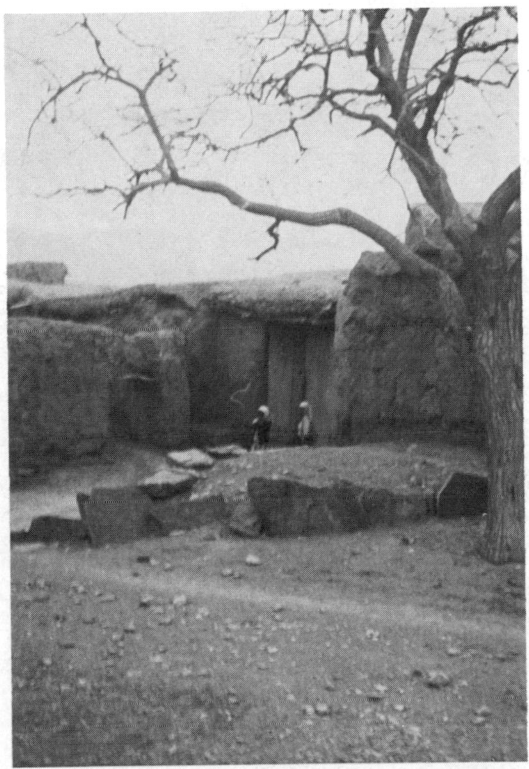

9. Children strolling around the deserted ruins of Moujān. Many inhabitants have left Moujān and many more will leave because the water supply is inadequate and because the gound contains too much salt

10. A last picture before our departure from Mouǰa̱n

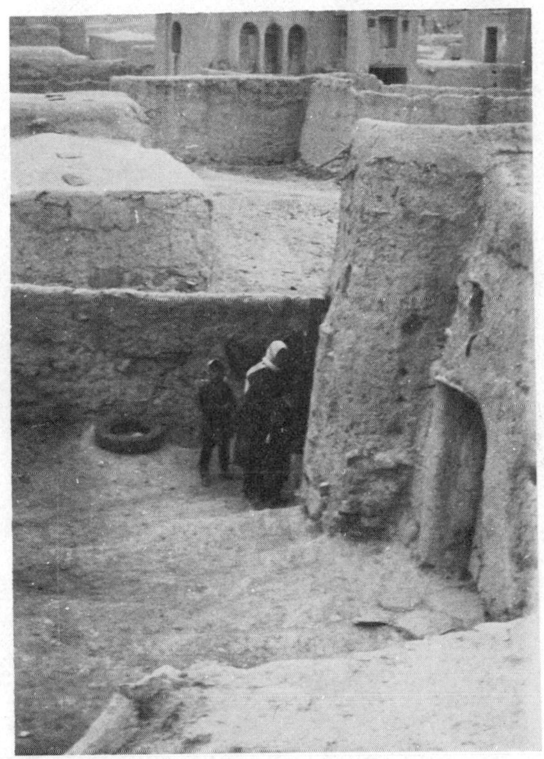

11. Our first visit to Xärrab. The weather was cold and so were the people. Only children could be seen.

12. The people of Mäzräʿä-ye Nou (Marzâno) helping us get through the muddy paths

13. Leaving Mäzräʿä-ye Nou

14. Our second visit to Xärrąb: the Persian village teacher; Mr. Yâdullah, father of the village chief; Mr. ʿEzzätolląh, chief of the village; Semih Tezcan, a member of the expedition.

15. Pictured left to right: a native of Xärrąb; the Persian village teacher; Wolfram Hesche, a member of the expedition; another villager; Hartwig Scheinhardt, a member of the expedition; Mr. ʿEzzätollah

16. Children of Xärrab in the courtyard of the chief's house

17. An enexpected meeting in the desert just outside Xärrab with the district officer of Khalajistan, Mr. ʿÄräbgol, one of our best friends in Khalajistan. Mr. ʿÄräbgol contributed greatly to the success of the expedition.

18. The very kind chief of Noudeh, Mr. ʿÄli Äṣqär Wäfa̱i, standing between two Khalaj men and Hartwig Scheinhardt and Semih Tezcan

19. A sport which gave us daily exercise in Khalajistan. There were many of those muddy little rivers on the way from Noudeh to Yängiǰé.

20. A flock of sheep and donkeys coming in from the fields into the big courtyard of the rectangular village Yängiǰé

25. People of Wenar̥eǰ, south of Qom

21. A typical assembly house for men, found throughout Khalajistan. This house stands in the center of the court-yard of Yängiǰé. The door underneath the balcony leads to a stall for sheep.

22. Kind and joyful people of Yängiǰé

23. The desert near the salt lake of Arāk

24. Second from right Mr. Ḥäbibollah-e Darestani of Darestan, who is responsible for selling gasoline. He seems to be something like the head of the village, because there is no official chief.

MAP

The following map, drawn by the three students of Gerhard Doerfer who undertook the Khalajistan expedition (Wolfram Hesche, Hartwig Scheinhardt, and Semih Tezcan) is cartographically rather crude. It contains, however, information not given on more precise official maps. It locates, for instance, many obscure villages. It also indicates conditions of roads and gives distances based on readings of the odometer. Moreover, it locates gasoline stations. In spite of its shortcomings, this map should be helpful to anyone wishing to travel in Khalajistan. Professor Doerfer, for instance, found it most useful when he undertook the second Khalajistan expedition in March 1969.

LEGEND

————	Excellent asphalt roads
- - - - - - - - -	Good roads, drivable the whole year
. . . .	Bad roads
Figures	Distance in kilometers
'	Distance interval markers
?	Location of village uncertain
*	Location of gasoline stations

Khalaj Villages Visited
(in order of visiting)

A. Mänṣur-ḁbḁd
B. Mouǰḁn
C. Sorxädé
D. Xärrḁb
E. Mäzrä̆ʿä-ye Nou
F. Kärdeyḁn
G. Xorḁk-ḁbḁd
H. Hezḁr-ḁbḁd
I. Fäiz-ḁbḁd
J. Noudeh
K. Yängiǰé
L. Xält-ḁbḁd
M. Tälxḁb
N. Wḁšqḁn
O. Ḥäsän-ḁbḁd
P. Säfid-ḁb
Q. Sär-e bänd
R. Kḁšé
S. Bon-čenḁr
T. Musi-ḁbḁd
U. Säqärǰuq
V. Zär-nušé
W. Dḁrestḁn
X. Moḥsen-ḁbḁd
Y. Näder-ḁbḁd
Z. Wenḁreǰ
AA. Säläfčegḁn
BB. Qäré-Su
CC. Bḁǵ-e yäk
DD. Seft
EE. Ispit
FF. Čḁhäk
GG. Mehr-e Zämin
HH Dermänek

Khalaj Villages Not Visited
(west to east)

(A) ʿÄli-ḁbḁd
(B) J̌älil-ḁbḁd
(C) Sär-e Rud
(D) J̌irḁġḁč
(E) Versḁn
(F) Zizgḁn
(G) Šḁné
(H) A̮ġuläk
(I) Mušäkeyé
(J) Bḁǵčé Weswḁr
(K) Äḥmäd-ḁbḁd
(L) Säfid-ḁlé
(M) Ḥosäin-ḁbḁd
(N) Qurqur
(O) Dḁǵḁn
(P) Šḁh-qḁlu

Non-Khalaj Villages
(generally west to east)

a. Kḁzem-ḁbḁd
b. Ferḁhän
c. Borz-ḁbḁd
d. Šḁh-ḁbḁd
e. Färnähin
f. Zolf-ḁbḁd
g. Fešk
h. Moässär
i. Gerekḁn
j. A̮šteyḁn (A̮hu)
k. A̮hu
l. Tärxorḁn
m. Čäšmé
n. Sḁleḥ-ḁbḁd
o. Nḁngerd
p. Rḁhgerd
q. Pougerd
r. Rästgḁn
s. Vešḁré
t. Dästgerd
u. Kondurud
v. Räḥmät-ḁbḁd
w. Ruḥ-ḁbḁd
x. Tḁǰ Xḁtun
y. Kärvḁn-säré-räng
z. Qälʿé-ye Čäm
aa. Virǰḁn

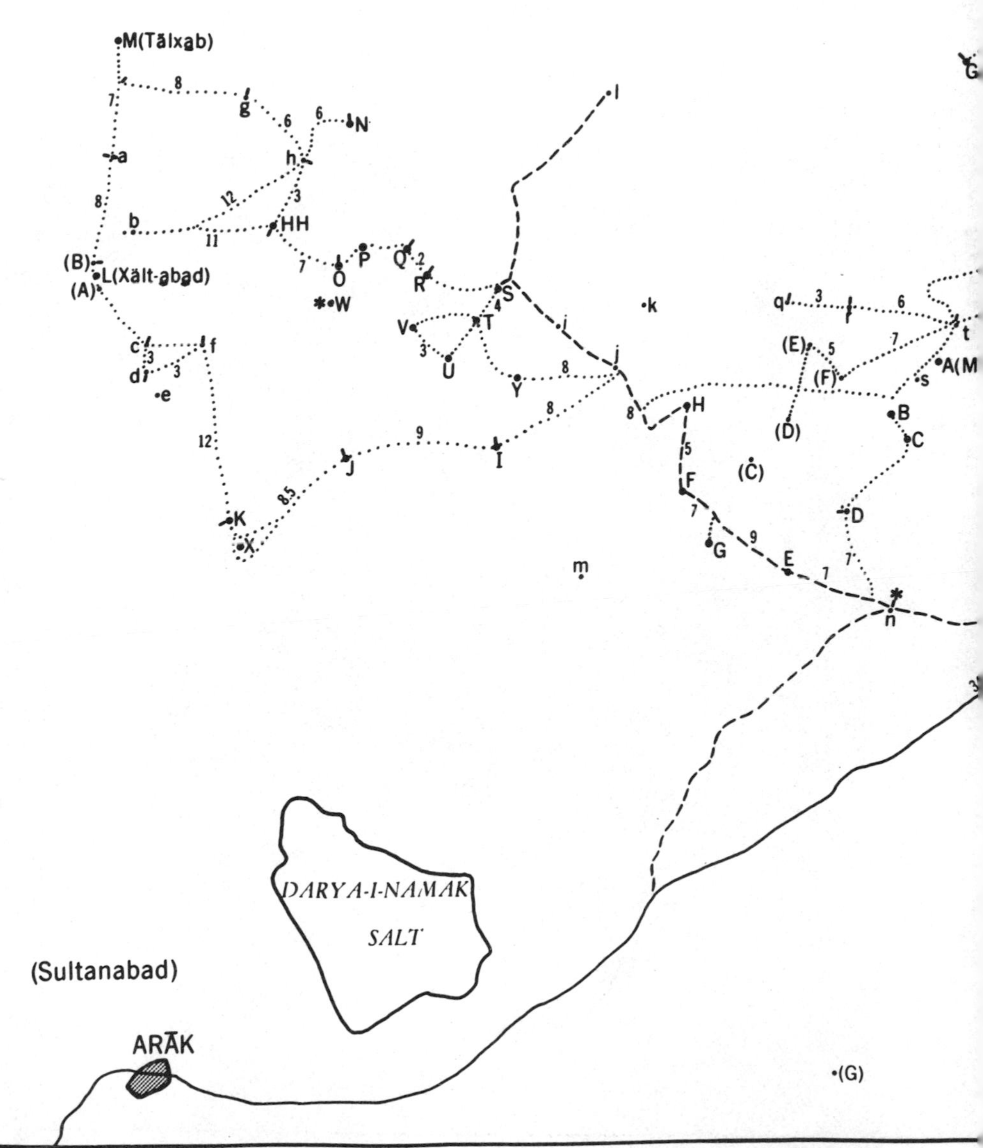
M(Tälxab)
N
L(Xält-abad)
(B)
(A)
HH
O
P
Q
R
S
T
U
V
W
Y
I
J
K
X
H
F
G
E
D
C
B
(E)
(F)
(D)
(C)
DARYA-I-NAMAK
SALT
(Sultanabad)
ARĀK
(G)